NO PATH HOME

NO PATH HOME

Humanitarian Camps and the
Grief of Displacement

Elizabeth Cullen Dunn

CORNELL UNIVERSITY PRESS ITHACA AND LONDON

First published 2017 by Cornell University Press

Printed in the United States of America

Library of Congress Cataloging-in-Publication Data
Names: Dunn, Elizabeth C., 1968– author.
Title: No path home : humanitarian camps and the grief of displacement /
    Elizabeth Cullen Dunn.
Description: Ithaca : Cornell University Press, 2017. | Includes bibliographical
    references and index.
Identifiers: LCCN 2017026508 (print) | LCCN 2017027518 (ebook) |
    ISBN 9781501712500 (epub/mobi) | ISBN 9781501712517 (pdf) |
    ISBN 9781501709661 (cloth : alk. paper) | ISBN 9781501712302
    (pbk. : alk. paper)
Subjects: LCSH: Internally displaced persons—Georgia (Republic) | Refugee
    camps—Georgia (Republic) | Humanitarian assistance—Georgia (Republic) |
    South Ossetia War, 2008—Refugees.
Classification: LCC HV640.4.G28 (ebook) | LCC HV640.4.G28 D86 2017 (print) |
    DDC 362.87/83094758—dc23
LC record available at https://lccn.loc.gov/2017026508

To Aaron Theodore Cullen Dunn
My son, companion, and teacher
and
To the memory of Tamuna Robakidze

THE AIRPLANE DANCE

The dance moved in circles, with airplanes:
some golden
some silver.

They went like this: a half circle
on the left side, going up
then down, over the roofs
... then up, on the right
golden, silver

How they spun as they fell
golden, silver ...

After that a neighbor's house was gone
and the house on the corner
and the house next door

And I was amazed
and shook my head:
look, there's no house! ...
look, there's no house! ...
look, there's no house! ...

—Nichita Stănescu, *Wheel with a Single*
Spoke and Other Poems

Contents

Note on Place Names in the South Caucasus

The issue of place names in the Caucasus is extremely contentious, and the form of the toponym generally indicates one's political sympathies. Thus to refer to South Ossetia as Samachablo, a toponym that refers to the territory as the property of the Georgian Princes Machabeli, indicates a Georgian nationalist perspective, to refer to it as the Tskhinvali Autonomous Region indicates sympathy with the Saakashvili government, and to call it Ossetia indicates sympathy with Ossetian ethnic separatism. Likewise, to refer to the capital of that region as Tskhinval indexes Ossetian sympathies, but to call it Tskhinvali, with the Georgian nominative case ending, indexes Georgian partisanship. In this book, rather than try to appear neutral while balancing a host of confusing toponyms, I have generally chosen the names used by the English-language press: South Ossetia, Tskhinvali, Disevi, and so on. The choice of names is expedient, not political: I use the names that English-language readers are most likely to be familiar with.

NO PATH HOME

THE CAMP AND THE CAMP

When the bomb hit the house Ketevan Okropiridze was pushing a heavy sofa to barricade her mother-in-law's bedroom, trying to protect herself and her family from the cluster bombs raining down from Russian planes overhead and the artillery coming from all sides. South Ossetia, the breakaway province in the former Soviet Republic of Georgia where Keti lived, had been under attack for more than four days. At the beginning of the war, when the Russian 58th Army first came across the Caucasus Mountains through the Roki Tunnel, the family had decided to try and survive the war in their own home. But the blast made it clear the house offered no safety. Late that night, with the tracer flares of Grad rockets lighting up the sky and the air vibrating with the sounds of rocket engines, gunfire, and cluster bomb explosions, they left. They dodged tanks and soldiers by picking their way through the gardens and the fields surrounding the village, hiding under the cover of trees in orchards. Finally finding transport in a packed minibus, they fled down the main highway toward Tbilisi, the capital. As they drove, a bomb hit the car in front of them and the air was filled with a cloud of earth and glass.

For Temo Javakhishvili the war's brutality did not end at South Ossetia's border. He left his village, Eredvi, late in the five-day war, fleeing toward the town of Gori. His son, Zviadi, lived in a five-story Soviet-era apartment block near the main East-West highway with his pregnant wife and their small son. But Temo never made it to Zviadi's apartment. Russian planes were bombing Gori, and Zviadi's building was hit. All the windows in the building were instantly blown out, and flames burst from the black holes where the windows once were. Zura, Temo's other son, tried to save his brother. As he crouched over Zviadi's bleeding body in the rubble outside the building, a foreign photographer snapped his picture. It became the defining image of the war, shown on television across the world and published on the front page of the *New York Times*: Zura cradling Zviadi's corpse, covered in blood and spattered with dirt, howling in grief and anger.

The night the war broke out Manana Abaeva could not walk. She had undergone complicated surgery on her left hip and had developed deep-vein thrombosis, a clot in the blood supply to her leg that caused the leg and foot to swell dramatically. If the clot were to break away from the vein in her leg and travel to her lungs, it could cause a fatal pulmonary embolism. But she could hear the fire of the Grad "Hailstorm" rockets, guns firing in the village, and the rumbling of the ground caused by tanks moving. As bombs began to fall on the village, her daughter helped her into a small Niva car crammed with the village's most infirm residents. The car set off along the road lined with Georgian tanks and troops, hoping to make it through the fighting without being fired on, carrying Manana away from South Ossetia and into an uncertain future.

The events of the war remain in dispute. Whether it began on August 6 with a Georgian invasion of South Ossetia or on August 7 with a Russian invasion, when each village was taken, what weaponry was used, and which side damaged which village are all facts hotly contested by Russia, South Ossetia, and Georgia. I have no means of independently verifying any claim, and settling debates or placing blame over the events of the war is beyond the scope of this book. But what is clear is that for Ketevan, Temo, Manana, and over twenty-eight thousand people ethnically cleansed from South Ossetia, the five-day war between Russia and Georgia in 2008 marked their entry into life in the humanitarian system. Their houses were bombed by Russian aircraft, looted by Ossetian irregular forces, and then burned. In some of the villages that were of strategic or symbolic significance the Russians bulldozed the burned ruins to make the point clear: the residents of the ethnically Georgian villages could never return. Huddled in kindergarten classrooms in Tbilisi or stuck in the tent camp administered by the Red Cross in Gori, they were brought into the humanitarian condition, a way of life determined by a complex web of international, national, and local institutions aimed at preserving life and alleviating suffering in the wake of violence (see Feldman 2012; Barnett 2010). No longer farmers, smugglers, teachers, or soldiers, their primary social identities were transformed as the UN High Commission for Refugees (UNHCR) and the Georgian government compiled lists of the displaced and assigned them official status. Now they were now first and foremost internally displaced persons (IDPs), refugees in their own country, part of the target population for the international humanitarian order.

The Georgian IDPs joined a global population of displaced people growing at an astronomical rate. In 2000 there were 21 million displaced people. By 2009 there were 43.3 million displaced people, two times as many as were displaced at the beginning of the decade. By 2016, more than 65 million people had been forced from their homes (Harild and Christiansen 2010, 2; Sengupta 2015). If people who are displaced by conflict or disaster cross international borders, they are formally designated as refugees and have a set of well-defined rights under the 1951 United Nations Convention Relating to the Status of Refugees. Officially they come under the mandate of the UNHCR, which assumes significant responsibility for their welfare. But refugees make up only 36% of the population of displaced people around the world. The rest, 64% of the world's displaced, are IDPs, people who have been forced from their homes but have not crossed international borders. Although IDPs should retain the rights accruing to all the members of their own countries, they fall into a "protection gap" because they are neither protected by international law nor, in practice, fully protected as citizens in their own countries. They pose a disquieting challenge to the nation-state system, which assumes that every person should be clearly assigned to one state or another: IDPs are, instead, neither the responsibility of the international community nor fully governed by the nation-state (see Cohen and Deng 1998). Although they are often considered exiles, people living on the margins of both their own societies and the international order, it is more fruitful to think of them as *insiles*, people caught in the interstices of an emerging system of humanitarian governance that confounds territorial boundaries (see Miéville 2009).

In one sense the Russo-Georgian War was short. The active fighting lasted only five days and the scale of the damage was comparatively small. But the war garnered an enormous humanitarian response from the international community, and thus placed the Georgian IDPs into the byzantine bureaucratic workings of the international humanitarian system. Over $4.5 billion in aid was given by international donors (Piccio 2013), with over $350 million earmarked specifically for IDPs. Six UN agencies and over ninety-two NGOs, many of them newly arrived in the wake of the war, joined forces to provide emergency assistance for the people ethnically cleansed from South Ossetia. Like all humanitarian aid to IDPs, this aid was supposed to be temporary, a short-term response to a catastrophic emergency. Emergency aid—the food, water, shelter, and medical care that agencies like the Red Cross and Doctors Without Borders portray in their appeals for donations—is aimed at the immediate preservation of physiological life. This emphasis on preserving life in the midst of crisis gives the humanitarian enterprise a rushed tempo, as humanitarian agencies move from war to war and disaster to disaster (Polman 2010; Redfield 2005; Calhoun 2008; Calhoun 2010). Yet for the Georgian IDPs, as for millions of displaced people around the world, the humanitarian system is not a temporary state of emergency and not only a series of life-saving measures but a way of life in which they must make do on a day-to-day basis over a long period of time. Around the world, once IDPs enter the humanitarian system they are often stuck there for decades and even generations—the average length of stay in a camp is now over seventeen years, which is hardly temporary. Sometimes crushed between institutions competing for sovereignty, more often left in the gaps of legal protection and service provision, and frequently pinned between warring states and marooned in the no-man's land of militarized borders, IDPs often find it difficult or impossible to leave the camps and settlements where they have been sent to live. This long-term confinement means refugee camps and IDP settlements are often not merely temporary encampments but rather enduring political problems. The Palestinians, for example, have been in refugee camps for nearly seventy years, and two generations have grown up in exile. Hutus and Tutsis both have been in camps for more than forty years. Dadaab, one of the world's largest camps for displaced people, in Kenya, is now entering its twenty-fifth year and contains more than three hundred thousand people, many of whom were born there and have never lived elsewhere. Even in Georgia displacement has become a multigenerational phenomenon: in addition to the people displaced by the 2008 war, the "old caseload," nearly a quarter of a million IDPs displaced from South Ossetia and Abkhazia between 1991 and 1993, remain in "temporary" housing. The "new caseload," people displaced from South Ossetia during the Russo-Georgian War of 2008, still hope to return to their villages of origin. But almost from the beginning of their displacement the camp has been not only a space for the delivery of aid but also of long-term residence (Agier 2011, 71). Although the Georgian government still pays lip service to the possibility of return, it has formally acknowledged that return is not imminent and, with the help of UNHCR, USAID, and other humanitarian agencies, has resettled the IDPs into thirty-eight new settlements where they are supposed to stay for the foreseeable future.

The first and most immediate question of this book, then, is why millions of displaced people around the world find themselves chronically ensnared in the humanitarian condition. In recent years the UNHCR has focused on the problem of protracted displacement and has sought to end it by calling for "durable solutions" for displaced people. Where the preferred solution—voluntary repatriation—is not a realistic option, UNHCR has advocated for forms of social reintegration that would make displaced people into full social

actors in the places they currently reside (Harild and Christensen 2010; Mundt and Ferris 2008; Brookings Institution 2010). Yet despite millions of dollars from donor governments and aid agencies meaningful social reintegration remains elusive. Why do displaced people remain trapped in what Agier (2011) calls "the continent of camps" for so long? How do they experience the aid they receive and how does it shape the ways they can reenter society? Why does humanitarian aid appear to leave them oscillating between dependency and abandonment for so long?

In this book I argue that the long-term limbo of displacement stems not just from the ongoing nature of modern conflict but also from the lifeworlds humanitarian aid creates. From the perspective of aid agencies and donor governments, displacement is largely a technical problem, which can be resolved by providing food, shelter, sanitation, medical care, and so on. Indeed some aid agencies have become highly specialized in providing that kind of assistance and have developed significant expertise in logistics and supply-chain management. But for refugees and IDPs themselves displacement is something beyond a technical problem of logistics and delivery. It is an existential dilemma posed by the destruction not only of their homes but also of the world they once knew, including many of their social relationships, their attachments to places, and the structures and practices they used to create meaning. Their attempts to use socially, politically, and spatially informed practices to make the world a relatively stable and comprehensible place once again tell us more generally about how people structure the things in experience, relate them to one another, and establish a basis for meaningful action. By focusing on people who sit in the ragged holes of a damaged society, I hope to show how social orders are built, broken, and constructed again out of the free-floating shrapnel of existence.

The problem of reconstructing a lifeworld that has literally been blown apart would be difficult enough. But IDPs do not reconstruct their lifeworlds unimpeded. Although humanitarian aid is meant to help displaced people begin their lives again, it often inadvertently puts them at a grave disadvantage in remaking a coherent and stable existence where they can make plans and where actions have a reasonable chance of achieving goals. Finnstrom (2008) argues that people in war-torn regions experience "a lessened control over ontological security in everyday life." I argue that this lessened control is caused not only by war but also inadvertently by the practice of humanitarianism and by the unplanned ways it impedes displaced people from reconstructing their own lifeworlds. The chapters that follow show that humanitarianism creates six states of being that pin displaced people in place: war, chaos, nothingness, pressure, authoritarianism, and death. A "state of being" is both a simple and a complex notion, one that I develop in more detail below, but as a first pass, I mean it as a mode of existing in the world that both incorporates and exceeds the world planned and administrated by the international humanitarian apparatus. I do not argue that displaced people's worlds are fully controlled by the humanitarian system. Rather, the states of being that displaced people experience are apart from the humanitarian system but intersect with it and are shaped by it, along with other forces such as religion and the nation-state. I want to distinguish carefully between what Feldman (2012) calls the "politics of life," and "the politics of living," that is, between the biopolitical techniques used by humanitarian actors to triage displaced people, provide social services to them, manage their economic activity, and govern them as a population, and the existential problem that displaced people face living in close proximity to that system. Rather than focusing on changes in policy at the international level, which often express intentions and aspirations rather than actual practice, or on the bureaucratic practices of aid agencies, which often show remarkable disjunctures with the way aid is given and used in IDP settlements, or even on the practices of aid workers, who are well-meaning but have a different perspective on aid than the beneficiaries of aid do, I have sought to understand the lifeworlds of the displaced from the practices of IDPs themselves, paying attention to how displaced people actually make do in the humanitarian condition and sticking as closely as I can to their understanding of the structures, agencies, and actors that both sustain and constrain them. My view, then, is not from the perspective of policymakers or aid workers, who often have a better understanding of the structural and political constraints around aid than displaced people do. Instead I have tried, to the best of my ability, to reflect a view of the humanitarian system from the ground of the camp and from the perspective of the people who live in it, even when this means perhaps perceiving aid differently than aid providers do.

What I ask, then, is how the practices of international actors, the dictates and programs of nation-states, the politics of local government, and the beliefs and practices of IDPs themselves intersect in ways that often trap displaced people in the suspended temporality of camp life. How do displaced people work against being stuck in prolonged liminality? How do they draw on memory, history, religion, and the social relations of their prewar lives as they seek to rebuild some sort of normal life in the spaces of the camp? What kinds of work—material, social, cultural—have to go on in order to socially reintegrate the displaced? And most important, why does the practice of humanitarian aid, which is aimed at facilitating that process, so often create a situation in which rebuilding a life and becoming a full member of society again becomes difficult or impossible? In asking these questions, I am trying to understand why the political and social constellation of life in the humanitarian condition leaves IDPs in purgatory, neither in a state of emergency nor able to act as normal citizens in the country where they reside.

To find out the answer to these questions, I spent more than sixteen months between 2009 and 2012 in the Georgian IDP camps. I arrived in Georgia five months after the war, on the day that the IDPs were moving from the kindergartens and libraries where they had been sleeping on the floor to thirty-six (later thirty-eight) new settlements. Thus I have been able to follow the process of postwar reconstruction almost from the beginning. That first year, which was the first year of their displacement, living in the camps was impossible for me: there was literally no room in the crowded cottages and none of the IDPs had food to spare. The political situation was still extremely tense and the Russians were only 30 kilometers from Tsmindatsqali, the settlement I spent the most time in. They were even closer in Khurvaleti, another camp in which I did research. It was literally inside the border, between the Georgian and Russian lines of control, about 500 meters from a checkpoint controlled by Ossetian militia and Russian forces. So I rented an apartment in the capital, Tbilisi, and commuted an hour and a half each way, five days a week, in the roving minivans called *marshrutkas*. After a few months, when I had made friends among the IDPs, I began spending several nights a week in Tsmindatsqali. In 2010 I lived in an apartment within walking distance of two settlements, and in 2011 I lived in Tsmindatsqali itself for nearly three months.[1] My job, as I reluctantly came to define it, was to accompany the IDPs as they lived as humanitarianism's beneficiaries, to understand what it meant to be the

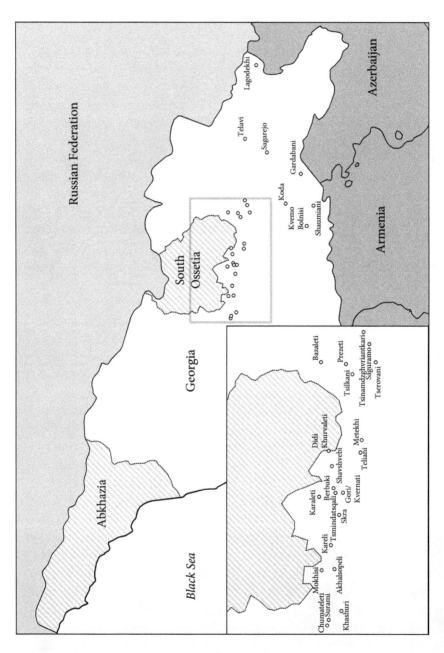

MAP 1. IDP camps in the Republic of Georgia

subject of humanitarian governance, to know the particular combinations of relief and suffering that humanitarianism engendered, and to see the resources and constraints it provided people seeking to remake some sort of tolerable existence.

What Is Humanitarianism?

Protracted displacement is often seen as the result of outside political forces: displaced people are prevented from returning to the towns and villages they came from until fighting has stopped and are also prevented from socially reintegrating into their host society by the host government. But in this book I show that the limbo of the camp is at least in part the result of the humanitarian enterprise itself, including the way it deals with material goods, handles information, and thinks about the role of displaced people in the system of aid governance. But before holding the humanitarian enterprise responsible, it is important to define what I mean by "humanitarianism," a word that has taken on several distinct meanings. Humanitarianism is often understood as a sentiment, an ethical impulse to help distant strangers. But it has become many other things, too: an ideology, a system of categorization, a massive industry, a set of bureaucratic practices, and, for many people, a way of life (see Bornstein and Redfield 2011b; Feldman 2014). Anthropologists have used several lenses to understand what the advent of humanitarianism as a globalizing force entails, including sovereignty and statehood, morality and ethics, suffering and precarity, and urbanization and the right to the city. In this book I use each of these lenses at different points. What has always startled me is how different humanitarian action looks from each of them.

The question of sovereignty opens a view of humanitarianism at a global scale. Humanitarianism's centrality to international politics is a result of dramatic changes in the international system since the end of the Cold War that have made it one of the new ordering principles of the international system. As a principle that allocates both power and money differentially among countries, humanitarianism divides the world's nation-states not into North and South, colonist and colonized, as during the eighteenth and nineteenth centuries, nor into East and West, or socialist and capitalist countries, as during much of the twentieth century. Rather, it divides the post–Cold War world into donors and receivers, states that are capable of adequately caring for their citizens and states that are not (Barnett 2010). This new norm in the international system, which stems from the United Nations' 2005 Responsibility to Protect initiative,[2] means that sovereignty is no longer absolute. Rather, under the aegis of global humanitarianism, the international community is increasingly willing to consider superceding a national government and intervening in various ways when a state cannot protect its citizens, including by making policy, providing material care for populations, and even by carrying out military action, such as the "humanitarian" bombings of Serbia or Libya.

The integration of humanitarianism as a moral value in global politics has driven great changes in the agencies that are tasked with providing aid, including international organizations in the UN system, donor government agencies such as USAID, and quasi-independent NGOs acting under contracts from donors. As humanitarian agencies use increasingly precise sets of rules about planning, implementing, monitoring, and evaluating humanitarian projects, they are less and less like the loosely organized do-gooders acting through voluntary organizations that once made up the humanitarian system (see Krause 2014). Now, whether they are ostensibly outside the state (like Save the Children, the International Committee of the Red Cross, and CARE International), above the nation-state (as the UNHCR claims to be), or resolutely within states (as ministries for refugees, departments of public health, and even armies used as humanitarian agents are), the agents of humanitarian action are bureaucratic organizations so tightly knit that it is possible to think of them as a single system aimed at the alleviation of human misery (Barnett 2010; Ticktin 2006; Fassin and Pandolfi 2010; Bryan 2015; Feldman 2008a; Feldman 2011; Polman 2010; A. de Waal 2010).

Anthropologists have argued that these changes have made humanitarianism a new form of sovereignty, a deterritorialized form of global governance in which aid agencies move from place to place in the wake of disaster and crisis to take over the policies and practices of national governments (Pandolfi 2003, 370; Fassin and Pandolfi 2010). Tracing the explosive rise in humanitarian aid—which has gone from an industry worth $1 billion in 1991 to one worth $18 billion in 2010—anthropologists have tracked the growth of an enormous new institutional system that includes the United Nations system, donor government agencies like USAID, for-profit firms like Chemonics, and ostensibly independent NGOs such as CARE International, Doctors Without Borders, World Vision, and the International Committee of the Red Cross (see, for example, Redfield 2013 or Bornstein 2012). They have tracked the detailed technical practices through which sovereignty is assumed and made manifest on the ground (Krause 2014). By creating international regimes of human rights law and policy (Hyndman 2000), creating standards for the provision of aid such as the SPHERE standards, using institutionalized mechanisms to determine who should live and whose life may be sacrificed (Fassin 2007; Ticktin 2006), providing healthcare to some and not others (Ticktin 2011), providing prepackaged, standardized "kits" of aid (Redfield 2008b), and most of all, by creating a set of bureaucratic procedures for funding and coordinating aid, international humanitarian agencies have come to assume new powers in the governance of the lives of the displaced.

In the wake of the war in Georgia, I too focused on the question of how the humanitarian system established new forms of sovereignty and so spent a great deal of time concentrating on the humanitarian system as a set of institutions that governed through bureaucratic and technical means (Barnett 2010). I conducted more than sixty semistructured interviews with representatives of the United Nations agencies, international NGOs, and government officials. I attended "cluster meetings" organized by the United Nations' Office for the Coordination of Humanitarian Affairs, which brought NGOs, donor governments, and Georgian government ministries together to plan and organize aid. I interviewed representatives of both international and local NGOs and rode along with humanitarian workers who were implementing projects. I helped unload heavy bags of flour and beans with World Vision, attended trainings for mental-health workers sponsored by the International Organization for Migration, helped conduct a "needs assessment survey" with CARE International, and rode along in an ambulance with a mobile medical team of IDP doctors. I also spent time, insofar as I could, with Georgian government officials who were addressing the new wave of IDPs. I interviewed officials at the Ministry of Refugees and Accommodation and at the Ministry of Health, Labor, and Social Affairs. When the Minister of Health visited Prezeti, one of the most outlying and desolate camps, I was there to watch him put himself in front of the television cameras while brushing off the IDPs who wanted to speak with him.

My aim was to see how humanitarianism, as an institutionalized system, governed the IDPs as a population. But as I soon discovered, defining humanitarianism in terms of institutions and bureaucratic practices is a limited optic. As I show in chapter 3, the anthropological work on humanitarianism seriously overestimates the international humanitarian system's capacity to establish sovereignty and to govern in the ways it claims (Dunn 2012b). This is not because humanitarians are full of nefarious intentions—on the contrary, they are generally sincere people who genuinely desire to help others and are motivated by a sense of professionalism and duty (see Malkki 2015). Nor is it because humanitarian projects are plagued with problems of ineffectiveness or corruption—they occasionally are, but it isn't that kind of failing that limits their capacity to govern (see Sullivan 2015; Sontag 2012; Polman 2010). Their limitations come because the world international bureaucrats envision and attempt to implement is not the whole of life for displaced people and does not wholly determine the framework in which they work to rebuild their lives after conflict and exodus. Many different actors and circumstances shape the economic, social, and biophysical trajectories of displaced people, whose own activities are also understudied and unaccounted for (Dunn and Cons 2013). For example, the role that nation-states play in managing the lives of the internally displaced has not been extensively studied (Barnett 2011), nor has the role that international aid to IDPs plays in state-building (and state-weakening) projects. With a few notable exceptions (e.g., Malkki 1996; Navaro-Yashin 2012), there has been little attention in anthropology to displaced people's own notions of "history" and "politics," to the ways they circumvent aid or adapt it to their own purposes, to the resources they bring to the process of rebuilding some sort of normalized life in the wake of catastrophe, or to the ways they appropriate and misappropriate aid projects to serve their own goals. In the end, seeing humanitarianism as a form of sovereignty says a great deal about how and why humanitarians act, but because it is an inherently state-centric view, it is a limited optic when it comes to the ways displaced people themselves experience war, displacement, or humanitarianism.

In order to learn more about the ways the IDPs themselves thought about displacement, I turned my attention to another way anthropologists have thought about humanitarianism: as action aimed at alleviating suffering (see, for example, Quesada 1998; Farmer 2004b; Rudoren 2013; Rieff 2003, 25). As a political ideology, humanitarianism is fundamentally premised on two key notions: first, that war and disaster generate suffering, and second, that suffering is unnecessary and can (and should) be avoided. What IDPs do, I thought, was suffer, and what humanitarian agencies did was to eliminate suffering. I thought then—as many humanitarians themselves do—that the effectiveness of aid could be gauged by how well it got rid of suffering. It is certainly true that displaced people suffer even in the Georgian settlements, which I once heard a Swedish diplomat call "the best refugee camps in the world." In the sixteen months I spent in the settlements, I watched Keti, Manana, Temo, and the other IDPs I knew in Tsmindatsqali suffer more deeply after the war than they did during it. As I discuss in more depth in chapter 6, they suffered physically in terms of rapidly degraded health and physical discomfort; economically in terms of poverty and unemployment; socially, as the occupations, village communities, and families that had made up their lives were fractured and as IDPs became stigmatized; and most of all morally, as justice and dignity were denied them. To understand the ways they suffered, and to understand how humanitarian aid did or did not mitigate their distress, I conducted more than fifty semistructured interviews with IDPs, listening to heart-rending experiences. Emotion pervaded the atmosphere: in interviews my interlocutors often wept or raged, and sometimes physically shook as they relived their war experiences or experienced the fear of making a political mistake that might endanger their families.[3]

As I kept returning to Tsmindatsqali, Khurvaleti, and Skra settlements, I began to know people personally and make friends, and I soon attached myself to a small group of IDPs from Ksuisi and Disevi, two villages in South Ossetia. The camps were open, with the exception of Khurvaleti, which was on the administrative boundary line with South Ossetia and therefore guarded by the Georgian military, but the IDPs and I were free to come and go at will from all of the camps. This gave me the opportunity to intimately observe people's daily lives and to see their hardships in detail and in real time. Manana Abaeva, who became my closest friend, would sit with me for hours while we picked wool to make mattress pads to ease the pain in her bad hip caused by the lumpy, cheap mattresses on the beds they'd been given. Mariam Sabashvili, who had been the director of a school in South Ossetia, taught me the history of the region as she held her grandson, who had been born in the camp just as Mariam's husband, Anzor, was dying. On occasional weekend visits to Tsmindatsqali from our apartment in the capital, my son too became involved in camp life, spending time playing with Manana's other kids and the pack of children who roamed the camp with them. Grabbing their plastic guns—not only pistols, but often replicas of automatic weapons—the kids would play Georgians versus Russians, replaying the war again and again. Life in the settlements was elegiac, soaked in an undercurrent of sadness and loss that was present even at happy moments like holidays and festive banquets.

Participating in daily life in the camps and establishing deep emotional relationships with some of the people there helped me to understand some of the profound bodily suffering the IDPs experienced in displacement. Whether watching Manana try to get around on her bad hip, or Eka worn down with yet another piercing headache brought on by her high blood pressure, or Temo struggle with his alcoholism, or visiting Dato, a man with cerebral palsy who was unable to leave his cottage because his wheelchair could not make it down the gravel roads, I became acutely aware that IDPs experienced life in the humanitarian system in a deeply embodied way, and came to know the specific ways that living as the "beneficiaries" of humanitarian action caused them illness, financial distress, confusion, and sadness. Their suffering was on the surface, and for a variety of reasons—including the belief that I might be able to get them more aid—it was important to them that I know how they suffered. Because suffering was a key part of their own narratives of displacement, it was important to them that I see and carefully document the physical hardships they confronted.

Focusing on suffering as the central problem of humanitarianism opens up a space for anthropological engagement that focusing on humanitarianism as sovereignty does not. In the first place, focusing on lived experiences of suffering transcends bureaucratic categories that seek to fragment distress.

The institutional structure of the humanitarian apparatus, in which various NGOs divide up the labor of aid, focus on particular functional areas, and assign bits of work as projects to different groups, constantly demands that the experience of IDPs be fragmented into medical, psychological, infrastructural, political, and economic areas in order to make them amenable to intervention. In the NGO meetings in Tbilisi, there was constant pressure to be working at the intersection of the subjects of aid and a sector of technocratic intervention: IDPs and health, IDPs and economic development, IDPs and shelter solutions, etc. Focusing on suffering, on the contrary, highlights the fact that all the aspects of displaced people's distress are of a piece rather than splintering pain into measurable attributes or domains of action. Suffering unifies the medical, psychological, political, cultural, economic, and even geographic elements that are institutionally and bureaucratically separated, seeing them instead as tightly bound together and reflecting or refracting one another (Kleinman, Das, and Lock 1994, ix). Most important, seeing suffering holistically resists the continual impulse of NGOs and government agencies to render social problems into technical ones that can be solved with the application of policy, procedures, and projects (Li 2007). Life in the humanitarian condition resists metaphors of rescue and remedy to present itself as an unappeasable existential condition that can't be simply patched up. Putting suffering as the focal point of research on humanitarianism enables anthropologists to carefully scrutinize the aid world's continual drive to fix or to break displacement down in ways that make it amenable to institutional action.

However useful the concept of "suffering" is in resisting splintering and technocracy, though, it is deeply problematic (see Ortner 2016). First of all, it replicates the key ideologies of bureaucratized humanitarianism and locks anthropologists into the same formulation of the problem that humanitarian bureaucrats have: one of efficacy. If humanitarianism defines suffering as a preventable tragedy demanding a direct response, it also demands that such a response must work (Bornstein and Redfield 2011b, 17; A. de Waal 2010, 297). But then the problem is that the only question one can ask about the humanitarian enterprise is "Does it work?" rather than "What kinds of social hierarchies does it lead to?" or "What kind of a world does it create for the people who must inhabit it?" Displaced people come to be defined solely in relation to the aid process, as "beneficiaries" whose job is to suffer and whose only value is in brute biological survival. What happens to them outside the context of the humanitarian encounter is outside the frame of the analysis, as are the strategies they use to attempt to recreate lives they feel are of value, and the communities, resources, habits, traditions, and meaning-making that goes on beyond the areas of life defined by the humanitarian project become irrelevant to the aid enterprise (cf. Malkki 1995 for a counterexample).

Viewing humanitarian aid through what Robbins (2013) calls "the suffering slot" has the unintended but insalubrious effect of replicating the ways that humanitarians constitute "beneficiaries" as victims. In the discourses and practices of aid, humanitarians strip away the specific histories and politics that caused displaced people to flee, constituting them instead as "ahistorical, universal human subjects" (Malkki 1996, 377). No longer treated as individuals with their own biographies and political standpoints, they are constituted as "pathetic victims": innocent, helpless, and suffering (Meyers 2011, 257). This rhetoric has been echoed in theoretical frameworks based on Agamben's (1998) "bare life" paradigm, which has become a mainstay in the academic analysis of humanitarianism. For Agamben, the limit case of the camp resident is the *muselmann*, a person so decimated by the camp that he has lost the ability to do anything more than exist as *zoe*, or pure animal life. Reduced to only bare physiological life, the social aspects of the camp resident become irrelevant. The bare-life paradigm has the virtue of highlighting the ways the displaced are forced to rely on their own biology as a primary means of interacting with the state or international institutions. It highlights the ways that new forms of biopolitical power operate. But in doing so, it replicates the definition of displaced people as passive and powerless, people whose status as pure victims stems from being stripped of sociality and reduced to pure biology. Even in cases where the ostensible attempt is to foreground the ways that displaced people do strategize and struggle within humanitarian regimes, the take-home point is often that the displaced have such limited agency that their struggles do little to improve their political, economic, or social situations. All they can do is suffer (see, for example, Agier 2010).

As Malkki points out, this paradigm means that "refugees stop being specific persons and become pure victims in general: universal man, universal woman, universal child, and taken together, universal family" (1996, 378). Worse still, they are often treated not as people at all, but as a mass, an incoming threat of natural disaster proportions, like a flood or a tsunami (Zetter 1991). Although many of the displaced may have contributed to resource conflicts underlying the political conflict, participated in the demonization of the opposing side, supported military action or been militants themselves or even combatants, once they become refugees or IDPs a profound silence is drawn over their pasts and they are made into pure, innocent, suffering humanity (cf. Fassin 2010, 47).

When the histories and biographies of displaced people are either eradicated or glossed quickly, and they are no longer understood in the context of a relationship to other people in their communities, they stop appearing as individuals and instead become metonyms for the entire mass of the displaced, which is treated as a mass both by the humanitarian agencies and by the anthropologists whose true object of study is not the displaced, but biopower itself (Fassin 2010). The result is that anthropological work on humanitarianism often produces a certain kind of moral sentiment: on the one hand, a well-intentioned but often maudlin pity for the suffering of the displaced, and on the other, a moral outrage against humanitarians and humanitarianism itself that often comes with a whiff of disdain and what Badiou has called the "self-satisfied egoism of the affluent West" (2002, 7). It can create two distinct forms of subjectivity: the first, a suffering human subject, and the second, an "active, determining subject of judgment—he who, in identifying suffering, knows that it must be stopped by all available means" (Badiou 2002, 9). Standing in this second subject position, the anthropologist and the humanitarian can find themselves arm in arm, sharing a sympathetic and indignant judgment that creates a shared politics of long-distance compassion (see also Fassin 2010). But the end result of using suffering as an anthropological epistemology is a problematic view of both suffering and of sovereignty. Whether locked into a politics of solidarity with the suffering displaced or denouncing the callous bureaucrats whose efforts to help are in fact part of a new politics of empire, anthropologists who have taken up the episte-mology of suffering as a lens onto displacement or humanitarianism have locked themselves into an analytic that identifies the protagonist, the victim, and the outcome of the story before it is ever told. This makes the analysis of biopower, which is the goal of this kind of anthropological research, hard to conduct. As Judith Butler writes,

> We must describe destitution ... but if the language by which we describe it presumes, time and again, that the key terms are sovereignty and bare life, we deprive ourselves of the lexicon we need to understand other networks of power to which it belongs, or how power is recast in that place or even saturated in that place (Butler and Spivak 2010, 42–43).

If, as I argue, both sovereignty and suffering are partial but insufficient frames, how should we understand humanitarianism—or, better, "life in the humani-tarian condition"—as a situation that alleviates, shapes, and sometimes causes the destitution of the displaced? What's a better lexicon for understanding the interlocking forms that power takes in a place like the Republic of Georgia—not only contemporary neoliberal biopower, which, no matter how ubiquitous, is never the only game in town, but also the jostlings of regional geopolitics, old-fashioned top-down authoritarianism, Soviet style cronyism, and the power that comes from circumventing or ignoring rules? How can we see the effects of these intertwined forms of power at multiple scales, from the international to the microscales of the camp and the body, and understand how actions at one scale might reverberate on another? And how do we understand the multiple subjectivities those reverberations might create beyond merely the twin poles of suffering and sovereignty? Focusing on the ways that displaced people are brought to camps for succor and then so often trapped there is a means of tracing out these networks of violence and care. Paying attention to particular regional histories and to the biographical trajectories of the particular individuals, like Keti or Manana or Temo, who have to work within the often conflicting structures of different kinds of power, contributes to that project. But understanding life in the humanitarian condition as a set of existential dilemmas that converge to make it difficult to leave requires more than just eschewing victimology or asking questions that go beyond issues of efficacy. As I argue throughout this book, it requires a shift in perspective from singularity to multiplicity, and from epistemology to ontology.

The Camp and the Camp

In China Miéville's brilliant novel *The City & The City* (2009), a young woman is murdered in Beszel, a dingy post-Soviet city of featureless concrete, rattling trams, and baggy suits. But the murder also occurs in Ul Qoma, a booming city in the exotic Near East, full of bright lights and flashy new buildings. It takes a visa to go "abroad" from one town to another. Yet the corpse is in Beszel and in Ul Qoma at one and the same time. The two cities are *topolgangers*: two cities in the same place, doppelgängers in a single topography. They exist in the same streets, parks, and even the same buildings, their residents carefully schooled to "unsee" one another. Citizens are trained to rule out certain aspects of reality although they are surrounded by it. But the city and the city are, occasionally, linked. There are "protubs" or inadvertent protuberances that citizens of both cities are trained to avoid without acknowledgment: a Besz drunk lurching into an Ul Qoman citizen, an Ul Qoman car careening out of control, an Ul Qoman's dog that runs up to sniff a Besz passerby.

A similarly odd and disconcerting doubling existed in the camp where Manana, Temo, and Ketevan, along with twenty-five hundred other IDPs from South Ossetia, were relocated five months after the August war. Like the other thirty-five new settlements built for the South Ossetian IDPs, the one they were sent to was on land nobody wanted. It was a low-lying, often muddy and occasionally swampy place, once part of an old Soviet agricultural research station. When I asked Temo who had owned the land before the war, he scoffed and said, "Owned it? The frogs owned it! If it had been good land, somebody would already have stolen it." The field on the west bank of the creek that ran through the old agricultural test plots was filled in with light-gray gravel roads. Then the cottages arose—all identical, all white, house after house. With no shops or churches or schools, no trees or bushes to variegate the landscape, and not even a bend in the road to break up the long march of houses, the settlement was so bleak and featureless it was disorienting. As one man asked on the day the IDPs moved in, "If I get drunk, how will I know where I live?" Even sober, I had

problems: whenever I did an interview in one of the cottages during the first year the settlement existed, I had to mark its location on a grid so I could find the people in it again.

On the frosty January day when the IDPs were moving into the settlement, I asked over and over what the name of the place was. "Name? It doesn't have a name," said Temo. I soon found out, though, that like almost all of the other settlements, it was officially named for its "host village," whatever the nearest collection of houses was called. The host village for the settlement where Temo and the others had been sent, though, had a particularly odd name. It was called Karaleti, after a village located on the curving road between Gori and Tskhinvali, the capital of South Ossetia—the same road the IDPs had fled down during the war. But the camp was 10 kilometers away from Karaleti, nowhere nearby at all. In fact it was right in a neighborhood in Gori, the provincial capital. Named for the bubbling spring that kept the surrounding ground damp, the neighborhood of Tsmindatsqali (Holy Water) housed not only the old Soviet agricultural station but also the military base where the Georgian Fifth Infantry Brigade and its attached fleet of tanks resided, and a host of dilapidated concrete apartment blocks filled with regular, non-IDP citizens of Gori. As in all the "new settlements," the people of Tsmindatsqali were perfectly free to come and go: the camp was not enclosed by any fence.

The camp and the camp: two zones occupying the same space and inhabited by many of the same people, but operating on very different logics. Karaleti was a blank slate built as the space where donor-funded humanitarian projects could provide services and govern the IDPs. It was a technicity, a town where human life was made into a technical problem that could be changed and manipulated through bureaucratic activity within the frame of projects. Time there came in staccato bursts: when the NGO workers blew into Karaleti in their white jeeps, everything happened at a breakneck pace, as if the IDPs immediate survival depended on completing this needs-assessment survey or that participatory development meeting *right now*. The IDPs in Karaleti were treated as a population to be managed. The camp was not a refuse heap for surplus humanity, but a recycling center: a place to transform the inert matter of a victim population, make it useful again, and send it back into the "normal" population (Arendt 1951; Agamben 1998; see also Bauman 2004). The blank emptiness of the relentless rows of white cottages became a screen on which the dreams of international agencies and NGO workers played out. On such a canvas, it was easy to project a bustling village full of farmers carrying the fruits of projects seeded by the NGOs, or to imagine a leafy suburb stocked with accountants, entrepreneurs, hairdressers, and other employees trained in donor-funded projects. The strange artificiality of the settlement and its oddly homogenous geography facilitated the insertion of Karaleti into its own future anterior time zone, as a town that existed not as it was but as it "will have been" once projects were "successfully implemented" (Frederiksen 2013; see also chapter 5).

In Tsmindatsqali, the camp superimposed on the same space, life was different. There were the same streets where the crunch of gravel under tires announced the few cars that arrived each day. The same faceless cottages housed people still stunned and shocked from their dramatic change in circumstance. But unlike Karaleti, a place where life itself had been rendered into a technical problem, Tsmindatsqali was a *place of being*, the terrain on which the IDPs had to work out new ways of existing in the world. Its central problem was not technical but existential. How to be the new kid in the fourth grade, for example, in a country where mobility was generally so low that most children stayed with the same group of kids from first grade until graduation? In some of the Gori schools IDP children were left to worry about permanently being stigmatized outsiders. In Manana's son Irakli's school, the school director separated the IDP children into their own segregated class. How to be beautiful in a society that put a high premium on hyperfemininity but in a situation where the IDPs weren't even wearing their own clothes? Sopo Tsuladze constantly bemoaned the shapeless orange housedress she was given to wear, saying, "Every time I get on the minibus, everybody stares at me—they know I'm an IDP." How to move around the city or the region when there was no job to justify the cost of transport? How to be hospitable in a culture where masculinity, femininity, kinship, and neighborliness were all played out in the ritual banquet (*supra*), but in circumstances where there was no food to properly host others? How to be a good neighbor when you now had to live next to people you neither knew nor trusted? Unlike the IDPs that the humanitarians envisioned as the residents of Karaleti, the real people in Tsmindatsqali were not isolated individual victims but a community whose dense sociality had taken enormous collateral damage in the war. Rebuilding those connections, both as they were and in new ways, made displacement a long-term problem rather than a short-term emergency that could be directed by NGOs or the government, or managed within the frame of a project. Displacement raised questions of postwar existence that fell completely outside the boundaries of technocratic humanitarian projects and yet constantly clashed with them.

The camp and the camp: two places on the same ground, inhabited by the same people in the same houses, built on the same roads, and yet distinctly different. One, seen by the aid workers and the nation-state, was a technicity on the margins where exiles live as victims, stripped of everything but a still-beating heart and still-breathing lungs, dumped as human garbage to be disciplined, managed, recycled, and eventually sent back into service once "socially reintegrated." The other, seen by the people who lived there, was a *place of being* where a distinct social ecosystem was violently displaced from its native mountains into the valleys, its connections and links disrupted and damaged but still existent, its people charged with somehow remaking their own social worlds. Both of them were in the same space but only tangentially and occasionally protruding into one another. Given the gap created by the separation of the two, how do we think about each camp in turn, and the differences between what the humanitarians envision and what the IDPs themselves do? Can the disjunctures and intersections of the camp and the camp explain why it is so difficult to break free of both? How do we think not only about each camp individually but both of them at once as well?

The key is to recognize that even though a single place appears to hang together in the same way all the time for all the people who interact in and around it, it can in fact be completely different in different moments because it is *enacted* in and through different practices (Mol 2002). How Karaleti is discussed, worked on, built, imagined, supplied, inhabited, and so on can be utterly distinct from how Tsmindatsqali is enacted. So to do an ethnography of Karaleti, I might be attentive to how international NGOs conceptualize humanitarianism, enact aid, and measure efficacy. I would be attentive to the technical problems that affect the aid process: the distribution of goods, the practical problems that aid workers believe displacement creates, and the projects aid agencies implement to remedy them (and, indeed, that is what I do in chapter 3). I would focus on the good intentions of the aid workers, which were manifestly real, and on the structural constraints they faced in doing the work they were deeply committed to. But from Tsmindatsqali, almost none of the aid workers' sentiments or the limitations the aid system placed on them were visible. From Tsmindatsqali, the humanitarian apparatus that engenders Karaleti appears not as a fully formed bureaucratic habitus but more as an oddly shaped, partially understood, mostly incomprehensible protuberance, much as Ul Qoma appears as a protuberance into Beszel. There is, of course, an enormous institutional structure behind the humanitarian effort: NGOs and ministries, requests for proposals and budgets, technical expert working groups and UN-sponsored cluster meetings, needs-assessment surveys and post-project evaluations, and on and on. These are the fields in which aid workers operate and in which much of their work takes place. But in Tsmindatsqali, only a fraction of that was ever seen. When the aid workers' jeeps rolled into the camp, it was as if one were lying at the bottom of a lake, watching boats pass overhead, seeing only a small white oval moving across the surface but remaining completely oblivious to the structure of the ship above it. Seen as a protuberance or a ship's keel, the projects and artifacts of humanitarianism lost their coherence. IDPs could not see what aid workers did as a product of noble ideals, or as part of a well-articulated plan that was known and understood by its ostensible "beneficiaries," or even the result of work-arounds devised by people trying to do good work in spite of a problematic institutional structure. Instead, because much of the institutional structure that humanitarian agencies were enmeshed in was invisible to the IDPs, much of what humanitarians did appeared to them as a set of unpredictable, transitory, fragmented, and often inexplicable practices that dipped in from a different world.

When I do an ethnography of Tsmindatsqali, and of the occurrence of humanitarian aid as experienced by its recipients, I see and unsee things differently from what I might see (or ignore) while thinking about the humanitarian project as it is enacted by humanitarians in Karaleti. I am not arguing with the humanitarians about what is true about the camp, as if there were one single truth about what happened there. Surely if I were to say (as I do in chapter 4) that the aid that was given was "nothing," the hundreds of humanitarian workers and employees of donor governments and ministry officials that were there could say, "Of course it wasn't nothing!" And they could pull out PowerPoint slide shows, photographs, and spreadsheets documenting all the things they handed out, and glossy four-color brochures showing what they did, and million-dollar budgets showing how much money was spent. Because of the aid industry's emphasis on monitoring and evaluation, aid agencies have baseline surveys and receipts and post-project focus group conversations documenting every step they took. It is obviously true that they did an enormous amount of work and delivered a great deal of aid. But that's only one truth. For the IDPs the aid that came was often not enough, or not exactly what was needed, or came in forms that actually impeded them from socially reintegrating. For them the projects weren't effective at poverty alleviation or social reintegration or peacebuilding, *or they wouldn't still be in the camp.* Most of the evaluation reports of NGO projects declared them a success. But why, then, did the IDPs remain poor and mired in the camps? If they could, wouldn't they leave for the city to work or to a village with enough rich land to farm and survive on? There must be another truth to consider, another state of being, one that doesn't take all the brochures and spreadsheets as either a form of action or material proof that action took place but instead asks how the things aid workers brought and the ideas they disseminated interacted with other aspects of life in ways that, as the IDPs told me, kept them alive but prevented them from really living.

Reassembling the Shards of War

So what is the central dilemma that IDPs face, if it is existential rather than technical? According to the IDPs I have worked with, the problem that war presents is the fragmentation of the lifeworld (see Nelson 2009). It is no accident that the central metaphor of literature about war is the explosion. War not only blasts the material world apart but also violently fragments time and space, as Kurt Vonnegut showed in *Slaughterhouse-Five*, and splinters the individual subject, as Ismet Prcić so brilliantly illustrated in *Shards* (2011). War is an event, a "pure break with the becoming of the world" that ruptures the network of material objects, social relations, and symbolic meanings that make the world appear as coherent, consistent, and meaningful (Badiou 2009, 99; Humphrey 2008, 360; see also Norris 2009, 9).

In this book I look at that network of objects, relations, and meanings through a framework proposed by the philosopher Alain Badiou. Badiou (2007) calls this web the "normal situation," and posits that it most often has a fairly (but not completely) stable internal structure: things and people are related to one another and distinguished from one another in ways that are the same from day to day. The normal situation is what creates place, as material things and spaces are linked in complex relations with one another (Navaro-Yashin 2012, 42). It creates subjectivity, as people are connected to one another and to social roles, and as the internal aspects of the person are linked through processes of discipline and governance (Biehl et al. 2007, 5). It creates meaning, as signs, symbols, and practices are related to one another in a relatively stable matrix. The normal situation is, of course, dynamic and changing—the web of connections is never fixed. But on a day-to-day basis, for most people around the world, the normal situation changes slowly enough that it creates a

phenomenological experience that is adequately predictable for people to cal-
culate risks and take actions that have foreseeable consequences. It is, for most
people, "a world that is in essence as rationally ordered as their thoughts about
it can be" (Jackson 2013, 31).

But the normal situation can be shattered by a capital-E "Event," in Alain
Badiou's sense of that word (Badiou 2006). War damages not only buildings
and bodies but also the way life was before the war. The traditions and routines,
places and paths, social networks and expected behaviors, symbols and personal
identities that once made up a world intimately known are all blown apart, separated from the context that gave them weight and reality and meaning. The connections between people, places, things, and meanings have been ruptured, and
the structure of sense-making gravely damaged. No longer is there a predictable
framework within which to occupy social roles, constitute economic value, and
engage in meaningful daily practice. No longer are people connected firmly to
communities or places. Without that structure, displaced people are confronted
with the free-floating shrapnel of existence: not just the protuberances of the
humanitarian project but also the scraps scavenged from their old homes, the
bits given out by kin and friends, the jobs and products obtained on the market,
the symbols and meanings handed down by the national government, and so
on. None of these are elements of a single ordering discourse (as humanitarian
projects are from the perspective of the humanitarians, or as statebuilding is for
government officials). Rather, they are elements brought into the camp without
having a preordained place in the structure of life.

My key argument, then, is that the work of the displaced is not just to wait or
to suffer. The work of the displaced is to remake the structure of their own lifeworlds. In the aftermath of a catastrophic event, displaced people must remake
themselves as coherent subjects by reforging relationships to places, things, and
other people. They must rebuild the normal situation. Doing so means confronting the void created by war and exile both individually and collectively, and
reassembling the fragments of existence into a structure that creates meaning,
affect, and place. It is a painstaking process that blends the elements that previously made up the lifeworld—not just possessions but also occupations, skills,
religious beliefs, and even the geographic features of their former villages—
with the elements of the humanitarian condition, including everything from
food deliveries and sanitation infrastructure to neoliberal market ideologies and
political symbolism, to recompose a mode of existence that is at least coherent
and somewhat stable, if not beautiful, happy, or comfortable (see Husserl
1970, 108–9).

The normal situation is not a foregone conclusion, though. In the chapters
that follow, I show how displaced people's attempts to create a normal situation

are constantly thwarted by the geopolitics, statebuilding goals, and bureaucratic practices of humanitarian aid. Despite its claims to the contrary, humanitarian bureaucracy is not based on the rational calculation, planned spatial arrangements, and ordering principles of what Foucault (2007) described as pastoral care. Rather, as I show in chapter 3, it is an *adhocracy* based on guessing, satisficing, and "winging it" that governs through a chaotic mode of domination (see also Nazpary 2001). As I show in chapter 4, the humanitarian condition is also full of existential voids, nodes in the network that aren't filled themselves, but merely point to all that has been lost. In chapters 5 and 6 I argue that because abandonment is part of the humanitarian temporal cycle of emergency and withdrawal (see Calhoun 2010), humanitarianism leads to black holes of expectation that create an ontology of crushing economic, political, and social pressure that kills and maims. Yet, as I show in chapter 7, life in the humanitarian condition also contains the potential for resurrection in one form or another. In the Georgian camps funeral rituals for those believed to have been killed by life in the humanitarian condition allowed IDPs to displace the humanitarian camp of Karaleti and rebuild their old villages as topolgangers on the soil of Tsmindatsqali.

What eight years following a single group of displaced people shows is that the most pressing problem in camps for displaced people is not just physical suffering but existential disorder and profound uncertainty as well. Although uncertainty may be a universal human problem, it is desperately acute for displaced people, for whom existential uncertainty about the near future is a central aspect of everyday life (Finnstrom 2008, 12). I argue here that the bewildering and often paralyzing nature of life in insile is not merely due to the fog of war but is also an integral part of life in the humanitarian condition. Uncertainty and confusion were problems largely overlooked by the humanitarians themselves, who were focused on technical solutions and who allocated the activity of organizing and planning to themselves rather than the IDPs. Yet for the IDPs themselves it was the unknown path to the future and the unpredictability of life in the humanitarian condition that made social reintegration such a perilous project. They were profoundly unsettled—not just spatially but also emotionally and socially.

So can the people displaced from South Ossetia successfully remake the normal situation, including themselves, their homes, and themselves as subjects, in the humanitarian condition? Will they do so along the neoliberal lines proposed by Western humanitarianism and development? Will they, instead, either cause or be subject to another outbreak of violence in the region, another round of the same ongoing war? Or will they be trapped in a long-term limbo, waiting for decades and generations?

WAR

The battle in the Caucasus in 2008 was, by all accounts, a very small war. At first blush it looked like a conflict between Georgia, a postage-stamp sized country that most outsiders knew little about, and South Ossetia, a breakaway province that almost nobody outside Georgia had ever heard of. Only a few hundred people were killed, not much infrastructure was destroyed, and the war seemed to be of negligible geopolitical consequence. All in all, it seemed highly forgettable: yet another of the ethnic skirmishes that had become increasingly frequent since the end of the Cold War, of little interest to anybody outside the region.

Yet from the first day I came to the IDP settlements, people of all political backgrounds took great pains to explain to me that this was no simple ethnic scrimmage. "It wasn't neighbors fighting against neighbors, not for the fifteen years between the two wars, when the Ossetians were shooting at us in the night, and not during the war this year," said Tamar Gigauri, an ardent Georgian nationalist from Eredvi. "It was a politically motivated fight started by Russia. We were close to our Ossetian neighbors before the war. Then our children started killing each other." Temo Javakhishvili, the man whose son was killed in a bomb blast, said much the same thing. "The NGOs want me to go to some peacebuilding class. But we're not the ones who need training in peacebuilding! Send Bush and Putin, that's who you should send," he said. "They're the ones who started it, anyway."

Far faster than television pundits or political analysts, the IDPs in the settlements understood that the conflict was a conflict of global geopolitical

importance. It was, they explained to me, a clash between the competing projects of the world's superpowers. And it was one that would rework the international order devised at the end of the Cold War in 1989. On one side was Russian
neoimperialism: the struggle to emerge from the humiliation of post-Soviet collapse, to regain a spot on the world stage, and to reestablish a Russian "sphere
of influence" on the territory of its historical empire. Underlying the Russian
project was a unique concept of human rights based on collective identity and
difference. On the other side was the institutional expansion of the European
project, including the enlargement of the European Union (EU) and the North
Atlantic Treaty Organization (NATO) and the continuing expansion of the
neoliberal rule of markets into former Soviet space. Premised on a notion of
human rights attached to individuals, European expansion had been the political centerpiece of the previous two decades of postsocialist transformation. The
2008 war was thus a battle about the limits of Europe, both in terms of how far
eastward expansion could continue and in terms of how much so-called European values could be applied to very different societies. Despite its appearance
as a small-scale ethnic conflict, the 2008 war signaled the end of the post–Cold
War interregnum and the beginning of a new world order in which the Russian
Empire would once again play a significant role. If the end of the USSR and the
expansion of the European Union were supposed to signal "the end of history"
and the triumph of Western liberal democracy (Fukuyama 1992), the war in
South Ossetia was "the end of the end of history": history roaring back with

a vengeance to challenge the fundamental precepts of post–Cold War sovereignty (see Asmus 2010).

In attempting to write a narrative that will explain the origin of this conflict, I am acutely aware that the historical narrative is deeply contested and that each side—the Russians, the Ossetians, the Georgians, and the Western Europeans—has a story about the war that describes different events on different dates and assigns motives to the other participants that have nothing in common with the other sides' own accounts of what happened. The narrative I tell in this chapter is necessarily shaped by the fact that my fieldwork was in Georgia, and since I was unable to enter South Ossetia I mostly heard the official narrative given by the government of Georgia. But even in the Georgian camp, there were always whispers of other, suppressed histories: Ossetian women would pull me aside and in hurried voices quietly tell me about atrocities carried out by Georgians. A few times Georgian women would pull me aside to give me opposing narratives: bitterly nationalist accounts of the atrocities committed by Ossetians against Georgians. More than once I heard virulently racist stories of the war from drunken Georgian men—men I knew had Ossetian mothers or grandmothers—that implicated both them and their Ossetian neighbors. And of course there was the Russian version broadcast on Russian television, told in Russian newspaper articles, and even made into a television movie. So in presenting the historical background and the events of the 2008 war, I have tried whenever possible to present all the conflicting narratives of a given historical moment. I was not present at any of these events, and so can only describe the same confused, hazy mess of history that all those who tried to make sense of it, from the Council of the European Union to the US Congress to independent historians, had to confront.

Ethnicity and Rights in the Russian Empire

Understanding either the local or the macrogeopolitical conflicts that played out during the 2008 Russo-Georgian War means understanding how ethnicity has been constructed in that part of the world, and how political and social rights have been carefully tied to ethnic identity there. The Caucasus, a small land bridge between Asia and Europe bordered by a mountain range with summits over 18,000 feet, has been multiethnic since antiquity.

Georgia boasts of visits from the ancient Greeks to the part of Georgia that was then ancient Colchis, voyages that were described by the geographer Strabo in the first century AD (Rayfield 2012, 27; T. de Waal 2010, 8). Ossetians also claim ancient roots in the region, arguing that they are the descendants of an Indo-Iranian group that settled in the North Caucasus around 350 AD. Sources vary on when the Ossetians crossed the Caucasus ridge to settle on the south slope. Some date this to the thirteenth century (Zamira 2005; see also Togoshvili 1985, cited in Saparov 2010, 100); others argue that the Ossetians did not arrive on the territory of what is now Georgia until the sixteenth or seventeenth century (see Totadze 2006, 44–45; Topchishvili 2009; Jojua 2007; Hunter 2006, 119). Whereas for most Western observers the centuries of Ossetian residence on the south slope of the Caucasus constitute enough time to consider the Ossetians legitimate inhabitants of the region, for some Georgian nationalists the Ossetians are still "guests" on the territory of Georgia who should be grateful that they are allowed to stay (Topchishvili 2009, 3; Sabanadze 2014, 122; Higgins and O'Reilly 2009, 568).

These two groups are only two among the more than fifty ethnolinguistic groups inhabiting the Caucasus range, including Kabardins, Abkhaz, Circassians, Lezgins, Svans, Mingrelians, and others. Yet the mere fact that the place has a large number of diverse ethnic groups isn't in itself an explanation of conflict: although Georgians and Ossetians have very different languages, they share a religion (Orthodoxy) and a wide array of customs, and they frequently intermarry. A more important factor has been Georgia's location at the edge of empires. Since at least the sixth century AD, Georgia has been wedged between more powerful states that seek to control it politically, including the Arabs, the Seljuk Persians, the Safavid Persians, the Ottomans, the Russians, and most lately, NATO and the European Union (Rayfield 2012, 55; Hunter 2006, 112). The Caucasus is not just a crossroads of empire, but a *crumple zone* of empire. Like the crumple zone in a car, which absorbs the force of a collision between powerful forces, the Caucasus is a site where the impact and force of expanding and colliding empires is most strongly felt.[1] For centuries, as empires have expanded they have met and battled on the terrain of the Caucasus.

In the eighteenth century the south slope of the Caucasus Mountains was forcibly incorporated into the tsarist empire. It was then that the principle of differentiated collective rights based on ethnicity, which is central to understanding imperial power dynamics in both the tsarist and Soviet periods, began (Burbank 2006, 398). Before the Russians took power the southern lowlands of the Caucasus range had been a feudal aristocracy, and the Machabelis[2] and the Eristavis, two Georgian princely houses, had laid claim to the territory of what is now South Ossetia (Vaneev 1956, 72 and 77, cited in Saparov 2014, 29). But in the late eighteenth and early nineteenth centuries, Russia began to absorb Georgian provinces, including Kartli and Kakheti, which included what is now South Ossetia, making them a governate or *guberniya* of the Russian Empire (Rayfield 2012, 259).[3] Georgians were not the only inhabitants of the newly absorbed territory. Roughly a quarter of the population was made up of Armenians, Greeks, Jews, Azeris, Abkhaz, Mingrelians, Adjaran Muslims, and Russians. The territory also included small groups in the highlands, among them Kists (Chechens),

Svans, and of course Ossetians (a significant proportion of whom were Muslim before incorporation into the Russian Empire, but who were largely converted to Orthodox Christianity in the late eighteenth century).[4] As had been true for centuries, ethnicity was mapped onto class. The Georgians made up the landed aristocracy as well as a substantial portion of the peasantry, the Ossetians and other highlanders were largely peasants, and the Armenians, who were concentrated in urban areas, made up much of the merchant class.

In the Russian Empire, ethnicity shaped people's relationship to the state and the rights they had as citizens of the empire in ways that it did not in Western Europe or the United States. The concept of human rights that was developed in the West in the late eighteenth and early nineteenth centuries was premised on the notion that rights inhere in the individual and that those rights are identical for each citizen, who is seen as equal before the law. In the Russian Empire, however, rights were based on a completely different set of principles. Rather than granting universal human rights that were the same for all people, the tsar granted rights to groups, usually defined on the basis of religion and ethnicity, and granted rights to individuals only as members of those groups. Different groups were thus assigned different bundles of rights: Ossetians, for example, had different rights than did Georgians or Kists. As Burbank writes,

> What was "natural" to Russian conceptions of law was not the possession of rights by individuals, but the practice of social regulation by groups . . . the law recognized and incorporated particularity and retained its claim to be the ultimate source of justice. (2006, 402)

Each set of rights corresponded to different kinds of state administrative structures because the Russian Empire incorporated local forms of government, customary legal systems, and educational institutions into the state at local and regional levels (Burbank 2006, 403; see also Beyer 2006 and 2014). Although later iterations of Russian imperial policy incorporated aspects of the Enlightenment-era conception of rights as it was used in the West, the Russian Empire generally treated the rights assigned to groups as manipulable and alienable rather than inalienable and assigned to the individual, as in the Western tradition. As Beyer writes,

> Rights belonged to people because, and only because, they were allocated to particular groups by the state . . . the state kept for itself the authority to assign, reassign and take away rights, duties and privileges from the groups that comprised the empire's population." (2006, 403).

A group's loyalty and service to the state, then, mattered enormously. A group that earned the pleasure of imperial administrators would be granted more rights and more autonomy to manage its own affairs, whereas uncooperative groups could be easily sanctioned.

This notion of governance based on difference shaped a distinctively Russian imperial notion of territory too. Unlike the emerging Western nation-state system, which held out the Westphalian ideal of an ethnically homogeneous population, a bounded territory and a state that governed both, the Russian Empire was never premised on the notion of a homogeneously ethnicized geography. From the very beginning the Russian Empire assumed that any given part of its territory held a mixture of ethnic groups. As Burbank writes, "the Russian imperial rights regime took place in a polity based on difference" (2006, 406).

Thus for the population of what is now South Ossetia—then about two-thirds Ossetian and one-third Georgian—both ethnic difference and the always tenuous relationship to imperial power came to matter a great deal. But the imperial regime often shifted its favor from one group to another, shifting the privileges that it granted to different ethnic groups as it did. For example, in 1804, a mere few months after all of Georgia was absorbed into the Russian Empire, Ossetian peasants rebelled against Russian military forces, who whipped them and threw them into pits full of dead cats, whey, and excrement (Rayfield 2012, 263). But just a few years later, in 1826, the tide turned, the Ossetians gained favor and were granted special privileges, including an exemption from the taxes and corvées that Georgian peasants had to endure (Rayfield 2012, 277).

Georgians received equally capricious treatment under the Russian Empire. In 1845 Viceroy Mikhail Vorontsov believed that the Georgians, more civilized than the Chechens and Ingush he was battling in the North Caucasus, should be ruled by consent rather than by force. He convinced Tsar Nicholas I to recognize the Georgian nobility, which tied them closely to the administrative structures of the empire (T. de Waal 2010, 45). Vorontsov also promoted cultural links between Georgia and Europe. He made it possible for Georgian students to study at universities in other places in the empire and established a theater in Tbilisi that imported ballet dancers and opera singers from Italy (Rayfield 2012, 288). The Russian belief that Georgia was an "oasis of European culture" in the otherwise savage Caucasus convinced the Georgians to turn toward Europe and to see themselves as a European country (Jersild 2002, 7; see also Rayfield 2012, 289; Manning 2012).

In the mid-nineteenth century, ethnicity, which was already linked to rights, was also linked to territory. The Ossetians were so restive that the Russian military authorities decided to create a special district, the Osetinskii okrug, a politico-territorial designation that endured for seventeen years before it was returned to other administrative units (Saparov 2010, 112). The term *okrug* indicated the intensity of rule: okrugs in the Russian Empire were districts ruled militarily, usually by Cossack armies (Saparov 2014, 30). This was the first time that the ethnonym "Ossetian" had been attached to a specific territory on an administrative map; notably, the okrug contained lands both north and south of the Caucasus ridge (Saparov 2014, 30). Inside the okrug the Ossetians had a special package of rights that gave them less autonomy than the Georgians, but more rights than the Abkhaz or the Chechens, who were being brutally suppressed by Russian forces (Rayfield 2012, 289; Gall and de Waal 1998, 309; see also Vaneev 1956, cited in Saparov 2014, 30). The rights of one group were not just different from those of another but were also obtained at the expense of the other group, which created enormous competition and jockeying for the favor of the imperial power.

The differences between the Georgians and the Ossetians were compounded by the arrival of capitalism and urbanization in the last quarter of the nineteenth century. Although Georgia was never fully industrialized, industrialization in Western Europe gave Georgians the chance to export minerals, wine, grain, and cotton, and they began flocking to Tbilisi to pursue business interests (Gachechiladze, Nadzhafaliyev, and Rondeli 1984, 67). Soon they made up 25% of the city's population (Rayfield 2012, 302). This created an educated urban elite that was soon connected with events and ideas from outside the country by newspapers such as *Droeba* and *Iveria*, which fostered a sense of the Georgian nation as inherently European. Meanwhile the Ossetians, still mainly concentrated in the highlands above the town of Tskhinvali, remained rural people isolated from capitalist development and the politics of the capital. Kept outside the burgeoning export trade in natural resources and agricultural goods, the Ossetians did not participate in capitalist development but remained peasants and pastoralists (as well as postal riders, thanks to their proximity to the Georgian military highway). Georgia's growing urban elite posed a problem for the Ossetians, even if they did not know it at first. In Tbilisi a group of young journalists led by Ilia Chavchavadze and Niko Nikoladze developed a Westphalian form of Georgian nationalism, which argued that each nation should occupy and control a territory that was its alone, and began demanding Georgian statehood (T. de Waal 2010, 36; King 2008, 3). Thus the rise of Georgian nationalism and the defense of Georgians' rights soon began to imply a threat to Ossetians' views of their national identity, their claims to territory, and their rights as subjects of the state.

The First Georgian Republic: 1918–1920

In the beginning of the twentieth century, as the Russian Empire began to show signs of weakness, nationalists were not the only groups thinking about the so-called nationalities problem. The Bolsheviks too were beginning to think about how to contend with the complicated politics emerging from nationalist movements. Joseph Stalin—who was born in Gori, Georgia, where Georgian and Ossetian national identities came into conflict—argued in 1913 that national and ethnic identities should be suppressed, since they could only prevent workers from understanding their common class-based interests and thus harm the workers' movement (Stalin 1954, 303–304 and 338; see also Hirsch 2005, 27, 43.) But Lenin, the leader of the Bolshevik revolutionaries, argued that for peoples oppressed by colonialism and empire, national identity was not antithetical to class identity but was actually *the same as* class identity and should be supported by the Communist Party because it was a "progressive thing of the future" that would speed workers through capitalism and toward socialism (Lenin 1916; see also Hirsch 2005, 29, 51–52). This was a politically calculated move on the part of Lenin, who quickly realized that the promise of national autonomy could rally non-Russian groups to the Bolshevik cause (Hirsch 2005, 53).

In February 1917 the Russian monarchy collapsed and the empire was no more. Within months Russia was in the midst of a bloody war in which the Bolshevik (majority) Party fought the Menshevik (minority) Party and other political forces for control of the government. For Georgia, like other non-Russian territories on the periphery of the empire, the collapse of the empire and the ensuing chaos in Russia offered a chance for independence (Saparov 2010, 100). The Menshevik Party, led by Noe Zhordania, won national elections and began forming the government of the Transcaucasian Federation, a new state that included Armenia and Azerbaijan (Jones 2005; T. de Waal 2010). But the new state lasted only a few months before it fell apart, leaving Georgia on its own to form a state. Zhordania himself thought that declaring independence was a weak position, an act of tragic historic necessity occasioned by the need to protect Georgia from the Ottoman Empire (T. de. Waal 2010). But he knew that once Georgia existed as an independent state, it was essential that both it and the Marxist doctrines of the Mensheviks leading it gain legitimacy and support among its populace. Just as Lenin had foreseen, political propaganda based on class interests did surprisingly little to forge legitimacy for the new government among peasants and urban workers. Instead the Menshevik government had to turn to nationalism to rally the population (Higgens and O'Reilly 2009, 569). This posed a huge threat to non-Georgian populations within the new boundaries of the First Georgian Republic, who could foresee a future in which they were decidedly unequal as citizens. So they rebelled. The Abkhaz set up their own national council and declared their membership in a federal North Caucasian republic of highland groups. The Ossetians soon followed suit, seeing a chance to displace the Georgians and seize lands for themselves. In a bloody battle the Ossetians at first captured Tskhinvali, but were repelled by Georgian troops (Saparov 2010, 102; Rayfield 2012, 326).

Faced with Georgia's superior military strength, the Ossetians soon decided to seek the protection of a powerful patron. In 1920 they pledged their loyalty to the Bolsheviks (Saparov 2014, 70; Welt 2014, 209). In response the Menshevik People's Guard of Georgia led a massacre, recapturing the territory by slaughtering thousands of people and forcing between twenty thousand and thirty-five thousand to flee into North Ossetia[5] (T. de Waal 2010; Welt 2014, 222; Sabanadze 2014, 126; Saparov 2014, 70). This event had a searing effect on Ossetian national consciousness: even today, nationalists refer to the 1920 rebellion and suppression as "the Ossetian genocide" (Saparov 2014, 74; Gazzaev 2010; Pavlovsky 2008). As Chigoev writes of that time:

> The Georgians aimed to physically destroy the Ossetians and/or to arrange their exodus to the North Caucasus. Over 18,000 Ossetians died in that war; close to 50,000 Ossetians became refugees and never returned to their motherland. And while Georgia never achieved its goal of complete liquidation or exile of the native South Ossetian population, the South Ossetian people suffered severe damage. (2011)

There is no evidence that the Georgians intended to eliminate the Ossetians as a group. But it is clear that the Georgians meant to expel the Ossetians from the south slopes of the Caucasus, going so far as to create a government commission for "resettlement" that had as its charge the full removal of Ossetians from the area (Saparov 2014, 74). This began a nasty cycle of suspicion and repression, where Georgia suspected the Ossetians of being Russian puppets and engaged in brutal tactics to rid itself of what it saw as an internal threat (Rayfield 2012, 327). The stage was set for a recurring pattern in which the Ossetians called on the Russians whenever they felt threatened by Georgian ethnonationalism. The local politics of ethnic rights had become tightly entwined with the politics of global empire in dangerous ways.

Soviet Ethnonationalism

In February 1921 Georgia's short-lived independence came to an end. Having taken over the government of Russia after a long civil war, the Bolshevik Red Army attacked Georgia, the Mensheviks' stronghold. With no imperial protector, the Georgians had little choice but to acquiesce to the incorporation of their territory into the rapidly expanding Union of Soviet Socialist Republics, which was politically organized on the basis of ethnonationalism. In the USSR, ethnic

boundaries were "ontologically essential, essentially territorial, and ideally political" (Slezkine 1994, 418). Like the tsarist government, the Soviets believed that
different nations should have different baskets of rights. But unlike the imperial
government, the Soviets tied those rights firmly to territory and demanded that
ethnographic and administrative borders coincide. Like multiple families living
in a communal apartment, each ethnic group was supposed to get a "room" or
territory of its own, with larger and "more cultured" nations given more territory and more autonomy (Slezkine 1994, 430, 434; Tishkov 1991, 604; Lapidus
1991, 701). Georgia had the status of union republic, one of fifteen in the USSR.
Within the union republics, autonomous soviet socialist republics (ASSRs) such
as the Abkhaz and Adjarian ASSRs inside Georgia had a significant amount of
autonomy, especially in cultural matters like publishing and education in the
local language. Beneath that were the autonomous oblasts, like South Ossetia,
whose rights were much more circumscribed but who still were permitted special
rights, such as a disproportionate share of seats on local soviets, media in their
own language, a greater number of school and university admissions, more jobs
in local factories, and so on (Slezkine 1994, 439).

Given the linkage between ethnicity, territory, and political power, it was
not surprising that the number of groups clamoring to be counted as a nation
within the Soviet Empire increased to more than one hundred. "The dictatorship of the proletariat was a Tower of Babel," writes Slezkine (1994, 439). It was
"the most extravagant celebration of ethnic diversity that any state had ever
financed" (414). The Soviets had not simply taken over a territory full of preexisting ethnic groups but had actually *made* ethnic groups by making ethnonationalism a salient and consequential principle of political power (Comaroff
1991, 672).

The notion that an ethnic group should be contained in a single contigu-
ous territory, however, did not match up well with the ethnic diversity and
intermixing of ethnic populations in the Caucasus. In South Ossetia the border included both ethnically Ossetian and ethnically Georgian villages inter-
spersed with one another, resulting in a population that was simultaneously
mixed and segregated (Saparov 2014, 84). Georgian nationalists often argue
that the establishment of South Ossetia was part of a revenge plot by Stalin,
who bore a grudge against the Georgian people and deployed a divide-and-rule
strategy aimed at keeping Georgia weak enough so that it could be dominated
by Russia (see, for example, Bonner 1995, 772; d'Encausse 1993; cf. Sabanadze
2014, 123, cf. Saparov 2014, 87). But it was neither personal grudge nor diabolic anti-Georgian political strategy that led Stalin to advocate for autonomous regions inside Georgia. It was the result of a USSR-wide policy to gain
support for socialism by fostering nationalism. Stalin, the man who originally

opposed nationalism as a principle of territorial organization and who had rejected his own Georgian national identity in favor of becoming Russified, ironically become the architect of Soviet ethnonationalism. As Rayfield (2012, 364) argues, Stalin somehow had transcended nationality: Even Stalin's son, Vasili, once told his sister Svetlana that "our father used to be a Georgian," implying that in becoming Soviet Stalin had a national identity that was something different from or more than Georgian. This tension between ethnonational and Soviet identities created lasting conundrums for both the Georgian and Ossetian residents of his home region.

The Fall of the USSR and the Return of Ethnonationalism

The Cold War, for all its tensions and strains, had the virtue of creating relative political and geographic stability. While the USSR had gained territory for itself and its satellite states during World War II, NATO and the Warsaw Pact had tacitly agreed after the war that the Soviet sphere of influence would extend all the way to the Berlin Wall, but no further. The boundaries of Europe were therefore largely stable for more than forty years. Inside the USSR ethnoterritorial relations were also quite stable. Ethnic groups that had named territories after World War II kept them, and smaller ethnic groups with aspirations to autonomy knew there were unlikely to be changes to the map of the Soviet Union. Inside the autonomous oblast of South Ossetia, ethnic relations were calm. Georgians and Ossetians worked together, lived near one another (particularly in Tskhinvali), and frequently became family to one another through intermarriage.

With the collapse of the USSR in 1991 the geographic stability that had existed since the end of World War II suddenly evaporated, leaving national boundaries and spheres of influence in Europe up for grabs. Soviet satellite countries, including Poland, the Czech Republic, and Hungary, raced to join NATO and the European Union. Soviet republics such as Latvia, Lithuania, and Estonia also left to join Western Europe. Russia, reeling from the collapse of its empire, could only stand by as the buffer zone that once stood between it and the Western democracies eroded. For the Russian government, the end of empire constituted an existential security threat (Mearsheimer 2014). But with an economy in freefall and a military weakened by aging weapons, there was little it could do to stop the exodus. In a series of agreements beginning with the Charter of Paris in 1990 and continuing through a series of agreements reached under the auspices of the Organization for Security and Cooperation in Europe (OSCE), Russia pledged to accept the right of all states to choose their own security alliances and agreed not to change borders through the use of force (Asmus 2010; 200). This agreement, and the territorial limits it implied, would become the key issue behind the 2008 war. As Western Europe expanded into what had been Soviet territory, where were the limits of empire? What would happen if the Western powers had access to strategic sites on Russia's very borders?

Nationalism, the vocabulary in which smaller groups sought to carve out power from the remains of the Soviet Union, made the problem of expanding and contracting empires even more difficult to address. With ethnonationalist movements erupting all across the former Eastern Bloc, it was no surprise that it was the political means through which Georgia, led by the radical nationalist Zviad Gamsakhurdia, broke away from the fragmenting remains of the USSR. His political program showed why the idea that rights belonged to ethnic or national groups was a more powerful political tool than the Western notions of democratization and universal human rights attached to individuals. But Gamsakhurdia's nationalist rhetoric was a double-edged sword: no sooner had he helped Georgia establish independence than he plunged it into ethnic conflict, civil war, and total economic collapse.

Ironically Gamsakhurdia did not start out as a rabid nationalist but as a dissident who, like many other Soviet-era dissidents, spoke out in favor of a European notion of human rights. In the 1970s he helped to found the Initiative Group for the Defense of Human Rights, became the first Georgian member of Amnesty International, and helped establish the Georgian branch of the Helsinki Group, a nongovernmental organization aimed at monitoring Soviet compliance with international human rights agreements (Zürcher 2007, 128). Like other advocates for human rights in the USSR, Gamsakhurdia was punished for speaking out against the state: he served three years of hard labor plus three years of exile for "anti-Soviet activities" (Zürcher 2007, 128). Yet as the power of the Soviet national government began to wane in the late 1980s under Gorbachev's glasnost and perestroika policies, Gamsakhurdia dropped his focus on universal human rights. Instead he articulated a vision of independent Georgia as a powerful Christian state led by the spiritually, culturally, and politically superior Georgians, with the national minority groups held to a subordinate place in the political system (Jones 2013, 59).

Three aspects of the post-Soviet situation made nationalism the overwhelmingly dominant mode of social organization in the post-Soviet space in the 1990s while severely limiting the space for a liberal notion of human rights. First, the destruction of the USSR destroyed or discredited many of the cross-cutting identities that had made the multiethnic Soviet society relatively stable. Although the state had once promoted a "Soviet" identity meant to supersede ethnonational identity, that was obviously gone after the demise of the USSR. Class- or occupation-based identities too became completely discredited, and any talk of people banding together as workers was seen as Soviet and propagandistic, and thus anathema (Yamskov 1991, 654). What was left behind was largely national identity, the one form of being that the USSR promoted heavily but did not incorporate well into Marxist dogma.

Second, ethnonationalism had the virtue of providing not only a theory of the relation of non-Russian groups to the Soviet state, but also a theory of their relations to each other at that historical moment as they became competitors for power and resources. Since the Soviet authority had constituted a system of nationalities that was structured like nesting dolls, one inside another, it became increasingly logical to assert that if a union republic could break away from the USSR, an ASSR or an autonomous oblast could break away from a union republic. Because the USSR had linked ethnicity, political power, and territory, ethnonational identity became the ground on which people fought for political power as the country dissolved into ever-smaller constituent territorial units. Post-Soviet ethnonationalism was "remedial" in that it aimed at redressing historical injustices inflicted by the Soviet regime while constituting each nationalist as a victim of that injustice (Sabanadze 2014, 127). Thus, like many other nationalities in the former USSR, both the Georgians and South Ossetians came to see themselves as culturally besieged, their very existence as a group threatened and territorial autonomy the only remedy.

Third, although nationalism was almost exclusively oriented toward mobilizing the population for independence, there was very little thought anywhere in the former USSR about who would govern afterward or how minorities would be incorporated into new states controlled by their titular nationalities. Thus, by its very nature, ethnonationalism posed the strong likelihood that those ethnic groups that could not secure their own territory and state would be almost completely deprived of political power and a role in the new state. Citizenship itself was jeopardized for all minority groups, and basic human rights, which in the post-Soviet space were organized on the grounds of nationality, not humanity, were deeply threatened. This made ethnic identity more important than it had been even in the imperial or Soviet periods. Because one's entire existence hinged on membership in an ethnic group, people were more invested in their ethnic identification and more willing to see people with different identifications as radically and frighteningly other (see Comaroff 1991, 670).

Zviad Gamsakhurdia launched a politics almost completely based on those three aspects of post-Soviet nationalism (Cheterian 2008, 169). As London's *Independent* newspaper put it, "The fall of the Berlin Wall in November 1989 heralded the rise of nationalism and ethnic exclusiveness. Georgia is living testimony to the destructiveness of this potent mixture and Gamsakhurdia was its high priest" (McCauley 1994). He promised to limit mixed marriages, enshrine Georgian as the official state language, and restrict the rights of non-Georgians, whom Gamsakhurdia posited as "guests" of the rightful Georgian owners of the territory (Barry 2008, A6). At a rally in the town of Akhalsopeli, Gamsakhurdia made his position clear:

> Can you not understand that at this precise moment a conspiracy against your people is being put into action? The enemy is right here, disguised in our midst. Give him the reply he justly deserves. Go for these traitors, pour the melted lead of the Georgian nation over them! We shall not permit ourselves to be abused. . . . We shall put an end to all these traitors, we shall put the truth under their noses, we shall work for the speedy dispatch of all foreigners living in our land. (Van der Leeuw 1998, 153)

The Ossetians had little choice but to respond with their own variant of populist ethnonationalism. In 1989 Adamon Nykhas, the South Ossetian Popular Front, began to offer up equally strong rhetoric, demanding more political autonomy vis-à-vis Georgia (Saparov 2014, 149). At first Adamon Nykhas demanded that South Ossetia should be upgraded to the status of union republic within the still-standing USSR. But on November 23, 1989 Gamsakhurdia, who had fostered intense discussions about the illegitimacy of Ossetian claims to territory, led a caravan of buses and cars holding twelve to fourteen thousand Georgians to Tskhinvali, the South Ossetian capital (Rayfield 2012, 378). The march was an enormous provocation. To the sixty-nine thousand Ossetians resident in South Ossetia, the marchers seemed like an invading force. Violent clashes ensued, killing several people and leading thousands of others to flee to North Ossetia.

In December 1990 the Georgian Supreme Soviet adopted a law preventing Ademon Nykhas from participating in parliamentary elections. The Ossetians replied by escalating their previous demands and declaring themselves a union republic equal in stature to Georgia. Gamsakhurdia, who had been elected chairman of the Supreme Council of the Republic of Georgia, was intent on preserving the territorial integrity of Georgia while leading it out of the USSR. He led the Supreme Soviet in denying South Ossetia's request for separation and abolishing its autonomous status. He declared a state of emergency and sent several thousand Georgian troops to occupy the territory. By December 1990, as the Soviet Union was falling apart, Georgia and South Ossetia were in a state of open warfare (Rayfield 2012, 380).

The war inflicted enormous damage on South Ossetia. Eighty percent of the dwellings in Tskhinvali were destroyed by 1992 (Zürcher 2007, 126). Approximately fifty thousand ethnic Ossetians were forced to leave Georgia and migrate to North Ossetia. But Ossetia was not Gamsakhurdia's only battleground. He was also was fighting other conflicts at the same time, including inside his own government. In August 1991, at the same moment that Mikhael Gorbachev was battling a coup attempt in Moscow, Gamsakhurdia faced a coup attempt from the leader of the Georgian National Guard and the prime minister. A ferocious civil war erupted. Gamsakhurdia fled to Armenia, but then returned and began fighting from his home region in western Georgia (McCauley 1994). But then, suddenly, on December 31, 1993 he was found dead with a single bullet wound to the head. Although his widow proclaimed it was suicide, rumors of his murder were widely circulated (Independent 1994; see also Rayfield 2012, 384).[6]

Georgia soon deteriorated even further as war broke out in Abkhazia. With Russian backing the Abkhaz ousted more than 220,000 ethnic Georgians from the breakaway province in thirteen months of brutal fighting (Rayfield 2012, 384). Left as IDPs, the Georgians in Abkhazia were sheltered in libraries, schools, Soviet-era Intourist hotels, and other public buildings, where they would remain for more than twenty-eight years. On both Rustaveli Avenue, Tbilisi's main boulevard, and on Konstantin Gamsakhurdia Street, a major thoroughfare ironically named after Zviad Gamsakhurdia's father, huge hotels were transformed into vertical refugee camps (Manning 2008). The Hotel Kartli in Gori was likewise full to the brim with people displaced from South Ossetia. These makeshift shelters were constant reminders to the Georgians of the loss of territorial integrity and the implosion of the state.

The coup d'état, civil war, and the wars in South Ossetia and Abkhazia left Georgia a postapocalyptic wreck (Rayfield 2012, 380). Even after Eduard Shevardnadze, the former Soviet foreign minister, was called back to be the Georgian head of state, the country remained a failed state. The economy plummeted, leaving Georgia with a GDP per capita barely higher than Sudan's (Jones 2013, 76; IMF 2015). Infrastructure fell to rubble and the hulks of wrecked factories, destroyed collective farm buildings, and crumbling urban apartment buildings dominated the landscape. Much of the country was run by illegitimate paramilitaries and organized crime. The power grid nearly collapsed and the country was without consistently available gas or electricity. All of the residents of the territory—including Georgians, Ossetians, and Abkhaz—were left in the desolated ruins of a decimated society. Indeed, when I first visited Georgia in 2002, before the Rose Revolution, the most striking visual feature of the country was its ruination. Tbilisi had pockmarked streets, buildings with bullet holes from the civil war still visible, and apartment buildings with pitch-dark hallways of crumbling concrete. The road to Batumi, on the western coast, passed through orange

groves where rotting fruit was falling off the trees and tea plantations choked with weeds. (Describing Batumi to a friend there after my first trip in 2002, I said, only half-jokingly, "Imagine Miami. Now imagine Miami in the Soviet Union. Now imagine Miami in the Soviet Union after a nuclear war.")

As Shevardnadze said at the opening session of parliament in 1992:

> Outside this chamber there is another Georgia where people are perishing, starving, where schools cannot work normally . . . where hospitals lack proper medicines and culture is on the edge of destruction (Shevardnadze 1992, cited in Jones 2013, 102).

The dissolution of empire and the rise of nationalism in Georgia was a calamity of epic proportions. But Georgia was not alone: a civil war in Tajikistan, war between Armenia and Azerbaijan over the disputed region of Nagorno-Karabakh, a war between the North Ossetians and the Ingush, and two savage wars in Chechnya were all similar conflicts based on ethnonationalist uprisings. These conflicts on its borders, particularly in Chechnya, gave Russia reason to fear for its own security and territorial integrity. But even worse, from Russia's point of view, was the fact that NATO and the European Union used local separatist movements as a means to expand and gain strategic footholds on Russia's borders. Russian politicians began to fear that the post–Cold War bargain in which it agreed to respect existing national boundaries would eventually mean that NATO would jeopardize Russia itself (Mearsheimer 2014).

The Rose Revolution

For nearly a decade Georgia languished as a failed state. Petty corruption was an endemic problem with police officers demanding bribes, armed paramilitaries staging roadblocks and demanding payoffs, and educators taking payments in exchange for higher marks (Rayfield 2012, 388). On my first trip to Georgia in 2002 I saw this myself. We were pulled off the road multiple times by police who demanded payoffs, and I saw a load of potatoes headed for Russia pulled off the road in order to pay a bribe to police officers on the Georgian military highway. Once when we were pulled off the road to pay a bribe our driver left the side door of the van open, and all of a sudden a snowball exploded in my lap. My face speckled with ice and snow, I looked up to see who had thrown it and saw a man in a black leather jacket holding an automatic weapon and another snowball. I sat quietly while he threw several more snowballs at my head (Dunn 2008).

Smuggling, particularly through South Ossetia's Roki Tunnel, was rife: millions of dollars' worth of everything from soap and canned food to narcotics, arms, and nuclear material transited Georgia's borders without the payment of any taxes or import duties and ended up at the bazaar in Ergneti, where both Georgians and Ossetians traded. The South Ossetian administration collected bribes with every passage through the tunnel (Freese n.d.). Throughout the entire period Georgia remained resolutely politically oriented toward Russia, even joining the Russian-led Commonwealth of Independent States in 1993.

In the late 1990s, however, Shevardnadze began to appoint ministers who would turn Georgia toward the West, including Nino Burjanadze, Zurab Zhvania, and a young lawyer named Mikheil Saakashvili, who had gotten a law degree at Columbia University in New York and had studied at the International Institute of Human Rights in Strasbourg. With them in his administration, Shevardnadze began the process of breaking out of the Russian orbit. He made overtures to NATO, which promised Georgia eventual membership (Rayfield 2012, 389). He permitted the building of the Baku-Tbilisi-Ceyhan pipeline, which allowed Western companies to get Caspian Sea oil without transiting Russia. Shevardnadze was pulling the same trick that Georgian leaders had pulled for centuries: navigating between one large empire and another, playing them off one another in order to gain space for Georgian autonomy. At the same time he continued to run the country as his personal fiefdom, selling off everything from ambassadorships to jobs in the traffic police, collecting bribes and making it nearly impossible for foreign capital to enter the Georgian market. The country was reaching the breaking point. In 2001, with an aging Shevardnadze unable to control his party, Mikheil Saakashvili resigned and created his own party, the United National Movement (UNM). In 2003 UNM led a coup d'état that was known as the Rose Revolution after Saakashvili, who had led twenty days of protests in the streets of Tbilisi after a disputed parliamentary election, burst through the doors of parliament waving a single-stemmed red rose, a mob behind him (Jones 2013, 107). When Shevardnadze fled in midspeech, Saakashvili strode to the podium and theatrically drank from his abandoned glass of tea, signaling that he had taken the *skami*, the seat of power.

The Rose Revolution was partly substantive transformation and partly theater. Saakashvili's elite American education taught him all the right words to say to enchant Western listeners. He cracked down on petty corruption among government bureaucrats and police officers and built police stations with glass walls to symbolize the state's commitment to transparency. Wanting to prove the efficacy of his reforms, he worked to raise Georgia from number 127 to number 9 on the World Bank's Ease of Doing Business index. Saakashvili spoke a language of democratization, accountability, and development that echoed the official proclamations of both the United States and the European Union. This had the salutary effect of convincing European and American leaders, particularly within the Bush administration, that Georgia was adopting so-called Western values. The result was a massive rush of funding: Georgia soon became not only the fourth largest recipient of US military aid but also the beneficiary of one of the Bush administration's largest development programs, the Millennium Challenge Fund (Rayfield 2012, 391). Saakashvili's demonstration of Georgia's westward orientation was most powerfully summed up in his continual declarations about Georgia's desire to "join Europe" by joining NATO and the EU. As he wrote in the Washington *Post*,

> In the course of the Rose and Orange revolutions in Georgia and Ukraine, respectively, our peoples chose to develop open, democratic societies and set out to reorient our economic and political ties to the West. We believe it is critical to our future safety and economic security that we integrate ourselves with Euro-Atlantic structures, which is why we are working to gain membership in NATO and the European Union. (Saakashvili 2006)

Saakashvili repeated this statement in interview after interview. At official functions the flag of the European Union stood next to Georgia's own national flag. On Rustaveli Avenue in Tbilisi, in front of the parliament building, stood a large placard with the EU's circle of stars. Like Ukraine and Moldova, who were pushing in the same direction, Georgia made no secret of its ambitions to become more Westernized, more "European," more integrated into the Western European economy, and more tightly woven into the security architecture that had emerged in the West after the Cold War. From the Russian point of view this was no benign expansion of human rights, moral probity, or good governance. It was a potential military advance by a competing empire into territory that the Russians, who did not agree that Georgia had a national right of self-determination, felt was still their legitimate sphere of interest.

Despite all his public proclamations, Saakashvili himself was no real democrat. To gain enough political power to forge a strong state, he played populist and nationalist cards, promising (in Georgian) to bring Abkhazia and Ossetia back under Georgian control. To deprive the South Ossetian separatists of income, he shut down the Ergneti bazaar and sent security forces to South Ossetia to cut off illegal imports (Welt 2010, 70). The move backfired spectacularly. With both Georgians and Ossetians opposed, fighting broke out, putting both Georgians and Ossetians on edge and ready for further confrontation. Next he tried using "soft" power to woo the Ossetians to the Georgian side and began funneling resources to the region. Georgian villages got new infrastructure and social services, including a new hospital, pharmacies, movie theaters, and even ATM machines (ICG 2007, 4). But Saakashvili refused to deal with the injustices of the past or Ossetian fears about losing cultural and political autonomy, and so his efforts gained little political ground (*Imedi* News 2007, cited in ICG 2007, 5).

The Precipice of War

By the spring of 2008 Russia and the Western coalition were rapidly approaching a serious clash. Between 2005 and 2008 Saakashvili had dramatically increased military spending from 1% to 8% of GDP (Tagliavini 2009, 14) and was buying American carbines and tanks as well as other weaponry from Israel. Over one hundred US military advisers were stationed in Georgia, with more American advisers in other branches of the government (Tagliavini 2009, 15). The European Union too was establishing a presence in Georgia, although its commitment to the region wavered. Fatigued and financially drained from rapid eastward expansion, many of the EU member states were not eager to expand into the weak economies and unstable polities of the South Caucasus. Stuck in its ambivalence, the EU did not offer Georgia a plan for membership, but instead offered an Eastern Neighborhood Policy program that offered closer political and economic links with the Western bloc while, at the same time, forestalling attempts to actually join the union (Tagliavini 2009, 16). Europe, it seemed, refused to give Georgia a yes or no answer, but instead left it without any clear on-ramp to either the EU or NATO.

For Russia this ambiguity spelled an opportunity to reestablish itself as a regional power. The Russians were still smarting from the 1999 conflict in Kosovo, where NATO had backed the Kosovo Liberation Army against Russian-backed Serbian forces, claiming military action was required to protect Kosovar Albanians from genocide and ethnic cleansing by the Serbs. This principle of international intervention was later formalized as the Responsibility to Protect (R2P), a norm adopted by the United Nations in 2005 that required the international community take action to protect civilians if their governments would not. Russia regarded R2P and its associated claims of "humanitarian" military action as humiliating and threatening intrusions by the Western powers in its geographical sphere of influence. When Kosovo declared independence in February 2008 and was immediately recognized by the United States and the majority of the members of the European Union, Russian President Vladimir Putin argued that the Western countries had set "a terrible precedent, which will de facto blow apart the whole system of international relations, developed not over decades, but over centuries. They have not thought through the results of what they are doing. At the end of the day it is a two-ended stick and the second end will come back and hit them in the face" (*Sydney Morning Herald* 2008).

In the late 1990s and early 2000s, when NATO began expanding into the former USSR, Russia did not have the force to push back against what it saw as NATO's expansionist tendencies. But by 2008, having used rising oil and gas revenues to modernize its armed forces, it did (Asmus 2010). South Ossetia, along with Abkhazia, was the territory on which these conflicting geopolitical aims would play out, with Russia encouraging the South Ossetian nationalists' ambitions and backing them militarily.

Deliberately aping the West's talk of humanitarian intervention, Russia began to lay the ground for military intervention by giving out passports to residents of the separatist provinces, arguing that they were necessary on humanitarian grounds to ensure Abkhaz and Ossetians could travel outside Georgia. The passports made it possible to grant the Abkhaz and the Ossetians special sets of collective rights within a polity controlled by Russians, just as during the Soviet period. Although they were entitled to Russian pensions and other forms of social welfare, Abkhaz and Ossetians were not required to pay taxes or serve in the Russian Army (Mühlfried 2010, 9). More important, once the residents of Abkhazia and South Ossetia were made into Russian citizens, the Russian Federation could claim that under the Responsibility to Protect, it had the grounds to conduct military action on what was nominally the territory of Georgia (Dunn and Bobick 2014). Citizenship was instrumentalized in the service of military action, territorial claims, and demands for power and status in the international system (Mühlfried 2010, 9, Asmus 2010).

In April 2008 at the NATO summit in Bucharest, Saakashvili directly requested a membership action plan (MAP) or a procedure that would allow Georgia to enter NATO. The alliance was openly divided about the prospect of admitting Georgia and Ukraine: the United States along with Poland, the Czech Republic and other postcommunist states, was strongly in favor. Germany, on the other hand, opposed admission on the grounds that it would create hostile relations with Russia and potentially draw NATO into an armed conflict it had no desire to fight (Asmus 2010). Trying to resolve the conflict, US President George Bush sought to reassure Putin that NATO expansion did not pose a threat: "I have always told Vladimir Putin, my friend, that . . . he doesn't need to fear NATO; he ought to welcome NATO because NATO is a group of nations dedicated to peace" (Bush 2008, cited in Asmus 2010). Putin, on the other hand, felt quite differently. He told the Georgians,

> After NATO is expanded further to the East, and Georgia is a member of the organization, you will have to follow the discipline of the bloc and will therefore be a threat to our nuclear and military capacity. . . . After joining NATO, your sovereignty will be limited and Georgia, too, will be a threat to Russia (Putin 2008, cited in Asmus 2010, chapter 3).

The decision made by NATO in Bucharest, which was yet another decision not to decide, was a fatal mistake. Rather than either reject Georgia's aspirations or send a clear signal that it backed Georgia by offering a membership action plan, NATO followed a compromise course suggested by Merkel and offered instead an anodyne pledge of "intensive engagement" with Georgia as a step toward eventually receiving a membership action plan. Merkel herself handwrote a pledge that read: "We agree today that Georgia and Ukraine shall one day become members of NATO." But this pledge was the worst of both worlds: it was neither a clear signal that NATO would defend Georgia from Russian aggression nor a clear signal that it would leave Georgia alone and refrain from antagonizing the increasingly suspicious Russian government. In signing such a vague pledge, Merkel set the stage for the war.

The Outbreak of War

For many commentators after 2008 the most important question about the war was which side shot first. Did Saakashvili rashly decide to invade South Ossetia, aggressively attacking Tskhinvali on August 7, 2008, thus forcing the Russians to come to the aid of their South Ossetian compatriots (Tagliavini et al. 2009)? Or did Russian forces invade through the Roki Tunnel on August 8, 2008, necessitating a military response in self-defense from an unwilling Georgian government (Barry 2009)? Was the war an impetuous miscalculation on the part of Mikheil Saakashvili, who foolishly believed that once the conflict had started the West would leap to his aid in beating back the Russians (Nemtsova 2008)? Or was the war part of a long-standing plan by the Russians, who amassed their forces on the north side of the tunnel under the cover of their Kavkaz 2008 war games, while evacuating women and children from South Ossetia nearly a week before the fighting broke out (Malek 2009; BBC 2008)?

In hindsight it appears that all sides—the Georgians, the Ossetians, Georgia's US military advisers, and the Russians—had been preparing for battle for most of the summer. The Georgians were linked to light arms fire and shelling in Tskhinvali in early July, and to a bomb blast in the village of Dmanisi in early July that killed an Ossetian military leader (Tagliavini 2009, 204). In mid-July, after Russian military aircraft flew into Georgian airspace, the Georgian military hosted a US-led train-and-equip exercise known as Immediate Response, which involved more than two thousand soldiers from the United States, Georgia, Azerbaijan, and Armenia (Tagliavini 2009, 207). The Russians responded in mid-July by moving more than eight thousand troops to the border regions, especially the north end of the Roki Tunnel, for its Kavkaz 2008 war games (Malek 2009; Tagliavini 2009, 207). The result of these tit-for-tat provocations was the dry tinder for war, which only awaited a spark from either side to break into flame. The question of who shot first, then, is largely irrelevant: both sides were ready and willing for war.

In early August[7] the Georgian Army moved to try and take control of the heights around Tskhinvali. With tanks and artillery—including BM 21S "Grad" cluster bombs that killed civilians as well as military targets—the Georgian Army advanced toward the south end of the Roki Tunnel, hoping to take strategic bridges and roads along the way to prevent a Russian advance

(Human Rights Watch 2009, 3). But the Russian response, swift and overwhelming, could not be forestalled. Claiming the need to protect its citizens—that is, the South Ossetians who had recently been given Russian Federation passports—from attempted genocide, Russia bombed the Georgians with cluster munitions, killing civilians and destroying homes as well as destroying Georgian military forces housed nearby. Georgian villages in South Ossetia were particular targets of Russian aerial bombardment because the Georgian Army was using them as forward posts. After the bombing both Russian forces and South Ossetian irregular troops stormed through the Georgian villages in South Ossetia, burning homes, beating elderly people with the butts of their guns, raping women, illegally detaining more than 159 ethnic Georgians, torturing many of the detainees, and forcing ethnic Georgians to flee from their homes (Human Rights Watch 2009, 3–4). Because these actions were taken with the intent of driving residents away on the basis of their ethnic and political affiliations, Human Rights Watch (2009, 4) has identified Russian and South Ossetian actions as ethnic cleansing. In 2016 the International Criminal Court also authorized an investigation into whether Russia had engaged in ethnic cleansing in Georgia and thus had committed a war crime.

As Russian forces routed both Georgian military forces and civilians, the war quickly spilled out of South Ossetia (and Abkhazia, where Russian military forces had taken the Kodori Gorge) and into Georgia proper. The town of Gori was aerially bombed, leaving apartment buildings in flames and bomb craters in the street in front of the statue of Joseph Stalin and the museum at his birthplace. Because of the poor quality of ordnance used by both sides, unexploded cluster bombs lurked in gardens and fields, making it impossible to harvest the rapidly ripening crops. (I had the chance to see a bomb casing myself when a friend who lived near the center of Gori found one—thankfully, already exploded—behind a bush in his garden.) Tanks rolled down city streets in Gori and Khashuri, and young Russian soldiers, underpaid and poorly equipped, begged local residents for food. Many of the people I interviewed said they had given the soldiers both food and alcohol, hoping that this would create a personal relationship that would ensure the givers' safety.

Over 145,000 people were displaced as a result of the war—at least 10,000 people inside South Ossetia and 135,000 people within Georgia proper (United Nations 2008; Tarkhan-Mouravi 2009). They streamed into Tbilisi seeking temporary shelter, camping out in kindergartens or libraries, living in squalor in abandoned hospitals or squeezing into relatives' homes. As the Georgian government struggled to locate the IDPs and register them, international NGOs and the United Nations system struggled to provide them with bedding, clothing, and food in a process that was chaotic, disorganized, and erratic (see chapter 4).

From August 8 to October 9 the Russian Army occupied not only South Ossetia and Abkhazia but also big sections of Shida Kartli and Akhalgori, two regions
agreed to be part of Georgia proper, not South Ossetia. It was not until October 9
that the Russian Army pulled out of the buffer zone and retreated behind the
ABL, or the South Ossetian administrative boundary line (RIA-Novosti 2008).
Only then did the Georgian government begin the process of hastily building
thirteen new cottage settlements for the IDPs, many of which were in the buffer
zone or along the ABL, which was controlled militarily by Georgian, South Ossetian, and Russian forces. (Other housing units were built out of old apartment
buildings and army barracks, and one new cottage settlement was added in 2009,
for a total of thirty-six new settlements.) In the thirteen settlements along the
ABL, 3,963 small cottages were built in a frenzy of building that lasted less than
three months. By January 5, 2009, less than four months after the war, the Georgian government was pushing IDPs out of their temporary squats in Tbilisi and
shepherding them into the new settlements. The people of Eredvi, Ksuisi, and
the other Georgian villages, people who had been farmers, smugglers, teachers,
construction workers, and small business owners, began their lives as beneficiaries of the international humanitarian order. It was an entirely new social status
for them, one in which the everyday routines of their old lives were profoundly
disrupted and reworked. The camps were a new world, one in which the logics
of humanitarian action were blended with the ever-present guns and tanks of
military occupation.

The Russo-Georgian War was, in many ways, the climax of a long history of
imperialism that swept up not only the Russian Empire but also the Ottoman
Empire, the USSR, and post–Cold War American hegemony. Yet despite the fact
that the conflict was embedded in a long history of imperial conflict, it fore-
shadowed the future as much as it was a culmination of the past. The war and its
aftermath signaled three very clear changes in the international system of power:
First, that the Responsibility to Protect doctrine could not be the basis for a new
international system of power, both because the West refused to consistently
uphold it and because it was a thin cover for less noble geopolitical objectives.
Second, that the United States and its allies in NATO believed "soft power" in
the form of humanitarian and development aid was an alternative to conflicts it
did not wish to manage militarily. And third, that the Russians had devised "war
without war" and "occupation without occupation" as new forms of warfare for
the twenty-first century.

First, the Responsibility to Protect doctrine was offered by the United States
and the United Nations as a human-rights-centered response to the failures of
the international community to stop genocide in Rwanda and the former Yugo-
slavia (Fassin and Pandolfi 2010). But when it was invoked in Kosovo the Russian

government did not agree that NATO intervention was humanitarian action, instead viewing the high-minded talk about protecting individual human rights with military action as a cover for the geopolitical ambitions of the United States and the European Union. When President Dmitry Medvedev and Prime Minister Vladimir Putin offered R2P as justification for the massive onslaught on Georgia and compared it to NATO's intervention in Kosovo, they did so with a snide wink. Overtly, they claimed to use the same notion of "humanitarian intervention" and the same concept of "human rights" that the West did, while at the same time revealing the similarity between US and Russian geopolitical ambitions. By following the United States in claiming that bombing can be humanitarian and warfare can be a form of care for a vulnerable population, Medvedev and Putin showed how R2P and other forms of so-called humanitarian intervention can be used to intimidate local populations, commit violence on noncombatant populations, and ultimately control the foreign relations and internal politics of surrounding states. Their claims to be humanitarians themselves were not genuine claims on humanitarian politics, but a way to parody the rhetoric of international humanitarianism and reveal the hidden realpolitik at its center (Dunn and Bobick 2014, 409). The Russian occupation of South Ossetia was thus not a genuine claim on humanitarian politics, but a way of mocking the sanctimony of the West and revealing the disingenuous force behind its supposedly noble intentions.

The Russian invasion of Georgia showed not only that the West applied R2P cynically, but also that it applied it selectively. When Russian forces ethnically cleansed Georgian villagers the villagers' human rights were clearly at stake. Their own government said openly that was unable to protect them and called for assistance. But the West stood by doing nothing. This revealed that the United States and NATO would only invoke R2P when it suited their geopolitical objectives, even in the face of a massive violation of human rights. R2P, which had been the ideological basis of a new organization in the international system, was thus too hollow to maintain a system of power that excluded Russian geopolitical ambitions.

Second, Western responses to the Russo-Georgian War highlighted an increasing unwillingness to engage in war. The United States, of course, was already fatigued by seven years of a failed $725 billion war in Iraq and a conflict in Afghanistan that was rapidly turning into a $1 trillion disaster. France, Germany, and Britain too had little interest in having a massive war with Russia, particularly given that they were dependent on Russian gas and oil, which the Russians were eminently willing to cut off. Western Europe had very little political appetite for a war with Russia, especially over a small country like Georgia.

Third, and perhaps most important, the Russo-Georgian War showed the innovative ways that a resurgent, newly powerful Russia had devised to conduct war. If Putin and Medvedev had learned one lesson watching the Americans in the quagmire of Iraq, it was that while wars were cheap, occupations were expensive. So Russia devised a way to have war without war and occupation without occupation (Dunn and Bobick 2014). Rather than having a full-scale war, Russia took control of breakaway provinces and occupied only a small chunk of land, leaving the rest of the country unoccupied and largely unaffected by war. But to the small perch of land they controlled, the Russians brought in enough tanks, planes, artillery, and troops to launch a full-scale invasion of the entire country. The Georgians were well aware that a massive Russian force was a mere 44 kilometers from Tbilisi and could invade at any moment. The omnipresent specter of future war constantly shaped the strategies of the Saakashvili government, Western donor nations, and the IDPs themselves in the postwar environment.

As the IDPs from South Ossetia were forced from their homes and into the humanitarian system, then, they were entering a situation that was extremely complex at multiple scales. On the local level they had to contend with municipal governments and host villages, who were often overwhelmed by the influx of new people and often unwilling to share resources. At the national level they had become the political responsibility of Mikheil Saakashvili, the same man who had arguably caused the war that displaced them, and who was now under fire from other postcommunist parties. And at the international level they had to somehow navigate between the soft power and unreliable protection of the Western donor nations and the brute military force of the Russians, who were perched only kilometers away. Understanding the new circumstances they faced, and how to survive the uncertainty produced by them, would soon become the central problem of their existences.

THE NORMAL SITUATION

When I first came to Tsmindatsqali and the other camps, the thing that struck me most powerfully was how motionless they were. As I describe in chapter 4, the people in the camp did very little in the first year. They moved slowly, slept a great deal, and, as in other parts of Georgia, seemed to be able to sit for hours and hours doing nothing at all. But it wasn't just the lack of activity that was puzzling—that is a common condition among the economically marginalized in post-Soviet Georgia (see Frederiksen 2013). It was the fact that it seemed to arouse no boredom, no restlessness, even among people who had been accustomed to a great deal of activity. There was a curious numbness in the camps, the sense that even as late as two years after the war the IDPs were in a state of shock, still ambulatory but somehow so overwhelmed and confused that they could not fully take in their new circumstances. They had somehow shut down. Where I expected collective grief, I mostly saw dissociation. Where I expected to see people dissecting the events of the war, I mostly saw people sitting in silence. Although many of the people I knew in the camps told me their stories of the war in the context of an interview—which was for them, I think, a way of giving testimony for the purpose of historical documentation—I rarely heard them discuss the events of the war among themselves, unbidden.[1]

Reading other narratives about war and its aftermath, mostly memoirs and fiction written by persons who had experienced war firsthand, convinced me that this haunting numbness was an integral part of the experience of war and forced migration. These literary renditions echoed the descriptions that my interlocutors in the IDP camp had given me not just of their wartime experiences but of their postwar experiences as well. For example, in *The Yellow Birds*, a novel about the American war in Iraq written by Kevin Powers, who served as a machine gunner in Mosul, we follow a returned soldier, Pvt. John Bartle, who has returned from the war and is falling apart. The novel flickers in time and space: from Kentucky to Iraq, from Germany to Virginia, leaving the reader as disoriented as Bartle, who tries to make a world that has become baffling make sense by struggling to put his fragmented experiences into some kind of a coherent picture. But as he says, this process is "like putting a puzzle together from behind: the shapes familiar, the picture quickly fading, the muted tan of the cardboard backing a tease at wholeness and completion" (Powers 2012). As Benjamin Percy writes in his review of the book, the fragmented structure is the main point of the novel: "The nonlinear design of Powers's novel is a beautifully brutal example of style matching content. War destroys. It doesn't just rip through bone and muscle, stone and steel; it fragments the mind as a fist to a mirror might create thousands of bloodied, glittering shards" (Percy 2012).

The idea that war destroys sense, that it fragments being in ways that make it difficult or impossible to move easily through the world, is replicated in Ismet Prcić's powerful novel *Shards* (2011). In the opening pages, we meet a character, also called Ismet Prcić, who is breaking into pieces. Having survived the Bosnian War, he has become a refugee and is being resettled in San Diego. In disjointed, fragmentary sections of the novel we hear about Ismet, a young boy in Tuzla experiencing the "the thought-collapsing, breath-stealing sound a spinning shell makes as it pierces the air on the way down toward the center of your town," Mustafa, a Bosnian Muslim fighter who responds with sadism and cruelty, and Izzy, a young immigrant trying to adapt to college life in California who soon begins to decompensate and descend into madness. It is only late in the book that we discover that these three are possibly the same person, maybe the same person as the author himself, a man who has been splintered into shards and for whom the world is becoming chaotic, incomprehensible, and meaningless.

Both Prcić and Powers pose what I came to understand as the fundamental existential question about war and life in a postwar condition, the question that the IDPs struggled most with. On the one hand, I didn't want to center my questions on the baseline question of survival, or "to be or not to be" in the sense of "will we live or will we die," although, as I show in chapter 6, that question became more important, not less important, the longer people spent in the camps. Nor did I want to ask about how sovereign power forced some people into a state of exception and a condition of minimal humanity that accounts only for their biological survival (Agamben 1994). Those questions seemed to me to be highly state-centric, focused mostly on the opinions and actions of a single governing power without thinking about other actors in the same space. Worse, the Agambenian perspective seemed seriously neglectful of the opinions and experiences of the people who were supposedly reduced to "bare life" but who did not in any way see themselves as that. But on the other hand, I also wanted to avoid psychologizing what had happened to the IDPs during the war and what happened to them afterward. It might have been easy to use the medicalizing language of "trauma" and to diagnose the people I interviewed with Post-Traumatic Stress Disorder (PTSD). But this would reduce the complex problem of existence to a medical rather than a moral conundrum. It would assume that "trauma" was an individual rather than a collective injury and that it was caused by the violence of war, not the experience of aid afterward. It made it look as if "trauma" was a self-evident label rather than one that was carefully socially constructed in a way that made the problem amenable to intervention by Western NGOs and their culturally inflected forms of psychotherapy, which saw debriefing and achieving catharsis as the basis of healing (Fassin and Rechtman 2009, 165–73). What I needed to understand was the way that war created an existential injury to a community, not a psychic injury to an individual.

The novels by Prcić and Powers suggested that the key question was precisely about what created the experience of fragmentation and shaped the struggle to find form for intensely chaotic experience. The novels combat convention, logic, and the linear structure of time itself to pose what I came to see as the essential problem faced by displaced people all over the world: Can they reassemble the shards of an existence blown apart by war in order to restore not only their own holism and integrity as subjects and social actors but also the holism and integrity of the world as they experience it? Asking that question quickly invoked a whole suite of other questions: How and why does war fragment experience? What is the nature of this fragmentation? Are the experiences of war and forced migration unique ontological experiences, and if so, why? And if they are like other experiences of violence, how so? What makes forced migration, in which people are pushed by extreme violence to abandon their homes, professions, and ways of life, different from other kinds of moves, such as labor migration or simply moving house? Does humanitarian aid help people put the shards of their experiential world back together or impede them from doing so, or both?

Trying to understand how war disrupted being meant understanding the nature of being itself—that is, trying to understanding how war causes experience itself to become and remain chaotic, even if that meant understanding first how experience is normally structured in ways that makes it seem largely unchaotic. I needed a theory that would let me see both stasis and change, moments of comparative experiential stability as well as moments of extreme experiential rupture. Here the work of the philosopher Alain Badiou proved to be surprisingly fruitful.

His ontology is complex, bulky, and difficult to follow. In contrast to the postmodern theorists, who see experience as intrinsically dependent on the particularities of history and culture, Badiou demands that we accept a generic account of experience stripped of all historical and cultural context (2006, xiii)—a demand that goes against every grain of my own thinking as an anthropologist. In order to make his theory generic, he expresses it mathematically, using Cantorian set theory, which took me months to learn. Badiou is curmudgeonly, cranky, and intentionally difficult—in short, an epic pain. I found myself arguing with him at every turn, challenging his premises, grousing about his Eurocentric claims for truth, modifying his theories, and rejecting huge chunks of his later applications of his theory to modern political events (e.g., Badiou 2013). And yet I found in his theory of ontology and multiplicity a framework for making sense of what my informants, as well as others who had experienced war, were telling me, and patiently working through his cumbersome theoretical apparatus gave me a schematic way of understanding how experience is structured and how it becomes radically unstructured.

Badiou starts by questioning the things we see in the world as fundamentally whole: objects, landscapes, people, and so on. Like many existentialists or phenomenologists, he begins instead by seeing the world as a priori multiple, as made up of aspects of existence and sensory impressions that are not intrinsically grouped together. William James, the psychologist, famously said that the world presents itself to an infant as a "blooming, buzzing confusion" (James 1890). For Jean-Paul Sartre, human beings enter the world confronted by a "plurality" that presents itself immediately as pure perception (Sartre 1943, 17). For Badiou things are both more abstract and more clear: being presents itself as pure unstructured multiplicity, and as nothing other than multiplicity (Badiou 2006, 24).[2] It is human beings who gather elements of perception into sets and then present them as the whole objects that are encountered in daily existence. Such a consistently organized multiple Badiou calls the "count as one" (see figure 1). An apple, a landscape, a son or a daughter—these are all "counts as one," multiples that are presented as wholes because they have been structured into something that appears as a single entity (see also Humphrey 2008, 366). Thus the sensory impressions red, round, shiny, sweet are grouped together, made into a set, and *presented* to us as the count as one (apple).

Badiou makes two key arguments about counts as one: First, the way the elements inside each "count as one" are structured is what makes something appear as whole. It is important to note that the count as one is an *effect* of structuration; it does not preexist it (Badiou 2006, 25; Hallward 2008, 101) (see figure 2). So what is interesting is the underlying structure that takes the multiple that is presented in experience and groups it in a fragile and contingent set (Badiou 2006, 25; see also Meillassoux 2011, 3; and Humphrey 2008, 366).

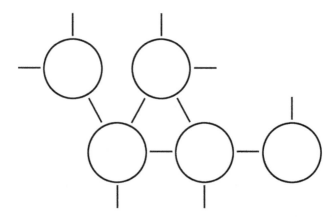

FIGURE 1. A dense network of counts-as-one related to each other. What happens when those links are broken? What happens when lots of new elements that are not yet integrated into this structure arrive?

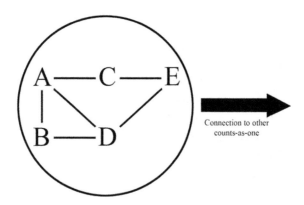

FIGURE 2. Structuration: each element is related to the others in a (mostly) stable way. Structuration makes the count-as-one present itself as (mostly) stable.

Presentation is the way things appear to us immediately in their concrete and specific form; it is what Badiou calls "the suture to being" (2006, 66). But it does not describe the way that these counts as one are related to one another in experience, or how we make sense or meaning of them. But since multiplicities are built of multiplicities, we can think about all the counts as ones that appear, and how they are represented, or organized in a structured way, to create a historically and geographically specific world saturated with meaning. The world itself appears as what Sartre (1943, 41) calls "an organized totality" because its elements are not only grouped but also set into relations such that they point to one another, creating a web in which the being and meaning of any element of experience is inextricably bound up with the being and meaning of others. Badiou calls this represented multiple of multiples a "situation" (2006, 25) and says, "ontology, if it exists, is a situation." That is, being itself is an artifact of structuration: that the world in which we find ourselves always appears to us in terms of not only whole entities rather than random and disconnected sensory impressions, but also of entities that are instrumentally, logically, or semantically related to one another. Readers who know Badiou's ontology well will note that here I have collapsed what Badiou calls "representation," which is related to pure being, with what he calls "appearance," which is the logical structuration of concrete and historically specific worlds. Badiou keeps representation and appearance apart because he views the logic of any particular world as distinct from the structure of pure being, which exists outside any specific context. Speaking as an anthropologist and geographer, I find this distinction mostly useless. Although it is essential for preserving the logical system that Badiou sets up in *Being and Event* and ensuring that it isn't contradicted or amended by *Logics of Worlds*, what concerns us here is not the consistency of a philosophical system or the ontological status of pure being, but the characteristics of a specific, inhabited world. For that reason I see no value in keeping representation and appearance separate: the state of the situation that structures representation is the logic of the world we inhabit. We exist not in isolation, but always in relation to the concrete situation in which we are embedded.[3]

Think, for example, of a classroom. The ensemble (teacher) (desk) (chalkboard) (students) (chairs) is grouped together into a set and presented as (classroom). There are other elements in that set as well: A person walking into a European-style classroom has immediate expectations about what activities will be carried on there (there will probably be reading and writing; it is less likely that there will be horseshoeing or skinny-dipping) and what behaviors are permitted (no yelling, no dancing, only the teacher can get up and move about, and so on). Or, return to the initial example, an apple: The count-as-one (apple) is a meaningful part of experience not just because it is the grouping of (red) (round) and (shiny), but also because, more important, the count-as-one (apple) is related to other objects in experience instrumentally, as things that can be worked with or on. Thus for the inhabitants of the Georgian villages in South Ossetia, (apple) was significantly related to (tree), (orchard), (pruning), (picking), (wooden crates), (truck), (Roki Tunnel), (cash money), and (Vladikavkaz bazaar).

Elements in experience are also related to one another structurally. Badiou names the structure that organizes what is presented into a meaningful order "the state of the situation," which is to being much like what Saussure's (1916) *langue* is to *parole*. The state of the situation is an underlying grammar, a structure that gives objects in experience meaning not by linking their appearance to some underlying necessary sense, but by placing them in a structured relationship to one another (see figure 3).

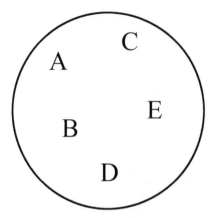

FIGURE 3. The count-as-one elements are grouped together in a stable way so as to appear as a single thing.

Thus the count-as-one (apple) is meaningful not just because it is the grouping of (round) (red) and (shiny), but because it is categorized, or placed in relationship to, elements like (banana) and (pear), but less closely tied to (dog) or (magazine). Elements in our lived, concrete world take meaning from both their practical use as well as from their relations to some elements and nonrelation to or conceptual distance from others.

The concept of the "state of the situation" argues that it is the way that these structured sets are related to one another that makes the lifeworld into a place experienced as continuous, predictable, and expected. What glues the world together, what makes it knowable and actionable, is not the presence of any particular element, whether it is a thing, a person, an idea, or whatever. What glues the world together and makes it appear as a seamless whole is *the structure that binds elements together.* Ordinarily, everything that is presented in experience is structured by the state of the situation and then represented. As a matter of course, the majority of things that we encounter in the world have a place in a structure that makes them comprehensible, meaningful, and possible to act with or on. This is what Badiou names "the normal situation": everything that is presented is represented, and everything represented is presented. As Hallward writes,

> A discrete world exists insofar as it holds together a certain configuration of multiple-beings which appear there, along with a certain range of . . . regulated relations between those beings (Hallward 2003, 300, paraphrasing Badiou 2006, chap. 2).

In the normal situation, we can move through the world relatively (but not perfectly) confident, acting mostly without having to reflect consciously on what things are or where they belong in relation to other things. But this one-to-one relationship between presentation and representation can be ruptured when the state of the situation, the structure that links objects in experience to a system in which they gain meaning by indexing one another, is ruptured. According to Badiou, the name of this rupture is "the Event."

War and the Event

What is created in this world, or made, can be undone, unmade; the threads of a rope can be unwoven. And if that rope is needed as a guideline for a ferry to a further shore, then one must invent a way to weave it back, or there will be drownings in the streams that cross our paths.

(Powers 2012, 100)

Novels about war, when written by people who have experienced it, are very often also about cracking up. Prćić's novel *Shards* is a case in point. Powers's novel *The Yellow Birds* is another. But so, too, is Kurt Vonnegut's classic novel *Slaughterhouse Five*, in which he describes the bombing of Dresden during World War II from the perspective of Billy Pilgrim, a man who has become "unstuck" in both time and space and who experiences being as nothing but discontinuous fragments. The novel shifts vertiginously in time and space, flitting back and forth between Dresden, Germany, the fictional town of Ilium, New York, and a zoo on the planet Tralfamadore, where the narrator has been imprisoned in a zoo for the benefit of his alien keepers. As in *The Yellow Birds*, these rapid, discontinuous cuts in time, space, and scene are meant to convey the disorientation caused by war, the sensation of being out of time and place caused by forced displacement, and the feeling that the world is coming apart—which seems to be an incredibly common reaction to the experience of war (see Hautzinger and Scandlyn 2013). So from the outset the problem posed both philosophically and anthropologically is why the experience of war is so damaging. What, precisely, does war damage, and what are the effects of these existential wounds? Using Badiou's framework, I argue that the chaos and fragmentation of war comes from damaging the state of the situation, or the structure that allows counts-as-one to be organized into a normal situation. War shreds the fabric of being.

One way to begin to understand the ontological problem that war poses is to begin from Badiou's concept of "the Event" (with a capital E), which is the central concept of his ontology. Yet it is exactly there that I depart from him, rethinking the Event in order to rethink the ways that people constitute the logics of worlds and (re)construct normal situations. Thinking through the Event in more concrete terms, I argue, is essential to understanding the experiences of war and social upheaval, as well as the process through which people become acting subjects.

For Badiou, Events are of world-historical importance. An Event occurs when an acting subject declares a truth so radical that it upends the normal situation, destroying the previously stable structure of knowledge and experience. St. Paul, for example, declared the revolutionary truth of Christ's resurrection, and in doing so superseded both Greek and Hebrew law and overturned social hierarchies. Paul's statement, "There is neither Jew nor Greek, there is neither bond nor free, there is neither male nor female: for ye are all one in Christ Jesus" (Galatians 3:28), was socially revolutionary statement, given the strong social hierarchies of the time. It was also an epistemologically revolutionary truth, one that could not have existed within the terms of the previous normal situation: within the confines of either Roman law or Jewish law such radical equality among persons was completely impossible. Most important, it was an ontologically revolutionary truth, one that tore apart not only the normal situation but also the structure that placed people and things into a new stable order (Badiou 2003; see also Humphrey 2008, 360). For that reason, the declaration of truth that sparks an Event marks a pure break with the logic that once animated the world, forcing those who acclaim that truth to reestablish a new structure linking presentation and representation and therefore forging a new normal situation. Declaring a truth and sparking an Event, according to Badiou, is also what constitutes a human subject: whereas those world-historical figures (oddly, in Badiou's account, always men) are true subjects, other humans are mere "somebodies." Once a truth has been declared, Badiou tells us, the world can never be the same again. This is a rare project, and the subjects that come into being by declaring truths are equally rare. Badiou names such notables as Vladimir Ilyich Lenin, Arnold Schoenberg, and Copernicus as subjects who declared revolutionary truths, sparked Events, and forced a reordering of the worlds around them.

My own sense is that Badiou sets a very high bar for both Events and subjectivity. If it takes something as monumental as the declaration of the resurrection, or the fact that the Earth revolves around the sun, to constitute an Event and to make the person proclaiming it into a subject, than there are very few of either. But what if we define the Event not by the declaration of a revolutionary truth, but by the destruction of the state of the situation, the structure that links presentation to representation? This shift in emphasis has two consequences: In the first place, it means that Events are not necessarily based on voluntaristic decisions by heroic subjects (cf. Badiou 2003; Humphrey 2008). Rather, a happening can become an Event even for people who do not subscribe to its fundamental "truth" or declaration, but who are forced nonetheless to deal with its consequences. This is a line of thinking Badiou would resist: he has fervently rejected the logic of victimhood, saying, "Ethics . . . defines man *as a victim*. It is this definition that we must proclaim unacceptable" (2002, 22). But to deny that Events have consequences that are *experienced by people who did not choose them* is to subscribe to a concept of subjectivity unduly premised on free will. Rejecting the Agembenian notion of the "passive victim" does not imply the opposite pole. Rather, as I show in later meditations, it should invoke a concept of "burdened agency," of people acting under strong constraint.

Second, if, as Badiou argues, an Event can only be decided in retrospect as people are "faithful to" or pursue the consequences of it, then a happening is an Event to all those who must contend with the destruction of the state of the situation, whether or not they "proclaim its Truth," as Badiou would say, or subscribe to the fundamental notion behind the event. Thus war, with its profound disruption to the sense and stability of daily life, is an event (perhaps with a small *e*, to distinguish it from Badiou's Event) for those who experience the massive ruptures it causes. This means that in contrast to Badiou, who thinks in the binaries of "normal situation" and "Event," we should think about "eventishness," a property that situations have more or less of depending on the degree to which they rupture the links that hold elements in experience together in stable ways. The Resurrection of Christ would be on one end of the scale, to be sure: it was a huge Event that continues to have repercussions two millennia later. But other events, perhaps reactionary rather than revolutionary, or ones that affect particular groups rather than declaring universal relevance, might also be thought of as events, even if less so than the ones Badiou describes. As I attempted to show in chapter 2, the 2008 war in Georgia was an event in that more limited sense: while it took up the long-standing logics of Russian imperial rule, it also marked a severe rupture for those whose lives were upended by being forced to migrate. In chapters 3 and 4, then, I attempt to trace some of the consequences of the "eventishness" of the 2008 war, of the kinds of ruptures it produced and the experiences of chaos and nothingness that were engendered when the structure that held the IDPs' worlds together was blown apart.

Defining the event in terms of the destruction of the normal situation rather than the proclamation of truth would account for the disorientation and fragmentation expressed by the fictional (or real?)[4] soldiers described by Prcić, Vonnegut, and Powers, and for the real-life experiences of war veterans with PTSD, as well as for IDPs and refugees, as I describe in chapter 4. As Hallward (paraphrasing Badiou 2006) writes,

> When something *happens*, when in the wake of an event, "being seems to displace its configuration under our eyes, it is always at the expense

of . . . the local collapse of its consistency, and so in the provisional can-
cellation of all logic" (2003, 301).

War is an event because it damages the state of the situation, the ordering
structure that mediates between presentation and representation, and in doing so
destroys the expected relations between objects in experience. It destroys logical
consistency, predictability, and sense. What is left is chaos, disruption, fragmentation, and confusion. The world goes crazy in war, and so people often feel as
if they are going crazy along with it. They experience a profound sense of the
uncanny as they encounter things that are presented but not represented, that is,
new objects in experience that have no place in the structure with which to make
sense of them, or things that are represented but not presented, that is, places
where objects should be but aren't, or things like devils and ghosts that can be
felt and thought but not seen or touched (see Navaro-Yashin 2012; Kwon 2008).
In chapter 4, for example, I look at the effects of objects given as humanitarian
aid that are presented but not represented, and that thus count as nothing for the
IDPs, even though the humanitarians most definitely see them as something—if
not as items of equivalent quality to what the IDPs lost, at least as things that have
ontological reality and that are better than nothing. In chapter 7 I look at the
reverse, or things that are represented in the structure but that are not presented
in reality. Focusing on the appearance of devils in the camp, I think through the
ways in which the ragged, frayed nature of the state of the situation shapes the
ways that the IDPs can engage in the domain of the political.

The problem of forced migration is not just about marginalization or precarity. Displaced people are not noteworthy simply because their suffering is more
drastic than the suffering other *misérables* endure, but precisely because their
dilemma is existential as well as material. For the displaced, the question isn't
simply about whether they will sink to the bottom of an established social order
(cf. Allison 2013; Bauman 2004), but whether there will be any sort of social
order for them at all. Displaced people are also characterized by their long-term
liminality, by endless waiting and a never-resolved ambiguity surrounding their
social status. In this state the world remains fundamentally disorganized and
difficult to comprehend. I explore this situation in more depth in chapters 4
and 5, but here it suffices to say that the enduring quality of this disorganization
of the lived world is not due to war, but to humanitarianism. It is an artifact of
the camp, and of what I call the "humanitarian situation." As I show in the next
two chapters, the very humanitarian structures that are meant to keep displaced
people alive act as "spoilers," rendering their attempts to organize the elements
in their new world into a chaotic mess and then leaving them in a state of nothingness, or a suspended temporal state in which it is impossible to engage in

purposeful action. It is this state of suspension, the condition of hanging over an existential void, that makes the displaced the central figures of contemporary life. Forced migrants illustrate the fragility of existence and the struggle to create a durable way of being.

The individual and collective work of people who have lived through war is to try and repair the state of the situation, to make sure that everything that is presented is represented and vice versa, thus to rebuild the structure that makes order. In doing so they have the hope of both reorganizing themselves as subjects and reorganizing the world around them into a world that is not crazy or fragmented, but stable and meaningful. This is not an easy job: as the Soviet-era proverb goes, it is easier to make fish soup out of an aquarium than it is to make an aquarium out of fish soup. But fish soup is what displaced people—who have lost even the material infrastructure and landscapes that might provide a base for reconstructing a normal situation—are given. So how can displaced people regroup elements of multiplicities and make them count as one? How do they reforge links between objects that are presented and the structure of representation in such a way that the world presents itself as stable? These are questions that plague everyone—they are central existential questions for all human persons—but they appear in an especially acute form for displaced people.

CHAOS

When most people think of humanitarians they envision altruistic amateurs operating without thought of personal gain to provide life-saving care for people affected by conflict and disaster.[1] Humanitarianism, we think, is a form of charity, a kind of concern for distant others (Pupavac 2010). But, as I mentioned in chapter 1, recent scholarship has shown humanitarianism to be something very different. First, as Didier Fassin and Mariella Pandolfi (2010) have argued, humanitarianism is politics. No longer innocent assistance, humanitarian aid has become a form of "mobile sovereignty" in which wealthy First World countries take over the functions of government in weaker "failed states" as a form of trusteeship (Pandolfi 2003; see also Fearon 2008). Often humanitarian aid is war by other means: by creating grateful allies and shoring up patron-client relationships between donor states and recipient states, aid is meant to create or maintain a strategic foothold in a region. (This, for example, was the US strategy in Afghanistan. In Georgia aid was clearly seen as an alternative to military action that would allow the United States to maintain its interests there.) Aid is thus often war by other means. This soft power, as it is called, does not come cheaply: whereas the total value of humanitarian aid worldwide was just over $1 billion in 1991, by 2015 humanitarianism had become an $25 billion industry (Fearon 2008, 65; Weiss 2013, 7; Global Humanitarian Assistance 2015).

That growth means humanitarianism has also become big business. Far from being simply the domain of good-hearted strangers, humanitarian aid has turned into "disaster capitalism": an increasingly lucrative and competitive market in which agencies must compete for funding (see Klein 2007). As the industry has grown, humanitarian agencies have become increasingly institutionalized, standardized, and professionalized (Barnett 2010). The humanitarian industry is now populated by a dense web of international agencies such as the United Nations agencies, donor government agencies like USAID or DFID, large international nongovernmental agencies such as CARE International or Oxfam, military units such as the US Marines, and even for-profit private military and security companies. They are linked together by contracts and subcontracts given out through competitive bidding. That means that humanitarian agencies, even nonprofits, now operate under the same market-based logics and calculations as for-profit agencies—a fact that often creates conflicting imperatives for ostensibly charitable organizations. Both governmental and nongovernmental agencies are under pressure from local and international market forces to put self-reproduction, or "staying in business," at the top of their institutional goals (Weiss 2013, 7). They are shaped by the same demands businesses face: the need for efficiency, the desire to rationalize and standardize their practices, and intense pressure to demonstrate transparency and accountability so that their donor-clients can make complex cost-benefit calculations about the value of aid (see Power 1997). In response they now use many of the management tools that for-profit enterprises do: advertising, marketing, spreadsheets, audits, and so on. If "the spirit of capitalism" is reshaping humanitarianism, it is in a deeply Weberian way, one in which morality is expressed through the rational pursuit of economic gain (Weiss 2013, 5; see Weber 1930.)

As I show in this chapter, the product offered for sale to donor governments in the humanitarian marketplace is *social order*. Humanitarian agencies claim that displacement, like other humanitarian crises, is a problem amenable to solutions based on techniques of rational administration that include planning, accounting, systems analysis, standardized forms of reporting, and standardized "kits" of services and material aid (McFalls 2010; Redfield 2008b). By using the same management tools used in other capitalist businesses, they say they can provide what Foucault (2007) called "pastoral care," or the government of a population through social engineering projects that provide safety, well-being, productivity, and a stable social order. In offering this product in a competitive market, these agencies claim that they can create geopolitical security for donor governments at the same moment they create existential security for displaced people. So in this chapter I first write an ethnography of Karaleti, a camp envisioned by humanitarian bureaucrats as a space where IDPs not only receive life-sustaining charity and are reintegrated into society, but where they can also be ruled by a "therapeutic mode of domination" in which new and improved social orders allow donor governments to rule outside their own borders (McFalls 2010; Pandolfi 2003).

But can humanitarian agencies really establish the kind of sovereignty for their donor clients that they claim to be able to? Do their businesslike technocratic methods really create new and better social orders out of the chaos of war? And do attempts to create social order create security for either displaced people or the nation-states they inhabit? In this chapter I argue that although humanitarian actors claim to govern by applying management techniques of seeing, counting, and rationalizing, in fact humanitarian aid is a process based as much on guesswork, rules of thumb, and satisficing as it is on rational planning. This, I argue, transforms bureaucracy into what I call *adhocracy*, a form of power that creates chaos and vulnerability as much as it creates order. Because the world that humanitarians create in Karaleti is not purely bureaucratic but adhocratic, it intersects with the dirty and uncertain world of its topolganger, Tsmindatsqali, to create existential disorder, confused thought, and a damaged material environment. This chapter, then, is the ethnography of protuberances from the world of the humanitarians into the lifeworld of the IDPs. It is the story of how the chaos of aid prevents IDPs from making plans for their own economic and social futures, blocks their ability to integrate into mainstream society, and leaves them precariously exposed to protracted poverty and violence.

Bureaucracy, Violence, and Care in the Republic of Georgia

When donor governments, mainly the United States and the European Union, pledged over $350 million in postwar aid to Georgia, ninety-two NGOs and six UN agencies rushed into Georgia to compete for the contracts funded with that money. In the archipelago of camps, humanitarian agencies offered the newly displaced immediate necessities, such as food, clothing, and household goods, but also offered projects such as microlending, small business development training, seeds and tools for agriculture, psychosocial counseling, and job training. Blurring conventional boundaries between emergency relief and development, these humanitarian projects were aimed not just to keep the IDPs from dying but to also make them live again as citizens, producers, consumers, and family members.

This new approach to aid, in which displaced people are not only kept alive but are also transformed into the new citizens of an improved social order, is intimately related to changes in the international system. Under the UN doctrine of "sovereignty as responsibility," the primary responsibility for providing for the welfare and safety of IDPs rests with their own governments. When those governments cannot meet those responsibilities, they should request and accept offers of aid from the international community (Cohen n.d., 3). The penalty for refusing aid is high: if a government fails to protect IDPs, and fails to allow international donor governments to do so, the international community can, under the Responsibility to Protect doctrine, decide to intervene, even militarily if necessary (Cohen n.d., 4). The act of protecting and providing, then, *is* pastoral sovereignty—and foreign governments assume much of it both by contracting for the provision of humanitarian aid and by rebuilding failed states into new ones that can provide it themselves (see Pandolfi 2003; Barnett 2010; Foucault 2007).

In Georgia the drive to socially reintegrate the IDPs rather than to let them linger indefinitely in temporary housing and social isolation came out of the country's history of state failure. Even before the 2008 war the state struggled to manage over 250,000 people displaced during the 1991–1992 civil wars in the breakaway provinces of South Ossetia and Abkhazia (Greene 1998, 289). These "first wave" IDPs flooded public buildings in Georgia in the early 1990s, taking up residence in makeshift conditions that often did not include running water, functioning sanitary facilities, or electrical power (Kharashvili et al. 2003, 26; Chauffeur and Gusep 2004). In the capital, Tbilisi, Soviet-era hotels, including the once-luxurious Hotel Iveria on Tbilisi's main boulevard, became frighteningly dilapidated vertical refugee camps where IDPs struggled to survive (Theodorou 2006; Kalin 2006; Sumbadze and Tarkhan-Mouravi 2003, 28). Like other run-down collective centers at some of the city's most prominent locations, the Iveria was a constant reminder of the Shevardnadze government's failure to provide security to both the IDPs and the general population in the face of increasing waves of poverty and economic collapse (Theodorou 1996, 6; Manning 2008). It was a gaping political wound encountered by the residents of the capital nearly every day.

After the Rose Revolution in 2004, the new government headed by Mikheil Saakashvili was eager to remove the aesthetic and political blight of the IDP collective centers from the urban landscape. In early 2007 the government adopted a neoliberal "national strategy" to privatize the collective centers and to remove the IDPs as a visible symbol of the state's failure to effectively turn them into the objects of technical policy (Government of Georgia 2007). As a flagship project, the Iveria Hotel was emptied of IDPs, leased to developers, and transformed into the glass-and-steel Radisson hotel and shopping complex. It was a "monumental embodiment of the political fantasy of [Saakashvili's] Rose Revolution" (Manning 2008). Yet, beyond the highly symbolic Iveria, more than 250,000 first-wave IDPs remained in the same squalorous limbo as ever, recalcitrant in the face of the state's attempts to bureaucratically manage their suffering.

In 2008, when war broke out again in South Ossetia, the IDP situation took on new urgency. With twenty-eight thousand new IDPs in addition to the old caseload, demonstrating the state's ability to care for IDPs became a test of political legitimacy at a moment when Saakashvili's sovereignty was in doubt owing to Georgia's massive loss of territory during the war. In order to reestablish authority he had to reassure a restive population that despite his loss of South Ossetia he could continue to lead the country and to provide military, political, and economic security for the population. The fate of the IDPs quickly became a metonym for the reestablishment of sovereignty on the geopolitical scale, and the new settlements quickly became symbols that were meant as the antithesis of the Hotel Iveria.

Although Saakashvili had failed to convince Western governments to engage militarily during the South Ossetian war, he engaged them on a massive scale by throwing open Georgia's doors to foreign donor governments, the United Nations, and international NGOs, who provided over $1 billion in aid in 2008–2009. In contrast to what Pandolfi (2003) described for former Yugoslavia, the humanitarian apparatus in Georgia did not violate national sovereignty or override an unwilling government. On the contrary, humanitarianism in Georgia was intrinsically a state-building project, one that promulgated "capacity building" for the nation-state as a means to deliver aid more effectively, bind Georgia more tightly to the West as a client state, and create a bulwark against Russian expansionism. Whatever the neoimperialist geopolitical ambitions of the Western donor nations were, they were consonant with Saakashvili's larger project of penetrating social milieux that had been outside state control since the collapse of the USSR. Like the Communists who had gone before him, Saakashvili's goal was reestablishing state control over minute, everyday aspects of social, political, and economic life (see Dunn 2008; Manning 2008; Schueth 2012). Controlling the social reintegration of the IDPs—and making sure that IDPs did not reintegrate enough that they could not be moved back to South Ossetia if the Georgian Army could retake it—was a key element in that project.

Modalities of Humanitarian Governance

By the time I arrived in early 2009, the rush of incoming NGOs that had initially focused on simply keeping the IDPs alive had begun to launch "post-emergency recovery" projects that covered almost every aspect of social life. In the properly governed spaces of the settlement, IDPs were supposed to become politically docile and economically productive subjects who ran their own businesses, farmed food for consumption and sale, maintained healthy bodies, and formed stable families (see Foucault 2007). As in many other postconflict situations, the government, international donor government agencies, and international NGOs in Georgia portrayed the vast array of humanitarian projects as apolitical charity. On television, on the Internet, and in the glossy reports of the aid agencies, the building of the settlements and all the projects to reestablish "normal" life that went on within them were seen as gifts of care from both the Georgian government and international donors, for which IDPs should be grateful.

On one occasion, for example, I traveled to Prezeti settlement, where the minister of health, Sandro Kvitashvili, had arrived with a phalanx of television reporters (many of whom were from the government-controlled stations). Kvitashvili, like Saakashvili, was also educated in New York City, and had a similarly slick veneer. In Prezeti, a frozen camp on a hill so desolate that wolves followed the children to school, Kvitashvili's polished English and crisp, blue gingham shirt stood out among the IDPs, who were heavily layered in drab sweaters and coats. But what impressed the IDPs I spoke with about Kvitashvili was not his appearance, but his smell: among the stale odor of unwashed bodies in the settlement, which had no indoor running water, Kvitashvili's expensive foreign cologne was an olfactory tracer of his presence and his difference. As he made a very brief tour of a cottage where a mobile medical team was visiting and gave a statement for the cameras, I watched reporters rounding up IDPs for interviews and telling them what to say. One reporter put her arm around an elderly woman and hustled her toward the camera while telling her, "Just say you're really grateful for the minister's help and for everything you've gotten."

For all the agencies involved in the UN's cluster system, the fact that social reintegration projects were managed through a series of bureaucratic systems was a point of pride. Those systems ranged from cluster-system coordination, formalized needs-assessment surveys, and international standards for aid to standardized accounting practices and quantitative outcome measures. For the Saakashvili government, which had gained international legitimacy through its efforts to combat corruption, the bureaucratic control of aid allowed it to claim that the aid process was well-regulated, orderly, and transparent. As Saakashvili said, "Responsible leadership and transparent governance are needed if you want your aid to be effective and change people's lives" (Millennium Challenge Corporation 2011).

How were these claims about care and transparency related? Why did creating social order seem, at least in the minds of both the foreign humanitarian agencies and the Georgian government, to require bureaucratic order? For critics like Maren (2002) or Polman (2010), the application of bureaucratic practices commonly used in business implies that humanitarians' declarations of altruistic motives are a sham. But bureaucratization is neither a straightforward way to more efficiently create social order, as the humanitarian agencies claim, nor a contradiction of altruism (cf. Calhoun 2008; Stein 2008; Krause 2014). Rather, sentiments of altruism, bureaucratic management, and the construction of spaces like the new Georgian settlements are three distinct modalities of care, each of which locate humanitarian action in a unique space and which enable particular forms of action.

In the first of the three modalities of care, the *affective modality*, humanitarianism presents itself as an ethical configuration (Ticktin 2006, 35). As a moral and emotional reaction to suffering, humanitarianism engages with notions of destruction and salvation that are both locally specific and derived from global discourses of morality and violence rooted in Western norms (Moyn 2010). Despite the emotive pull of these discourses, they are not transformed into action until they are institutionalized in NGOs, UN agencies, and government ministries. This transformation into the second modality, the *bureaucratic modality*, renders suffering into an organizational or logistical problem that can be rationalized in a Weberian sense (Calhoun 2008; Barnett 2010, 81). Yet mere bureaucratic rationalization and the creation of new social institutions is not enough to help displaced people. Instead, the products of the bureaucratic modality, its reports and PowerPoint presentations, its proposals and spreadsheets, its projects and reports, become aid when they are transformed into a third modality, the *material modality*. In this mode humanitarian projects are transformed into new material objects like food, furnishings, and medicines, and most especially into new spaces of habitation, production, and consumption. An IDP settlement is thus the material manifestation of the meanings attached to care and compassion (including political ones), the specific ideologies and forms of sovereignty within which those sentiments were transformed into bureaucratic architectures, and the ways bureaucratic institutions use specific techniques to perceive need, assess risk, and provide assistance.

While the aim of such projects may be to govern all of social life for the displaced in a kind of benevolent totalitarianism, the actual reach of aid projects is determined by the negotiations, slippages, and deviations from plan that occur in the transformations between affective, bureaucratic, and material modalities (e.g., Redfield 2005; Ticktin n.d.; but cf. Feldman 2008a.). Like many other attempts to improve the human condition, humanitarianism's mobile sovereignty often falls short of its stated goals as it attempts to use bureaucratic means to shape the behavior of the target population and constitute security (Li 2007; Scott 1998).

Managing Aid: The Cluster System

To manage the massive flood of aid entering Georgia, the United Nations provided its Office for the Coordination of Humanitarian Affairs (OCHA) as the lead agency, promising a streamlined bureaucratic method for converting offers of help to the war-affected population into material assistance. By August 11, a mere four days after the outbreak of the war, OCHA had arrived and had set up a "cluster coordination" mechanism for organizing the many NGOs and millions of dollars in aid that had begun to flow into the country. The cluster coordination system is a recent bureaucratic innovation, put forth by the United Nations in 2005 in the wake of its inadequate response to the Darfur crisis (ICVA 2005). It is designed, in the vague terms of the UN document describing it, to "ensure sufficient global capacity," "identify predictable leadership," "strengthen account-ability," and "improve strategic field-level coordination and prioritization" (OCHA n.d.-a).

Ticktin (2006, 35) argues that humanitarianism attempts to depoliticize human suffering by rendering it into a moral problem—that is, by transform-ing a political problem into an affective one. In Georgia it soon became clear that the cluster system sought to render political problems apolitical. But it did so here not by shifting to the ground of values, but by transforming compas-sion into bureaucracy and rendering suffering into a purely technical problem (Li 2007). Via the cluster system OCHA established a division of labor among agencies, appealed to donors for funds, and coordinated the delivery of services to the displaced. The cluster system rendered suffering technical by breaking human needs into nine categories managed at the level of population: shelter, food security, water and sanitation, health, logistics, early recovery, protection, security, and telecommunications. Each of these functional areas was assigned to a UN agency known as the "cluster lead": The World Health Organization han-dled health, for example, while the World Food Program managed food supply. While OCHA coordinated the entire aid process, the cluster leads were supposed to gather donor agencies, international NGOs, local NGOs, and government ministries working on that particular issue and coordinate all the "partner agen-cies" to ensure the aggregate of needs is met, that two NGOs aren't providing the same services to the same group of IDPs, and that there aren't gaps in the provision of aid. The cluster leads were also supposed to coordinate the funding process by dividing up the labor to be done, coordinating the development of project proposals, and aggregating them into a joint request for funding from donor governments known as the "flash appeal." Each project was carefully recorded on a master spreadsheet coordinated by the cluster leads and distrib-uted to all the participants in the cluster.

The aid system thus had a grid or cell-like structure designed to superim-pose order on the chaos of agencies offering help by breaking down the complex basket of needs of a widely varying group of displaced people into a fungible bundle of biophysiological needs and assigned to corresponding bureaucratic structures. Individuals themselves were bureaucratically standardized, stripped of the social ties forged in village communities and the social identities tied to gender, age, residence, and health status. With the exception of children (who became the focus of particular attention from UNICEF), all displaced people were assumed to be identical individuals with identical needs. The same allotments for caloric intake, medical care, sleeping space, and clothing were made for each individual, now the anonymous unit of humanitarian need. As the IDPs streamed through the tent camp in Gori en route to the kindergartens and other public buildings where they would stay for the first four months, humanitarian agencies passed out cots, woolen blankets imprinted with the UNHCR logo, meals designed to meet basic caloric requirements, and standardized "hygiene kits" with a washcloth, soap, and toothbrush. Through the process of standardizing aid, each IDP was turned into an anonymous, standardized example of humanity, a *homo humanitarius* as generic as the *homo sovieticus* that preceded him (see Arendt 1951).

At the same time that the refugees were standardized as a population, however, the individual was broken apart bureaucratically. Physical needs for food, shelter, water, and the repair of the body were considered separately and largely without relation to one another. People's needs as social beings—the need to know where family and friends were and to be near them, the need to worship, be educated, or have meaningful work—were all left aside in the rush to meet basic biological needs (see Turner 2005, 312; Rieff 2003). IDPs with specific personal, occupational, generational, and place-based identities were thus transformed into a population assumed to have uniform needs rather than a collection of individual sufferers.

Reducing the IDPs to standardized victims had the salutary effect, at least from a bureaucratic perspective, of making it possible to resolve their problems using standardized "kits" of aid. As Redfield (2008b, 123) points out, humanitarian agencies have long relied on kits, repositories of implements that may be useful in alleviating suffering. Like the medical kits carried by doctors, the larger-scale humanitarian kits assembled by humanitarian agencies are prepacked and portable, stockpiled for fast-breaking emergencies. They are highly standardized for various types of disasters: massive displacement, endemic disease, famine. Some of the kits contain material necessities, such as tents, cots, and blankets for one thousand people, an isolation hospital to treat five hundred cholera sufferers, or equipment to build latrines for five thousand displaced people in a temporary camp. But other kits are as replete with concepts and administrative tools as they are with material items: microloan projects, work-for-food programs, domestic violence prevention trainings, and peacebuilding seminars often come in prefabricated "kits" of ideas and activities that are as prepackaged as kits for cholera prevention or demining. As "immutable mobiles" (Latour 1987), these project kits were seen as eminently portable, as suitable for one country or disaster as another.

OCHA's job, then, was to use the standardized modular kits offered by the various humanitarian agencies and funded via the flash appeal to assemble a new social order in the settlements. In Georgia that edifice had to provide long-term security to the IDPs while at the same time engaging Western donor governments in ways that facilitated national security. To do this, the bureaucratic structures of the cluster system had to be transformed into a third modality of care—a *material* mode, in which the grid-like structure of the cluster system could be quickly written onto the built environment to create a space where humanitarian kits could be deployed.

In early October 2008, just a few weeks after the bulk of the IDPs had moved into kindergartens and other public buildings in urban areas, the Municipal Development Fund of the government of Georgia broke ground at thirty-six IDP settlements.[2] Working twenty-two hours per day, construction companies hastily tossed up small cinderblock cottages or renovated government buildings into tiny standardized apartments. These new settlements were the material embodiment of the clusters' spreadsheets. Although the cottages and most of the apartments envisioned people in nuclear family groups rather than as individuals, they assumed a homogeneous set of needs for each nuclear family and disregarded the ties of extended family that predominate in Georgian social relations. In the cottage settlements each family was assigned an identical amount of space, no matter if it was three people or six, and each cottage was furnished identically.[3] ("Why did they only give us four stools," asked the mother of a family in Tsmindatsqali, "when they know full well that there are five people living here?") Families were often broken apart and housed in distant settlements. With the sole exception of Tserovani settlement, which had a preexisting main street from when it was a Soviet *kolkhoz*, there was no room set aside in the settlements for schools, churches, or even bathhouses—a serious lacuna, given the lack of indoor plumbing in many settlements. Clearly the object was to get bodies under roofs, bodies that were considered as little more than individualized shelter-needing biological units.

The neat grids of the settlements seem to display the same "state simplifications" and "high modernist ideology" that Scott (1998) so brilliantly described. The bureaucratic reduction of people into bundles of biophysical needs, the architectural reduction of spaces for social interaction, and the transfer of rationality from the white cells of the spreadsheet into the white cells of the settlement's grid all seemed to evidence an attempt to control people by making them visible and legible. This was a clear contrast to the solution proffered for the wave of IDPs who had been displaced in the 1990s, who were squirreled away haphazardly in public buildings. Yet "bare life" did not sum up the forms of existence in the settlements. Along with the provision of infrastructure, medical care, and basic necessities like food and clothing, many of the "kits" humanitarian NGOs had to offer were conceptual rather than material, and aimed at social reintegration rather than the mere continuation of physical life. While Heifer International funded the distribution of livestock, for example, the International Organization for Migration brought out standardized psychosocial aid programs aimed at providing emotional support to people who experienced violence. CARE International not only brought firewood but also brought an array of economic development programs including business training, vocational education, and microlending. In each of the thirty-six settlements—but particularly Tserovani, which was closest to Tbilisi and which thus became a demonstration site to be shown off to both the public and visiting dignitaries—projects were launched to transform the built environment in ways that would interpellate the IDPs as active, productive subjects. In Tserovani, soon after a police station was built as a visible marker of state sovereignty and discipline, other buildings indexing a more complex form of engagement with the state and with the local economy were erected. A glossy new school was built to educate IDP children. Next door a large municipal building was built to house the governments-in-exile of the displaced villages. Across the street a line of small shops was built to replace the metal grocery kiosks and bazaars that served the destroyed villages. In the center of the new retail row a sign announcing the imminent construction of an Internet café signaled the IDPs would soon be connected to the global flow of information. As the months went on a few small factories began to encircle the

perimeter: a commercial bakery, a paper mill, a commercial chicken farm. All of them were built with hundreds of thousands of dollars in subsidies to private entrepreneurs from USAID and other donors.

The Georgian government was adamant that these new dwelling places were "settlements," or *dasaxleobebi*, rather than "camps" or *banakebi*. Settlements were meant to be something radically different from refugee camps, which were seen as a technology for excluding people from the polity, warehousing them, or constituting them as surplus humans (see also Agamben 1994; Ticktin n.d.; Redfield 2005). Tserovani was not meant to reduce the IDPs to bare life or to act as a holding tank for an unwanted and useless population. Rather, it was expressly designed to recycle the IDPs, to reconstitute them as productive social beings and to reengage them as citizens of the nation by enmeshing them in webs of circulating ideas, products, people, and money. Clearly the form of sovereignty operating in the settlement was not premised on a state of exception (as an Agambenian framework might have it), but on a more productive form of biopolitics that used neoliberal technologies of development and aid to make the IDPs live, but then turned their existence into a debt owed to the state that could be gratefully acknowledged but never repaid (see Schueth 2012 see also chapter 6). Humanitarian aid thus created not just a public symbol of the West's willingness to guarantee Saakashvili's sovereignty vis-à-vis Russia, but also a form of citizenship in which people were made simultaneously responsible for themselves and eternally dependent on the state. In theory at least, the humanitarian penetration of everyday life would enable a new way for the state to manage the population—one that did not depend on oppression and force, as it did during the Soviet period, as much as it depended on the careful shepherding of IDPs and the cultivation of their indebtedness and dependence on the Saakashvili government.

Adhocracy and the Production of Chaos

From the standpoint of donor governments and the international NGOs, social reintegration—or at least the reconstitution of a new social order in the camps—seemed like a well-organized and logical project. The linkage between humanitarianism and statebuilding seemed like a straightforward way to constitute social order and security. But behind the orderly facades of the spreadsheets, meticulously designed cluster system, and identical cottages, the IDPs did not experience a sense of security or well-being. From the settlement, the NGOs and the state could be seen only partially, and the social order they attempted to construct presented itself as something fragmentary, confusing, and arbitrary. Many of the IDPs lived with a chronic sense of fear, an all-encompassing sense that the future was unknown and that they were constantly at risk of further violence or disaster. As Vano Grigoladze, a man from the village of Tamarasheni, told me:

> The Russians have taken my future. They've taken my path. Before I had walnut trees, a beautiful house.... Now, I don't know what will happen. There's nothing here, there's no path forward. We're afraid. For fifteen years (in South Ossetia), they were shooting at us. We lived in fear. Now I'm afraid that if the Russians come back, they're going to take all of Georgia. That is the Russians' way: to pretend they are your friends, then turn around and shoot you. So who is going to help me? I am afraid of dying, and nobody should die too early. I don't know when I was born and I don't know when I'll die. In between, it's been nothing but war.

In sixteen months of research in the settlements, I heard a variation of this speech over and over, from men and women, IDPs from every village, and people of all ages. In this lament, regional, national, and local levels of vulnerability were all mixed up together: the Russians had taken away all forms of security, and neither Saakashvili nor the international NGOs had been able to restore social order.

The litany points to the abyss between planners' visions for social reintegration and beneficiaries' experience of it. Despite the intense bureaucratization of aid, the acutely stylized forms of planning and the carefully thought-out contents of each humanitarian project, beneficiaries do not necessarily see reintegration projects as productive of a nurturing social order that facilitated their resumption of their familiar, everyday lives. Nor do they automatically see attempts at social reintegration as an oppressive totalitarian order (cf. Agier 2011). Instead the new humanitarian order often presents itself as an extension of the chaos of war—a kind of permanent disruption that renders life unpredictable, leaves people at risk of violence and poverty, and prevents them from making their own plans for new lives. The chaos of aid prevents IDPs from re-creating a "normal situation," or a network of relationships between people, objects, and places that would make a lifeworld stable enough to act within.

Producing the Chaos of Aid

Why does the cluster system produce a sense of chaos for its beneficiaries rather than a sense of order? Why did the system for organizing humanitarian aid, which was supposed to restore the normal situation, instead constantly disrupt it? Looking at the copious spreadsheets, notes, maps, and grids about Georgia archived at the UN's ReliefNet site, a computer archive open to all the participants in the cluster system, the social integration project for the new IDPs seemed to be well planned. Via its designated "response coordinator," the minister of health and labor, the government of Georgia claimed that it could tell the international agencies what the IDPs needed and how it should be delivered. For their part, the international agencies gave the appearance of having the means to fulfill the government's plan quickly and efficiently. However, I argue that the bureaucratic mode of humanitarian action is not just characterized by epistemologies of planning and order, but is fundamentally reliant on other forms of knowing, including guesswork and improvisation. Context is all important: while individual humanitarian agencies see themselves as "a mobile strike force" that could deploy kits without regard to the specifics of any particular emergency (Redfield 2008b), the kits' poor articulation, with vague overarching plans for meeting the IDPs' needs and the foreign aid workers' ignorance of the particular needs of a specific population, meant that projects were often transitory, confusing, and useless. This epistemological fuzziness casts doubt on claims to create security and order through political acts of spatial composition and challenges the idea that humanitarian activity can render political vulnerability into a technical problem.

In Georgia the first hints of just how disorderly the aid process would be came within a week of the war. In the first place, despite the fact that the government of Georgia's response coordinator was supposed to work with OCHA and the cluster leads to develop the flash appeal, or the master plan for the aid effort that could be sent to donors to request funding, there was never any central planning agency or coherent plan for aid to the displaced. On the government side, rather than a single spokesman for the government, there was a parliamentary committee, a group in the Chancellery, a group at the Ministry of Refugees and Accommodation (MRA), a group formed by the Tbilisi municipal government, and a special group formed by the prime minister, all claiming to represent the government in the cluster planning process. None of these agencies, though, had the capability to make a master plan that would organize the work of all the agencies offering aid. As Julia Kharashvili, who coordinated relief efforts at the MRA, said:

> The MRA had no opportunity to make a plan. There were only three people here who even spoke English. My telephone was ringing non-stop. We would work until two or three in the morning, go home to sleep three hours, and come back. I hardly had time to shower or dress, I'd get the neck of my shirt on and [my arm into] one sleeve, and the phone would ring again.

Likewise, on the side of the international aid agencies, there was a noisy plethora of voices and negotiating partners. While OCHA claimed to be coordinating the international response, many of the ninety-two NGOs involved in the cluster system were devising plans of their own and negotiating independently with the government; still other aid agencies that were not participating

in the cluster system were carrying out activities on the ground without informing either OCHA or the government of their activities. Thus, from the earliest
days after the war broke out, there was an enormous pluralization of regulatory
activity and regulatory authority that undermined the supposed rationality of
the system. This is an endemic problem in humanitarian situations around the
world. As Weiss (2013, 96) writes, "A cartoonist could not have come up with a
better design for futile complexity than the current array of UN organizations
and international NGOs."

Indeed, for displaced people themselves, the welter of UN agencies, international NGOs, ministries, local government agencies, and funders is most often
totally incomprehensible. Seen only fleetingly as they passed through the settlements on sightseeing visits with dignitaries or came for a few hours to hold a
meeting or distribute aid packages, the humanitarian agencies in the Georgian
camps seemed to come and go without any explanation. For the first few months,
the IDPs lumped all of them together as *mtavroba*, the government. (For example,
I would ask Elena Chochieva, my round, red-haired neighbor in Tsmindatsqali,
"Who brought you this food package," while pointing at a World Food Program
bundle containing bags of beans with the USAID logo, and she would answer,
"*Mtavroba.*") Later they began to make the distinction between *mtavroba* and
arasamtavrobis organizatsiebi, or nongovernmental organizations. But any finer
distinctions remained beyond most IDPs' ken: even as the NGOs plastered cottages and food bags and telephone poles with their logos, most IDPs never sorted
CARE from World Vision from Save the Children. (The exceptions to this were
the IDPs who became something like professional beneficiaries. They angled to be
invited to participate in NGO projects, hoping to gain stipends or resources, and
over time became quite knowledgeable about the local landscape of aid.)

The fact that the humanitarian agencies bring projects in the form of prefabricated kits pushes the humanitarian system[4] further into chaos rather than adding
order or rationality. According to David Kacharava, who led the health cluster on
behalf of the World Health Organization, the process of developing the flash appeal
was done almost entirely on the fly, as aid agencies pulled whatever kits they had on
hand off the shelf without much concrete knowledge of what these particular IDPs,
in this particular postconflict situation, actually needed. As Kacharava told me,

> The Ministry of Health did not even participate. Some of the partners
> (international NGOs and donor agencies) were calling us from the
> airport the night before the flash appeal was due, saying "we want in."
> They didn't know Georgia, didn't know the situation, didn't know what
> anybody else was doing. They just cut and pasted some old projects
> together. They literally just took out the words "Indonesia" or "Congo"
> and put in "Georgia." Some of the projects were total bullshit.

NGOs and donors were faced with a situation in which they had to very rapidly predict the actions of hundreds of other actors without any central plan to refer to. To decide what projects to offer or fund, they had to make fast guesses about what IDPs needed, what the other NGOs were doing, and what the government would approve. This required epistemological tools that went beyond acknowledged tools for bureaucratic rationalization such as standardization and gridding. Instead it required a set of covert epistemological tools that included imagining, rules of thumb, and satisficing. These tools transformed what first appeared to be a well-planned and orderly system into something with a markedly ad hoc character.

One example of an alternate epistemology was imagining. In selecting which kits to bring, workers often had to imagine what the situation on the ground might be like—offering to bring water to counteract an imagined dearth, or bringing in medicines to counteract the endemic disease they believed would emerge. In the absence of anything more than cursory "rapid assessments," aid agencies had to imagine what the IDPs needed or would like to eat, wear, and sleep on. Although some haphazard information was provided in the cluster coordination meetings, aid agencies often had to guess what the other aid agencies were doing, estimate what resources other actors had and where they were operating, and even where the IDPs would go next. The result was aid flowing in that was unneeded or inappropriate, while real needs were often not met.

For Julia Kharashvili, the official from the Ministry for Refugees and Accommodation, the problem was that each NGO imagined need differently:

> One hundred organizations a day came to us to say, "I want to do something to help. We'll bring tents." And then the next people would say, "We'll bring tents, but in a different color." Some organizations would say, "We'll bring water." And I would tell them that we had water in Gori, there was no need for anybody to bring it in. But they would say, "It's an emergency! You always need water in an emergency!" and they'd bring it anyway. A lot of times the aid they had to give didn't match what we needed. So they might bring one hundred tents when we already had enough tents but needed eighty mattresses.
>
> This kind of aid has a high dollar value, but that doesn't always meet people's real needs. Everybody brought what they could, but it often duplicated what the government already had in its emergency stocks. And then I was left trying to account for what had happened to all this money, to all these things that we didn't want or need. UNHCR sent used clothes, for example, but they were often secondhand clothes in really big sizes, bigger than people here wear. The Japanese sent clothes and shoes, too, but in really tiny sizes that we couldn't do anything with except give to children. What we couldn't use we just had to throw away.

Even months later, the mismatch between the material aid delivered in response to imagined need and the IDPs' real needs was evident. In the cottage of Vakhtang Baratashvili, an elderly man, a bed was stacked with used toys: dolls with tangled hair, ratty stuffed animals, and some grubby things made of injection-molded plastic. I was startled and asked if he had children living there. "No," he said, "they just gave those to me." He was given shoes as well, which he kept neatly stacked in one of the bedrooms. None of them fit, he complained, even though he'd told the aid workers his size. Bending down, he poked his finger through the hole in the shoe he was wearing. "It would be nice to have a pair that wasn't falling apart, or at least an awl and a needle and thread so I could repair these."

Inappropriate training and technical assistance revealed the extent to which humanitarian kits operated on the basis of rules of thumb, knowledge gained in one specific context that had been generalized to apply to all crisis situations regardless of their nature or location. The idea that water was needed in every emergency showed how epistemologically powerful these rules of thumb were, as did the "bullshit" projects developed for Indonesia or Congo that were assumed to be equally necessary in Georgia.

In many instances the application of rules of thumb in ways that ignored local contexts led to spectacular misallocations of aid dollars. For example, the health cluster identified low rates of breastfeeding as a key problem, made "promoting evidence-based feeding practices" one of three goals of the cluster under the flash appeal, and requested $680,000 in funding for infant-feeding support programs to be carried out by seventeen mobile teams (OCHA 2008c). Infant feeding programs were developed in Africa, where bottlefeeding is widely promoted but can be dangerous because of erratic supplies of formula and contaminated water. Georgia, though, is a post-Soviet country, one that experienced

industrialization and urban development. There were even fewer infants in the IDP population than in the already disproportionately aging Georgian population as a whole because young people had been migrating out of Georgian villages in South Ossetia to look for work. Breastfeeding in Georgia was widely accepted, formula remained easily available throughout the crisis, and there was high-quality running water in all the places IDPs were placed. Yet breastfeeding support was deemed urgent because humanitarian agencies' experiences in other locales suggested it should be urgent. In the race to develop projects and get them funded through the flash appeal, a model based on a totally different context was applied to Georgia and hundreds of thousands of dollars in aid money was devoted to prevent a problem that never existed. Meanwhile there were other problems for which no rules of thumb had been developed, such as diabetes in elderly IDPs living on high-glycemic-index bread, macaroni, and sugar delivered to them by the World Food Programme. These went unseen and largely unaddressed.

The same problem reappeared in projects to improve the IDPs' mental health. Many of the NGOs competed to create photogenic "child friendly spaces," brightly painted rooms where children could play, draw, and paint. Six other NGOs quickly devised psychotherapeutic programming for children, opportunities for the children to reenact their traumatic experiences or to depict them in artwork. Yet as the MRA's Julia Kharashvili pointed out to me, psychosocial aid to children was not the most pressing need:

> So many people wanted to do psychosocial assistance for children, even more than wanted to do humanitarian aid. But really the most traumatized people were often the elderly. They stayed behind to guard their houses, and they were often taken hostage, beaten, thrown into prisons, or forced to bury the corpses of the dead. But nobody wanted to help them. Our appeals for that kind of help were like a voice shouting in the desert. We kept rejecting international organizations' plans because there are local organizations here that are well-trained and well-qualified. The internationals would have to work through translators, and really, what kind of psychological help can you give that way? We begged the international agencies not to send their own people, but to fund the trained Georgian therapists we had here.

This kind of misplaced funding was well-intentioned, to be sure, but showed a significant disjuncture between the help on offer and the actual needs of the population because it was almost always the result of using rules of thumb developed in another part of the world as heuristics for aid planning in Georgia.

Above all, humanitarian epistemologies were based on satisficing. Satisficing refers to the process of making decisions that are "good enough" rather than optimal (Simon 1955; see also Byron 2005). Under the pressure of time, and with poor information to go on, aid workers often designed projects that seemed to help "well enough" rather than making the largest possible contribution. Bringing water when it wasn't needed was an example of this kind of satisficing—it looked good to donors and fulfilled the aid agency's mandate for emergency assistance, and so was "good enough," even though the IDPs didn't actually need water. Satisficing was also driven by ideological concerns external to the situation in Georgia. When donors had pet projects or concepts (around ideas of gender, age, and other forms of vulnerability, for example), those clearly spurred aid agencies to cobble together "good enough" projects that provided some small help to the target population, even if the money might have been spent to make a bigger difference to a more vulnerable group. As a UNHCR official said, "The NGOs have their sexy projects, and they try and squeeze them in." Under the business logic of the humanitarian marketplace, then, IDPs were soon seen not as the beneficiaries of humanitarian aid, or even as customers for the product that NGOs produced. Rather, they were the means of production for NGOs as they sought to meet the requirements of their real clients, the donors (see Feldman 2008b).

The largest problem with the OCHA-led cluster-planning system, though, is not that individual projects are poorly designed or inappropriate to the situation. It is that because the project kit is the fundamental unit of action rather than a master plan, the aid system remains patchy and erratic, and thus cannot constitute a seamless social order that produces existential security. OCHA is, at least in theory, supposed to use the cluster system to assemble modular kits into a coherent plan of action to reestablish social order that could be detailed in the flash appeal. However, as a unit of social practice, off-the-shelf humanitarian kits have a markedly idiosyncratic character: although they can be replicated from site to site without regard for local particularities of place, they are not standardized with respect to one another, and thus are remarkably difficult to organize, arrange so that they do not overlap, or map neatly onto the spatial coordinates where the "beneficiaries" of aid live. OCHA claims that the flash appeal, and its successors, the common humanitarian action plan and the consolidated appeal process, act as "A snapshot of a situation that identifies who does what and where" (OCHA n.d.-a). But because OCHA has no power to dictate what donors fund or what projects NGOs projects carry out, neither the flash appeal nor the common humanitarian action plan nor the consolidated appeals process ever function as any kind of master plan. Rather, aid remains a loose concatenation of kit-based projects proposed by NGOs themselves without respect to any planning or coordination mechanism. Chaos is not just something created by the war, against which the institutional structures of bureaucratic care have to struggle, but an intrinsic property of a system in which various organizations obtain funding by proposing self-contained projects ad hoc. This is not therapeutic management or pastoral care, in the sense of a visible sovereign meticulously planning for the welfare of a population. It is, instead, adhocracy, a system that uses rough-and-ready ways of knowing to quickly arrive at improvised solutions.

Adhocracies rely on what Tilly (1996) called "the invisible elbow," an imprecise means for getting by or making do by making reasonable guesses about actions in a complex world. Not surprisingly, it often leads to mistakes. Tilly, contrasting this mode of governance with the assumed accuracy of market rationality, describes it like this:

> For the invisible hand, let's substitute the invisible elbow. Coming home from the grocery store, arms overflowing with food-filled bags, you wedge yourself against the doorjamb, somehow free a hand to open the kitchen door, enter the house, and then nudge the door shut again with your elbow. Because elbows are not prehensile, and in this situation not visible either, you sometimes slam the door smartly, sometimes swing the door halfway closed, sometimes miss completely on the first pass, sometimes bruise your arm on the wood, sometimes shatter the glass, and sometimes—responding to one of these earlier calamities—spill the groceries all over the floor (593).

Tilly's point is that given constraints on information and the enormous difficulty of predicting what other people are going to do, most social actors are muddling around most of the time, doing the best they can but not very well. In the complicated world of humanitarian intervention, where hundreds of agencies attempt to plan action in the midst of rapidly changing events, agencies routinely make provisional plans and then attempt to alter their behavior quickly as they obtain new information. Far from being omniscient benevolent sovereigns or rational businessmen, their power is sharply limited by the fact that they are mostly bumbling about, acting on the basis of partial knowledge, inappropriate analogies, and very loose rules of thumb.

Although government officials and foreign-aid workers alike are willing to acknowledge just how much bungling and improvisation there was, they attribute it to different causes. One UN official saw the lack of rational planning and the need for on-the-fly responses not as a flaw in the cluster system, but as a problem of the Georgian character:

> The clusters are very ad hoc. Even where we have structures, it stays ad hoc. Part of this is the Georgian mentality—they are adhoc-ish. I'm afraid

that even good structures here will reduce but not overcome this adhoc-ishness. It's Georgia, and you have to play it their way. If there is an acute situation, you have to put away your structures and just help. That way you gain the ministry's trust, so they listen to you the next time. It's extremely personalized.

But adhocracy was not just a distortion of the cluster system introduced by irrational and inappropriately personalistic locals. Rather, it was a problem endemic to the cluster system that could be seen in the missteps and slippages of aid planning. These were not evidence of a deficit of modernist bureaucratic rationality, but rather signals indicating the presence of other forms of knowledge—practical forms, like guessing, imagining, and satisficing—that were important alternative bridges between the affective and material modes of care.

Materializing Adhocracy

The ad hoc character of the aid process not only permeates humanitarianism's bureaucratic mode but profoundly shapes its spatial mode as well. Rather than creating the secure, productive environments that might reintegrate displaced people as citizens, adhocracy creates a material environment that rapidly decays, leaving displaced people with the burden of repairing the mistakes made by epistemologies of guessing, imagination, and analogy. These chaotic, crumbling environments—slums in the making—leave displaced people demoralized, more vulnerable to violence and disaster, and more likely to be poor. The IDPs are thus reduced to a struggle for survival, not as a result of calculated action but by barriers to calculation inherent in the system.

In Georgia, although the settlements gave the appearance of being carefully planned, they were in fact rapidly cobbled together. According to officials at UNHCR, the settlements were constructed completely outside the cluster system, unbeknownst to any of the people working within it to plan for resettlement. On its own, the government's Municipal Development Fund quickly drafted plans for the new settlements and hired construction firms to begin work. The government notified UNHCR, which believed the IDPs would stay in the kindergartens for the winter, only after ground was broken at Tserovani. According to another UNHCR official, this haste was for reasons of statecraft: it was to show donors that the Georgian government could "do it better and faster" and thus to elicit cash donations to build the Georgian government rather than allowing international agencies to manage resettlement. Haste, she said, was an integral part of the chaotic and improvisational character of Georgian adhocracy.

They say, "Once we settle the refugees, then we'll take the next step. We'll do schools for all the villages later." They are always saying, "We'll cross that bridge when we come to it." But by that time, half of the beneficiaries are already in the river!

In the end, the UNHCR official argued, the settlements were built without an extensive planning process as the result of snap decisions made by government officials:

> Resettlement is like a water system: if you build it right, then if there's a leak, you can replace the bad pipe and the system will work again. But if you don't design the system right from the beginning, when it's broken you can't fix it. I'm worried that the government hasn't planned and that things are going to break down in ways that can't be fixed.

Things did indeed begin to break down quickly. Within weeks of the cottages' being built, the adhocratic institutional mode of care began to manifest itself spatially, and chaos began to inscribe itself on the built environment. In the rush to build thousands of cottages, the construction firms contracted by the Georgian government bought wet materials and often had not given them time to dry before continuing construction. Soon after the IDPs moved into their new quarters the buildings began to disintegrate. Wooden floorboards laid tightly together shrank, creating gaps where snakes, ants, and grass entered IDPs' homes, terrifying and disheartening them (see chapter 6). Wet plaster on the walls contracted as it dried, leaving the cottages with crumbling walls. The hasty design of the cottages had failed to include ventilation for the cottages' tiny attics, so breath and steam from cookpots condensed on the interior lining of the roof and fell back into the houses, leaving large brown water spots and holes in the ceilings. In Manana Abaeva's kitchen, as in many other people's cottages, the walls were covered with black spots of mold.

In the settlements without indoor plumbing, outhouses over pits served as toilets. However, the pits were often dug into clay soil, and waste began to rise in the pits rather than percolating down through the ground. Because the IDPs were expected to provide for their own food by planting the land around each cottage with vegetables, the human waste coming up toward the surface risked contaminating the crops and posed a serious health threat. Because no area had been designed to drive a truck up to the latrines, it was soon impossible to remove the waste without destroying the crops the IDPs labored to grow.

The built environment of the settlements thus reflected not only the statist urge to create discipline by ordering people in rows and making them visible to authorities, the drive to make people more secure by giving them the means to produce their own food, or the goal of having people sell surplus crops as a way of integrating them into local markets. It also revealed the impetuousness, satisficing, and guessing that was bound up in humanitarianism as statebuilding. In place of rationally produced security, there was disorder and uncertainty. Cracks in information were transmuted into cracks in plaster, and the gaps in planning mutated into the gaps in the floors where insects entered to eat the sugar and flour delivered as food aid. The storms that continued to buffet the IDPs were more than metaphorical: in the hard rains of spring and summer, water pounded through the cottages, soaking the clothing and furniture NGOs distributed. Manana Abaeva called me after the first flood in tears: the water had destroyed the winter clothing and coats her family had purchased using the entire "winterization payment" from UNHCR, and there was no more money in the offing. In the summer heat waves, vegetables grown with seeds provided by the UN's Food and Agriculture Organization and painstakingly canned a few jars at a time spoiled as the temperature soared in cottages designed without cool basements. In both Tsmindatsqali and Tserovani, gardens and newly bought possessions were damaged in storms that came up from below: the land for the settlement was apparently only available because the water table there was so high that spring rains turned the camp into a swamp. Epistemologies of guessing and satisficing, transmuted into institutional adhocracy, had lived material correlates that shaped the benefits IDPs could derive from the aid they were given.

The chaos of aid not only made security and social reintegration in the present difficult, but also made it nearly impossible for the IDPs to develop a rational plan for the future or invest their own material resources in their new settlements. Even well into the second year of displacements, humanitarian projects were arriving erratically, landing in some settlements but not others, offering different things to different people without clear criteria for who received aid and who did not. Heifer International might offer sheep and bees in Tsmindatsqali but not ever come to Koda or Gardabani, for example. CARE had a multimillion-dollar social reintegration project for the settlements in Shida Kartli province but never came to Mtskheta-Mtiani. In the context of the Shida Kartli project some IDPs were offered thousands of dollars of agricultural equipment while others, whose "business plans" were judged unacceptable for reasons their authors never understood, were left out. "Figuring out what we're going to get and when is like predicting the March weather," said Temo Javakhishvili's son, Zura, illustrating his frustration with the inexplicable and erratic nature of the aid process.

This is a problem endemic to humanitarian aid. Without knowing what kind of aid might come in the future, displaced people are hesitant to invest their own meager resources in improving their living standards or in starting small businesses. Without knowing if social reintegration projects such as livestock distributions or microcredit schemes might arrive at their specific locations, displaced people are unable to make decisions about which way to proceed in reestablishing themselves economically or socially. Their passivity and their dependence on aid, much decried by the humanitarians and the government, is not a moral failing or the result of emotional trauma. It is a product of adhocracy, a mode of governance that claims to be devoted to their social reintegration but in fact impedes their ability to join the local economy and discourages them from becoming attached to their new homes (see also Jones 2014, 12).

In Georgia the nation-state too was riven with cracks resulting from the institutional production of chaos. While the huge influx of humanitarian aid temporarily propped up the economy, the foreign direct investment that had allowed Saakashvili to claim it was providing the population with increased economic security plummeted from $2 billion in 2007 to less than half that, $759 million, in 2009 (Geostat 2010). As the economy slowed, Tbilisi was paralyzed for months by street protests organized by the opposition, which accused Saakashvili of recklessly attacking South Ossetia, bringing down the invasion, and creating the new wave of IDPs. As Saakashvili's one-time patrons, the United States and the European Union, distanced themselves and began a rapprochement with Russia, Georgia found itself increasingly isolated. With Russian tanks perched at a forward base in Akhalgori, a mere 35 miles away from Tbilisi, the Russian president Dmitry Medvedev pointed out the obvious threat to Georgian security, saying, "This is a direct signal to those . . . who get idiotic plans in their heads from time to time" (Felgenhauer 2009). Thus, despite the massive effort at statebuilding and the creation of security, Saakashvili was far from being able to exercise his responsibility to protect his own state, much less the Georgian population. During the hot nights of August 2009, a year after the war, the precariousness of the state was obvious most of all to the IDPs in the settlements just a few miles away from the de facto border, who lay awake in their beds, feeling the ground rumble as tanks prepared once again for battle. Although no attack came that summer, sniper fire back and forth across the border reminded everyone how unstable the situation was and how possible war remained.

Adhocracy and Domination

In her pathbreaking study of Hutu refugees in Tanzania, Liisa Maalki refers to the refugee camp as "a standardized, transferable device of power" (Maalki 1995, 53). The camp here is seen as a technology that aims to quarantine people stripped of political and social significance—people "who had lost all other qualities and specific relationships, except that they were still human"—in order to constitute new forms of sovereignty under the pretext of humanitarian action (Arendt 1951, 336; see also Ranciere 2004, 298). As Agier (2015) says, the figure of the absolute victim, anonymous and suffering, "determines the meaning given to the space of the camp itself insofar as it is created and run according to the rule of humanitarian government" and thus becomes the subject of a sovereign power that can merely let live or make die.

Yet, as the transformation of camps into settlements shows, the trend away from warehousing displaced people in spaces of exception and toward socially reintegrating them suggests humanitarians often seek to restore displaced people as social beings rather than reducing them to bare life—to make them live, that is, rather than letting them die. Intergovernmentals such as the United Nations agencies as well as donor governments now often do so by actively intervening in state formation, partnering with states that seem to have the potential to become liberal democracies in order to push those states to transform the spaces the displaced inhabit and make them into vehicles for the reestablishment of productive social order. "Building capacity," in the lingo of the humanitarians, stands for the transfer of bureaucratic practices linked to capitalism into the institutions of foreign governments.

But refugee settlements and the bureaucratic structures that enable their creation are not just technologies for the creation of order, but are also technologies for the production of chaos and disorder. To the Georgian IDPs sitting in their leaking cottages, wondering when aid would be delivered and if they could even use what came, the experience of humanitarianism was less one of being restored to full citizenship, or even one of therapeutic domination, than of a swirl of incomprehensible activity—aid coming down from the sky and then just as unpredictably vanishing. Life inside the humanitarian bureaucratic order was less about oppression and disempowerment than it was about disorientation and bewilderment. As an elderly woman in Tserovani said, "To put it simply, we're just very confused."

It might be tempting to label this a case of bureaucratic failure. It would certainly be easy to see the shortcomings of the aid process in terms of deviation from the ideal-typical model in which administrative practices create order, and then prescribe more of the same—better, improved technocratic management practices—as the remedy for the supposed "failures" of the humanitarian project. This is certainly the impulse that led to the cluster system in the first place, and that leads to the unremitting cycles of "new and improved" theories of aid management (see Dunn and Cons 2014). It might also be tempting to see a covert plan behind these "failures," a will to dominate that cares less about whether the IDPs receive usable shoes and watertight homes than it does about disempowering them, monitoring their movements, and creating new spaces for state incursions (see Ferguson 1994).

However, both these explanations miss the point. "Failures" in aid delivery are not aberrations from a rational-calculative practice. Nor are they mere covers for more nefarious activity, such as attempts to dehumanize the displaced, render them surplus, or make it possible to kill them (see Bauman 2004). The failures of humanitarianism stem from the epistemologies of the aid process. The same modes of knowing and not knowing that are integral to the endeavor of transforming the concrete spaces of the refugee settlement and alleviating suffering are the same ones used by capitalist businesses throughout the world. The chaos of aid is not a mere technical failure, but an outgrowth of the rationalizing practices that bureaucratic organizations use to grasp the world of the displaced and the ways they seek to govern it. Because chaos is intrinsic to the aid industry, it limits both humanitarianism's ability to create sovereignty and power and to repair the existential ruptures that war causes in the lives of the displaced.

NOTHING

On the frosty January morning I first walked into Tsmindasqali settlement, Temo Javakhishvili was drunk and agitated. He had just moved into the new "cottage" given to him by the Georgian government, a small cinderblock bungalow built on a damp piece of swampland, furnished with twin beds, a flimsy table, four small stools and a television blaring away on top of a cardboard box used for a stand. He paced back and forth on the bare pine floorboards, muttering and sometimes yelling. Zura, his eldest son, and I tried to comfort him, but he grew more and more upset. Shouting in a slurred voice, he removed his thick glasses over and over to compulsively wipe the lenses. "Nothing! They gave us nothing!"

Temo's distress was understandable. He had been violently ejected from the village of Eredvi in the breakaway province of South Ossetia during the war between Russia and Georgia in 2008. His house had been bombed by Russian aircraft, looted, and finally burned, possibly by his own neighbors. It was Temo whose younger son was killed during the bombing of Gori, and Temo's sons whose photograph, the eldest cradling the dead body of the youngest in front of a building in flames, had become the defining image of the war. His losses were enormous, the grief and emptiness in his life only temporarily anesthetized by becoming blind drunk, which he did often. Yet, on that first day, it was not the destruction of his family or the loss of his home that seemed to bother him most. It was the food aid package that had been delivered to him in his new cottage. "They gave us nothing! It's New Year's! The most important day of the year, the day when we hold our biggest *supra* (ritual banquet). But they just gave us some macaroni. That's it! Macaroni, and beyond that, nothing!"

In the first year I spent in the camps, I heard a variation of this lament over and over in virtually every interview and conversation. At Koda, a settlement made of renovated Red Army barracks housing 1,351 IDPs in small apartments, I joined a group of men gathered around a backhoe digging a trench for a new sewer line. A middle-aged man walked up to me and, probably mistaking me for an aid worker, struck up a conversation about what Koda had been given in aid. "We have nothing!" he said. "People just come here to us, and lie and lie and lie. . . . Maybe people in other settlements get something, but we have nothing at all." Yet, all around me, I could see the visible artifacts of aid: the freshly painted apartment buildings, the backhoe and the pipes for the new sewer line, and bags of food aid from the World Food Programme now for resale at makeshift kiosks (see also see CARE 2010; Jönsson and Ackerman 2009; Dunn 2012a). Yet even living in spaces carved out by humanitarian agencies and the nation-state, surrounded by donated objects, the man was adamant that he had received nothing at all. His plaintive litany was repeated in almost every interview I held with people in all the other camps: "They do nothing for us. The government and the NGOs are not helping us, they do nothing for us. We are alone, we are abandoned, and we have nothing."

Why did so many of the IDPs feel they had nothing? It was a startling sentiment, given that humanitarians are so focused on *doing something*. Humanitarianism's moral imperative to act rather than to stand idly by in the face of suffering is such a strong ethic that it is embedded in the most fundamental charters and codes of conduct of humanitarian organizations (Calhoun 2008; Bornstein and Redfield 2011b, 17). As the charter of the International Committee of the Red Cross says, for example, "The humanitarian imperative comes first . . . as members of the international community, we recognize our obligation to provide humanitarian assistance wherever it is needed" (ICRC 1995; see also Nockerts 2008). This drive to *do something*—no matter how ineffectively, no matter if the action isn't what is needed or required—is so powerful that I have often heard both humanitarians and students respond to criticisms of aid in the same way: "Well, something is better than nothing."

Is aid really something, as the aid workers say, though, or is it nothing, as their beneficiaries argue? Is something—however the aid workers define it—really better than nothing? These questions challenge the fundamental assumption of humanitarian aid: that the cataclysm of war creates voids in the material and social worlds that can be filled by humanitarian aid programs. At a fundamental level, contemporary humanitarianism assumes that nothingness is created by war, but can be filled with the objects and programs of aid. Arguments about aid thus center on whether humanitarians deliver aid properly, not on whether they should deliver it at all or what kind of world it creates. This makes the debate over aid a purely technocratic one: Both humanitarians and their critics agree that if only aid can be delivered more efficiently, at lower cost, with more account-ability, with more participation from the beneficiaries, or in a more transpar-ent manner, it would not only sustain life for another day but also replace the objects and activities that war destroyed and get displaced people and their soci-eties functioning again (see, for example, Rieff 2003; Zetter 1991; Sontag 2012; Easterly 2006).

These arguments mistake the reason that displaced people feel they have nothing and propose the wrong solutions to the wrong problem. The issue is not that aid agencies do nothing or give nothing.[1] As I argue in this chapter, the issue is that humanitarian aid *makes nothingness*. Nothingness is the central feature of life in the humanitarian condition: for those living in insile, it is the central existential category through which displaced people understand their new lives in the settlements, their new social status as displaced people, and their new political relationships to the state and the international community. For displaced people, the "something" that humanitarians deliver isn't better than nothing. It *is* nothing.

In this chapter I show that the reason that humanitarian aid makes noth-ingness is that it creates voids in the fragmented network that should link peo-ple, things, and symbols together into what Badiou (2006) called "the normal situation." As I argued in chapter 1, remaking this network is the fundamental existential task of displaced people. The normal situation is what could knit the fragments of their old lives together with the new ideas and things brought by the humanitarians together into a lifeworld that makes sense and is reasonably pre-dictable. But despite the best intentions of the humanitarians, the humanitarian condition impedes this process by creating three kinds of voids in the structure of daily life. First, at the level of material objects, humanitarianism delivers what I call *antiartifacts* that do not count in the eyes of displaced people, but only point to the things they once owned but have lost. Second, in the sphere of daily activities, humanitarianism does not replace the tasks and habits and practices that were disrupted by the war, but instead creates *black holes* that evacuate prac-tice and create long hours of doing nothing. Third, by keeping displaced people immobilized at a crossroads, stuck looking at multiple possible futures without the possibility of committing to any of them, humanitarianism creates a void in time, an *absolute zero* that freezes temporal horizons. From the IDP's point of view, these voids in the normal situation are empty of meaning themselves but constitute an affective atmosphere of mourning, grief, and loss that inhibits action and destroys meaning, and leads to a state of being that keeps people unsettled rather than allowing them to socially reintegrate.

Having Nothing: Zero

In the wake of the Russo-Georgian War, distributions of material aid had taken up much of the NGOs' efforts to help the IDPs. Indeed, at the cluster coordination meetings sponsored by the UN's Office for the Coordination of Humanitarian Affairs (OCHA), the NGOs reported that as late as seven months after the war they were still spending the bulk of their time doing distributions of food, clothing, medications, and so on. With humanitarian agencies arriving day after day to hand out everything from plastic basins to sanitary pads to bread, there was lots of stuff around. Some of it was useless, some of it was serviceable, none of it was particularly good quality, but still, it was something.

So, surprised by IDPs' claims to have received nothing, I began by asking aid workers at a UN-sponsored cluster meeting why the IDPs might deny that they had received anything of value. To my surprise, the aid workers at the table erupted in anger. "They're lying," said an aid worker from the NGO Caritas, lurching across the table at me and pointing his finger. "They aren't telling you things so that they can get more aid!" "They aren't telling you they've received things, not because they can't tell you, but because they won't tell you!" said an irritated woman from the Georgian Red Cross, who clearly regarded me as stupid and naïve.

Indeed, from the perspective of the aid workers, who were intently focused on the central problem of distribution, it was impossible to think that the IDPs had nothing. Humanitarian work is premised on the notion of the war as a cataclysmic Event, in Badiou's (2006) sense: as a rupture in the normal situation of being that evacuates normal life, particularly as it is constituted in and through the material world. The void that is produced, at least in aid workers' views, is first and foremost a loss of property. Filling that void with new property—that is, distributing the cots and pots of humanitarian aid—is seen not only as a means to sustain life or to remedy the condition of propertylessness, but to also heal the rupture of the event and to reestablish a new normality. To deny that one has received anything, then, is to reject the entire premise of humanitarianism, at least in aid workers' eyes.

As I began spending time with IDPs in the new settlements, however, I began to seriously question the idea that they were merely strategically angling for more aid. Indeed, no matter how many "hygiene kits" with razors and washcloths, no matter if they'd been given a small cottage or secondhand clothing or free food, people still felt as if they had nothing. The problem of nothingness became paradoxically even more acute as the government released an updated "state strategy for IDPs," which set the same goal of "social reintegration" for the 2008 IDPs that had recently been set for those from the 1992–1993 war in Abkhazia (Government of Georgia 2009). The apartments and cottages in the settlements were meant to be real communities rather than temporary shelter. But at least in the early months after the war, they were nearly bare. There were twin beds, four little backless stools, a few dishes, and a television, but little else. People began moving in some of the objects they'd been given in the collective centers, using them in creative ways to meet functional needs and to try and break the unrelenting plainness of their new abodes. Wool blankets with the UNHCR logo soon became carpets, and stickers given out by NGOs such as CARE International or Save The Children became a kind of decor, plastered up on walls and doors to add color. One family even hung a giant yellow stuffed bird, given out by one of the limp "toys for traumatized children" programs, on the wall to cheer up the room. But the donated objects did little to alleviate the pervasive sense of emptiness.

What are these objects that are both something and nothing, that are there but somehow do not count? What is it about humanitarian aid that disallows it from being the expression of care and solicitude that governments hope it will be, and prevents it from being the material foundation for resettlement and development that the NGOs want it to be? What kind of ontological status do the material objects handed out as humanitarian aid have in the lives of the displaced? These donated objects fill up space but don't seem to have positive ontological value: they are there, but somehow they don't exist. Rather, they signal the absence of everything that has been lost, pulling the sentiments of compassion and altruism associated with the donation into a void from which value seems unable to emerge.

One particular object, delivered in excess, illustrated this problem. As part of humanitarian food packages offered by the World Food Programme, IDPs were offered large quantities of macaroni. It was plain semolina macaroni, the same kinds of noodles in various shapes that one might find in an American grocery store, intended primarily to ensure that each IDP received 2,240 calories per day, the WFP's standardized measure for daily caloric needs. Each person was given the same ration: 1.5 kilograms of macaroni per month. This was enough for 26.4 servings of noodles per person per month, or macaroni almost every single day. Macaroni is not a staple food in Georgian culture. A Russian import, it does not occupy a place in the grammar of Georgian cuisine, which is based on highly spiced dishes often involving walnuts, pomegranate, cilantro, fresh vegetables, beef, and chicken. Although people eat macaroni, they rarely incorporate it into dishes as elaborate as the ones that predominate in Georgian cuisine. Instead it showed up as an oddly plain dish of pasta boiled in plain water, then fried in oil and perhaps sprinkled with sugar if served for breakfast. For many Georgians

macaroni is not food: it is just calories, something that poor people eat so as not to starve. "Look, it's UN help, it's to keep you alive," said Keti Okropiridze, my neighbor who had fled from Eredvi. "But there's no comfort in it."

As the first winter of displacement wore on, I was surprised by the contrast between macaroni and another form of food that was soon circulating widely: jars of fruits, vegetables, and other foods that were homegrown and home canned. One afternoon I was in the Skra settlement, perched on a twin bed shoved against the wall in lieu of a sofa, and talking with a ruddy-faced man named Aleko Mentashvili. As we drank *chacha*, high-test Georgian grappa that burned all the way down, we ate terrible bread made by Aleko's wife from flour given out by the WFP. There was something wrong with the flour and the bread would not rise, so everyone in the settlement was stuck eating bread that sat in the stomach like a lump of concrete. "It's not fit for animals," Aleko complained as we got progressively more drunk, his normally pink face turning flaming red. But then, with a flash of an idea, he rose unsteadily and wobbled into the kitchen. Returning with a small jar and a spoon, he said, "taste this!" It was honey, sweet May honey, fragrant with plum blossoms and fresh cut grass. He spooned out the dregs of the jar onto a plate, and we all dove in. "Where'd you get that?" I asked, knowing that honey was 25 lari a kilo, far out of Aleko's budget. "It's *mine!* It's from my bees!" he said.

I was confused, since Aleko's house was in the village of Tamarasheni, which had been utterly destroyed. Aleko had been famous all over the Didi Liakhvi gorge as the "bee guy," the man who had more hives and made more honey than anybody else in the region. In Tamarasheni, he had a full kit for managing almost a hundred bee boxes: a hat with a sweeping veil to protect his face and a smoker he had made out of an old coffee can, which he used to force the bees to leave the hive. He knew the bees so well that sometimes he could reach into the hive and remove the frames of hexagonal honeycomb without being stung. He would take the frames to an old Soviet washing machine, little more than an agitator in a barrel, which he had rigged as a centrifuge. There he would spin the honey out of the comb and into jars, which he presented with pride to his friends and relatives. Aleko's honey was, in large measure, the crystallized form of his identity, the product that defined him in local society more than even his status as a veterinarian.

When Aleko was displaced, and the bees were lost, his relatives from villages inside Georgia proper made the kindest gesture they could think of: they brought his honey back to him. As we drank on that cold day, Aleko scraped up one last spoonful and held it out to me. "This is the last honey from Tamarasheni," he said, his eyes overflowing with sadness and drink. I declined it, and Aleko ate it slowly, savoring the last taste of his land. It was as if his displacement had not been complete as long as the honey remained, but with the last of it gone he became truly unmoored in space, a person who was now from nowhere.

Eating the food that boomeranged back to the displaced—honey, jam, bottled fruit, and even homemade "white lightning"—became a ritual in many cottages

I visited. Almost always they were accompanied by beautiful, idealized, and elegiac descriptions of the house and the land they had come from. Judging from the few photographs people had gotten back from relatives along with the jars, the villages in South Ossetia were not much to look at: ramshackle brick houses, scraggly gardens, unpaved, rutted dirt roads, and unmowed clumps of tall grass everywhere. But to those who had lost them the houses and the land were paradise lost. Whereas macaroni, a hollow tube around a center of nothingness, could only trace the outlines of what had been lost and point to the space it once occupied, foods from familiar places truly filled the holes left by what had been lost, if only for a moment.

The meaningfulness of food tied to known people and places was so profound that people in the camps began to take terrible risks to get it. In August, when the fruit and vegetables planted in the meager plots around the cottages began to ripen, Manana Abaeva got me to borrow a friend's Niva, a small Russian jeep, so that she could make some real food. "Come and help me get my jars," she said. "Let's make jam." We bounced over potholed roads through the countryside until we ended up at the village of Mereti, right on the South Ossetian border. The trip, which was only 30 kilometers, took over two hours. At the first checkpoint on the Georgian side of the border, we had to explain what we were doing to armed guards. With an automatic rifle at the ready, a guard in his camouflage uniform carefully scrutinized my passport, and the car, which had diplomatic license plates. "*Why* are you going to Mereti? What are you doing here?" Less than a kilometer from the border, in full view of Russian tanks and snipers, Mereti was hardly the place for an idle drive. "Go to the post in Koshki. Talk to the commander," he told us, waving his weapon in the direction of a village on the boundary with South Ossetia.

We drove along the rutted road, littered with the remnants of pavement and full of potholes. At the end of a two-track lane we saw a small bunker with corrugated metal roofing, piled with sandbags meant to stop bullets. Inside the enclosure men in camouflage uniforms were lolling around. On a makeshift wooden table there were metal bowls full of food; the ground was littered with cigarette butts. A tanned man who was a solid slab of muscle came out and squinted at me. "Really, why are you here?" he demanded, looking skeptical as Manana and I described our plan to make jam. As he realized that we were not spies, but merely foolish enough to be making preserves in a conflict zone, he threw his head back, laughed, and offered us coffee.

When we finally made it to Mereti, Manana and I had lunch with her cousins, who could return to Mereti after the war because it was in the no man's land between the Georgian checkpoint and the Russian checkpoint, in a pleasant garden under a grape arbor. Manana pointed to the round green hills nearby, past the Russian checkpoints at the border. "See up there?" she said, pointing to a church standing alone on the hill. "That's our village, Disevi." "They destroyed everything, but not the church," she said, explaining that the soldiers feared divine retribution. "They didn't even steal the icons," she added, walking away and leaving me to wonder how she knew anything about the village after the war. After lunch Manana disappeared down into the cellar of her cousin's house, reappearing later with a huge bag of empty glass jars on her back. "Where on earth did you get those?" I asked her. "From my house!" she crowed, proud that she'd been able to rescue them from the wreckage and laughing at my bafflement.

In fact Manana's husband, Zviadi, had risked his life to cross the border under the noses of the Russian FSB (Federalnoy Sluzhba Bezopasnosti, the Federal Security Service, formerly known as the KGB). Zviadi knew the hazards of coming back so soon to dig through the rubble of the house. Although open combat had ceased, unexploded ordinance was everywhere. Roaming bands of Ossetian forces were still out looting. Russian soldiers, who had not been paid or fed in weeks, were scavenging for food and *chacha* in the abandoned villages. One IDP I knew, a woman, had tried to sneak across the border on foot through the fields to harvest food from her garden and had been caught by soldiers, forced to drop the food in the mud, and pistol-whipped. Others who tried to cross the border on foot had been imprisoned or shot. It seemed an enormous danger and risk, given how little was left of the house. "The money we had in the house, our gold jewelry, everything was gone," said Manana. The looters had stolen not only electronics and furniture but had even torn out pipes, wiring, and the metal roof to sell as scrap before setting the house on fire. "Zviadi cried for two days over how everything had been ruined. He got raging drunk the first night. But he picked through what was left, got into the cellar, and got my jars out. He brought them here to Mereti and then left them here because we couldn't take them to Tbilisi."

Home-canned food was thus worth risking the social embarrassment of recalling a gift or worse, going back for it and being shot by border guards or the Ossetian irregulars who still roamed the destroyed villages. Macaroni, on the other hand, seemed to be worth little. Better fed to swine than eaten, unless absolutely necessary. What made the two foods so different was provenance. Macaroni was food given out by nobody. The WFP and the NGO that delivered it, World Vision, appeared only as an anonymous agency that none of the IDPs I interviewed could remember the name of, saying only that it came from *mtavroba* (the government) or *gaero* (the UN, a generic term often used for all aid agencies). It was made by nobody, at least nobody any of the recipients knew, and it was made nowhere in particular, in some anonymous factory outside Georgia.[2] Home-canned food, by contrast, came from familiar lands and was prepared by people known and beloved: mothers, grandmothers, aunts. Rather than being transported by unknown agents and handed out by anonymous aid workers, the jars of home-canned food circulated in the deeply elaborated networks of kinship central to Georgian sociality, reforging the ties of family that had been splintered by war and the fragmentation of extended families into separate settlements. Home-canned food was thus something that was something by virtue of being emplaced and attached to persons.

The donors of the macaroni wanted it to create social ties too. USAID, the donor of some of the macaroni, which proudly labeled it as "a gift from the American people," might have liked for it to serve as the material representation of American generosity. WFP, which organized the food packages, and World Vision, which distributed them, might also have wished for the macaroni to stand as a gift, a concrete symbol of organized compassion. As anthropologists who study aid have pointed out, aid is not just a no-strings-attached charitable gift that express humanitarian sentiments of care, concern, and generosity. If the receivers also see aid as a gift that they cannot reciprocate, they are deeply indebted and become structurally inferior clients to their humanitarian patrons (Harrell-Bond 1992; see also Mauss 1954). Humanitarian aid, therefore, is often seen by its donors as a form of "soft power" that binds recipients to them in power-laden and unequal relationships of dependency and gratitude (cf. Nye 2005).

But for the Georgian IDPs, macaroni didn't represent any of that. Like other forms of humanitarian aid, from the perspective of its recipients it wasn't an artifact of humanitarian aid, but an antiartifact, something that did not represent its own character or the substance of what it was. Antiartifacts do not stand as metonyms of the projects that produce them, nor do they embody the affects or wishes of their makers, purchasers, or donors. They do not create links in the network of meaning that makes up the normal situation, connecting people and objects and places to one another. Instead they are placeholders. Much as the zero in the figure 505 holds open the place where something of value might go while acknowledging the emptiness of the place it creates, antiartifacts signal the existence of a category that remains unfilled. They represent not what they are, but what they are not; not what is present, but what is absent. As such, antiartifacts came to embody the experience of life in displacement. They did not represent what was there, but only pointed to everything that had been lost. They literally counted as nothing.

Doing Nothing: Imaginary Numbers

In his study of the concentration camp, the philosopher Giorgio Agamben says that people in camps are reduced to what he calls *zoe*, or bare life (Agamben 1998;

see also Ramadan 2013). In a state of bare life, people are considered purely as biological beings rather than as social beings. That is, they are reduced to social nothingness, deprived of political rights and hence of social being. Camps, in this view, are designed precisely to turn people into something that is no more than human—organisms that breathe and whose hearts beat, but that have no import beyond mere biological existence (Agamben 1994; see also Arendt 1951).

The Agambenian paradigm has been extremely important in the study of humanitarianism and state care (see, for example, Redfield 2013; Ticktin 2011; Povinelli 2008; Agier 2011). But the very existence of IDPs, who at least technically retain their citizenship and are always potentially included in the political sphere of the sovereign state, challenges the notion that camps are only spaces where displaced people are reduced to being "merely human." IDP camps today are not designed merely to sustain life. They are meant to create what Foucault (2007) called "security," that is, to stave off the possibilities of social blight (like prostitution, drug running, or black marketeering) by pushing people toward gainful employment and proper kinship roles (see Ramadan 2013, 68; Edkins 2000; Hyndman 2000). In theory at least, today's camps for displaced people do not govern them just by containing them or by excluding them from the polity, but instead manage them by channeling their daily activities in positive and productive ways. Whether by engaging the IDPs in recreational activities like children's soccer leagues and puppet shows, enrolling them in ostensibly sanitized political activities like women's peacebuilding seminars, or trying to reinsert them into the market through vocational training, business planning courses, or grants for entrepreneurial activity, IDP camps today are supposed to offer something to do. Through this structured and limited set of opportunities, humanitarians seek to direct the energy and time of the residents in ways that make them economically productive as workers or entrepreneurs, socially productive as good spouses and parents, and most of all politically productive as recipients of international largesse and as citizens of the nation-state (see chapter 7).

Despite this turn in philosophy, though, the most salient feature of everyday life in most IDP camps is not doing something, but doing nothing. Time itself is a void, a set of empty hours with nothing to do and nothing to wait for that point only to the activities that people used to do rather than the ones they might engage in now or in the future. But it was not just that life in an IDP camp was boring by its nature. Rather, the projects the NGOs themselves designed, meant to motivate and energize the IDPs, became black holes, spatial voids into which energy simply disappeared without even the faintest trace. Rather than energizing and motivating the inhabitants, the activity-based projects made people frustrated at first, and then simply listless.

In IDP and refugee camps around the world, humanitarian NGOs offer an impressive list of "schemes to improve the human condition," to use Scott's (1998) phrase. In Georgia there were breastfeeding support classes, microcredit loans and business planning seminars to encourage small business development, agricultural tools and seeds for farmers, and small demonstration factories (at one settlement). There were also puppet workshops funded by the Open Society Foundations, "life skills" classes, sporting events for children funded by NIKE, and workshops for psychosocial rehabilitation for the traumatized (American Friends of Georgia 2010; United Nations 2008; CARE 2010). Formulated under the neoliberal principle of "sustainability," they were meant to energize the IDPs, to push them away from continued dependence on aid, and to give them a sense of being responsible for their own destinies. A CARE in the Caucasus's annual report (2009) approvingly quoted an IDP: "We have to get up from the 'warm bed' of humanitarian aid and learn how to rebuild our lives in this new environment."

At cluster meetings sponsored by the United Nations, where NGOs reported on their projects and activities, the settlements were presented as veritable hives of activity, with program after program designed to rehabilitate, reenergize, and reintegrate the displaced. Yet in reality the settlements were nearly always as quiet as tombs. They were eerily quiet, devoid of the normal hubbub of life that characterized cities like Tbilisi or Gori, or even other Georgian villages. There was little noise outside during the day. The odd group of people who stood outside to talk spoke in murmurs. When people walked, they often walked at the painfully slow pace that people use when visiting museums. One day when I sat outside in Koda settlement to take a few quick notes, a dog knocked over a sheet of metal. The noise was so startling that everyone outside—five or six men talking in a group and two women walking along a path—were visibly startled. The camps were places where normal rules were suspended, where people weren't supposed to make any real decisions or pursue their old activities, where the place wasn't theirs but yet there was no other place for them. In such circumstances the eerie stillness and silence were the only real options.[3]

The exception to this strange silence was when workers from the NGOs or the UN agencies would arrive. They would drive in from Tbilisi in large four-wheel-drive vehicles, almost always with six or seven people, foreigners and Georgian employees based in the capital. Then they would run around summoning IDPs to attend a meeting they had planned but not announced in advance. The meetings were held at a breathless pace in large canvas tents set up by UNHCR, or later in the NGO-built "community centers" that were locked to keep the community out except when the NGOs came. The meetings were nearly always held in accordance with the NGOs' predetermined agendas, with little space for the

IDPs to raise issues that mattered to them outside the framework of whatever project was at hand. Then the NGO workers would load back into the jeeps and zoom out as fast as they had come, and the settlement would once again descend into sleepy silence.

At Tsmindatsqali settlement, where I spent the most time participating in daily life, we spent long hours in the day doing nothing. Most people were unemployed; those few that had jobs were in the employ of the government.[4] Women had some chores to do in the mornings, washing laundry by hand in plastic washtubs, preparing food, or weeding gardens, but it was little in comparison to the workload they had in South Ossetia, where there were large houses to tend, land to work, and livestock to look after. Men had even less to do: a few hours a day in the garden plots or spent making small additions to the cottages exhausted most of the possibilities for productive labor. Most of the day was spent watching hours and hours of television. Lots of people slept for hours during the day. Men played cards sometimes in an empty cottage they jokingly called "the casino." Manana Abaeva, Mariam Sabashvili, Eka Gelashvili, and some of the other women on our corner made small, low stools and dragged them outside to sit and talk aimlessly with the neighbors. But the time was long and empty, and the boredom was stressful for people accustomed to long days of physical labor.

Many of the people in Tsmindatsqali originally welcomed the arrival of the NGOs and would turn out in droves for whatever meeting was called, just to have something to do. But people soon became jaded, tired of attending yet another meeting in which nothing happened and from which nothing was gained. At one psychosocial aid meeting I attended at Berbuki settlement, sponsored by the International Organization for Migration, approximately forty-five women were initially rounded up to participate in the workshop. The first half hour was spent having each woman in the circle introduce herself and say "something she liked." "I'm Nino, and I like music!" said the facilitator, modeling for the participants the introduction that was desired. The IDP women shifted in their chairs, unsure of what to say. "I'm Keti, and I like my family," said one. "I'm Guliko, and I like spending time with my new neighbors," said another. Finally, when the introductions reached the top of the circle, a woman said what had been on the others' minds: "I'm a displaced person. I don't like anything. What is there to like?" Her comment pointed out the flaw in the facilitator's thinking: in the absence of knitting needles, yarn, musical instruments, and other supplies that cost money, IDPs did not engage in hobbies. As the introductions wore on and as the participants became visibly bored, women began to stand up and leave. By the time the facilitator introduced the main event of the workshop, a "theater of the oppressed" event designed by IOM officials in Italy, there were only eight IDP women left. Soon the six facilitators outnumbered the participants. By the end of the workshop only a single woman remained.

On another occasion I was with a bespectacled British man who was working under contract to CARE International to do a baseline survey of the IDPs' needs, as he approached the IDP community coordinator (*mamasakhlisi*) in

Tsmindatsqali settlement. The *mamasakhlisi* flatly refused to round up IDPs for a community meeting. "I can't get thirty people to come to a meeting anymore," he said. "They're tired of you wasting their time." This seemed ironic, given that most of the IDPs had nothing but time. But his statement pointed out people's resentment at what High (2006) has called the "participatory corvée," the enormous waste of person hours on rituals of participation when in fact decisions about development projects had already been made by the NGO staff and the donors. As the NGOs soon discovered, it was harder and harder to get people to participate in the programs that were supposed to benefit them, even ones where they stood to gain financially, such as microcredit schemes. "It's too much effort for too little gain," said the *mamasakhlisi*. Indeed the low numbers of IDPs served by each individual project showed how few "beneficiaries" felt investing time and energy in the NGOs' projects would benefit them. For example, two microcredit projects that were part of CARE International's $3 million SIIMS (Stabilization and Integration of IDPs into Mainstream Georgian Society) projects for IDPs and people in the "adjacent area" had only fifty-six participants out of more than twenty-eight thousand potential beneficiaries.[5] As Elena Chochieva, Manana Abaeva's usually bouncy Ossetian neighbor in the camp, told me glumly, "We're just so tired of talking and talking and seeing nothing change."

The glowing images of busy IDPs grateful for the chance that the NGOs gave them to rebuild their lives—photographs and slightly canned "voices" that appeared in the glossy four-color brochures put out in English by the NGOs themselves—thus seemed to me to be about some other settlements, not the ones I had been spending my days and nights in, the Karaleti of the aid workers' imaginations rather than the Tsmindatsqali we inhabited on long, boring afternoons. The topolganger the NGOs described—an imagined duplicate of the camp on the same terrain as the one the IDPs inhabited—seemed to be full of imaginary quantities of people served, their imagined qualities (industrious and busy, as presented in the elaborate brochures; lazy and conniving, as presented in the cluster meeting), and their imagined enthusiasm. With the exception of the little kiosks that sold cigarettes and sundries, and one man who used speakers he got from an NGO to work as a wedding singer, I very rarely saw any of the small businesses, "community-sponsored organizations," or self-help groups at work in the absence of the NGO workers' presence.[6]

Perhaps one reason that the camp inhabited by the NGOs had so little to do with the camp inhabited by the IDPs was that the intersection of the two topolgangers was so fleeting and brief: the world of the IDPs only appeared in highly artificial "rapid needs assessment tools"—short surveys that only requested answers to surveys with predetermined questions—and in the brief moments that NGO officials spent in the settlements. In the first year of displacement, at least, there was little unstructured time for NGO workers to listen or to learn from IDPs what was really needed—like a bridge to get tractors to the orchards, or glass jars for canning, or medication for hypertension (see chapter 6). The relationship of the world of the camps imagined by humanitarian workers and the real world of day-to-day life in the camps experienced by the IDPs was, perhaps, the very thing that produced nothingness. The projects that made so much sense in the imaginary camps inhabited by humanitarian workers made so little sense in the real ones occupied by the IDPs that they seemed to be utterly nonsensical, and soon the IDPs began to feel that any effort they contributed to them was just sucked away to no effect.

The fact that most of the time in the IDP camps is spent doing nothing belies the NGOs narratives, which argue that their programs energize IDPs and make them independent. As displaced people themselves become disenchanted with the gap between the dreams the humanitarians hold out and the reality of what help is delivered, they become increasingly unwilling to donate time and energy, the only resources they have, to participating in programs that benefit the NGOs but do not substantially benefit IDPs. It is that difference between the imagined and the real that creates zero, the problem of doing nothing. The lassitude of the camps is not a natural feature of displacement that humanitarians have to overcome, but something institutionalized humanitarianism itself produces.

Being Nothing: Absolute Zero

What is the line between doing nothing and being nothing? At what point does the fact that aid doesn't seem to count to displaced people get transformed into a narrative about how "ungrateful" they are? When does the contrast between the aid workers' frenzy of purposeful activity—doing needs assessments, responding to requests for proposals from donors, writing reports, and making brochures—and the IDPs' listlessness become a question of character rather than of circumstance? In Georgia, where stereotypes about regional character abound, the Georgian employees of the NGOs soon began to argue that the torpor of the camps was the fault of the IDPs' themselves and of the defects in their characters. "That's just how they are up there. Just slow," one NGO worker told me. "It's hard to get them to take responsibility for themselves," argued another, telling me that Georgians from South Ossetia were passive, phlegmatic, or downright sluggish.

But as I spent more time in the settlements, I saw the lack of activity and the almost deathly quiet in the camps during the day not as something intrinsic to the people, but as state of being created by tensions that pulled people in opposite directions. There was a matrix that kept people frozen, that drained them of their energy, much as the molecules in a quantity of matter are completely drained of all their energy at absolute zero, -273 degrees Celsius. It was not only the gap between what the humanitarians promised and what they delivered that rendered the IDPs so passive. Rather, it was the fact that life in the humanitarian condition is premised on a tension between four political forces that creates temporal uncertainty—an enormous void in people's ability to predict what might become of them. Displaced people are often unable to step in any direction because they are trapped in-between four mutually exclusive futures—conflict, return, resettlement, and stasis—that are each equally likely. This leaves them frozen, unable to take the leap and gamble on any one of them.

The first possible future, an omnipresent danger, was another war. With the Russians firmly entrenched in South Ossetia and poised along the border, geopolitics were never very far away. Everyone knew that the conflict was at best frozen rather than truly resolved, and as the first anniversary of the war approached, tensions on the border with South Ossetia began to rise again and it was terrifyingly clear that the conflict could flare up again at any moment. Just a few miles from the settlement, Georgian and Ossetian soldiers were firing at each other. As always seemed to be the case in this conflict, nobody could determine which side was the aggressor and which the victim. The Georgians blamed the Ossetians and the Ossetians blamed the Georgians, but the European Union Monitoring Mission (EUMM) could not get close enough in their heavy blue armored vehicles to determine which way the shells and mortar fire were heading. In the village of Plavi Ossetian border guards came down the hillside and across the border one night, got drunk, and began firing in the air. The next day a fourteen-year-old boy saw something hanging in a tree, pulled it down, and the thing—it was a detonator—blew his arm off (Vartanyan and Shwirtz 2009). In Khurvaleti, which was tightly wedged in the no man's land between the Georgian line of control and the Ossetian border on the bluff above, Ossetian forces streamed down the hill and through the camp to attack soldiers at the Georgian checkpoint (International Crisis Group 2009, 9). Some people in the camps and villages along the border began sleeping in their gardens, fearing they might be crushed in their houses in the event of an aerial attack. In Tsmindatsqali settlement, which was a few kilometers from the border, we lay in bed at night feeling the ground vibrating underneath us as tanks and armored personnel carriers moved over the earth at the Georgian military base across the road. The anxiety level in the settlement was so high that nobody slept well. The sight of a helicopter in the air was enough to send the children in the settlement—my son and Manana Abaeva's among them—diving for cover.

Although war certainly seemed likely, the fear of violence stood in opposition to another improbable-but-still-possible outcome of the displacement: return home. Aleko Mentashvili, the bee guy, embodied what every single IDP I knew told me when he said: "The big problem isn't how we're surviving here. The problem is when we'll return. We don't know when that will be, but we just keep the hope that we'll return. Our hearts just aren't here. Nothing makes us happy here" (see also Vashakidze 2008). Aleko, more than any IDP I met in any of the settlements, was doing his best to settle in for the long run in the camp: as one of the earliest to figure out that the overflowing bags of macaroni could be used to slop hogs, he was one of the only people in camp to buy a piglet and build a small rickety pen for it out of scrap lumber. But when I asked him if the fact that his village, Tamarasheni, had been destroyed changed his willingness to return, he told me:

> Maybe we have to prepare as if we will be here for a long time. In Tamarasheni, everything was good. The air was good, the bees thrived, there was clean water. But now the houses in Tamarasheni are gone. They're only walls. The Ossetians stole the metal from the walls, all the things we had there. I don't think they bulldozed it, like they did to Kurta, but it's destroyed. We hear things from the old women who can go back to their own houses secretly, like thieves in the night, because they are less likely to be caught by the militias. But even if my house is completely gone, even if there's nothing left but the foundation, I would go back. I would leave everything I have here and go instantly, if they only told me I could return.

There was thus enormous tension between two poles of possibility, one centered on the question "will we go home?" and the other on the question, "will we die soon?" The uncertainty surrounding either future made any activity in the present almost nonsensical. There was little sense planting an orchard near the settlement or adding a room onto the cottage if return were imminent. No sense in starting a business in Gori or buying new equipment for a workshop if the war could break out again at any moment. With material needs so high and money in short supply, any investment in an unknown future seemed like a bad use of scarce resources.

The tension between war and return was cross-cut by another axis of uncertainty, one that stretched between the chaos of aid and the mysteries of power. Neither the Georgian government nor the NGOs gave out much information about what programs were planned or what aid was forthcoming. In the first year in the settlements, there were no bulletin boards and no widely distributed newsletter (although there were a few issues of a newspaper that some people got but others had not heard of). There were few posters put up around the settlements to announce projects aimed at the IDPs. When the government issued vouchers for health insurance in January, for example, no information about how to use them was given out until late May, leaving IDPs wondering what was covered and what was not. They often avoided being treated for serious conditions such as hypertension and diabetes, fearing that they might incur bills they could not pay, and so often waited until they had life-threatening conditions and had to call an ambulance. The NGOs, too, rarely announced or explained their programs. The United Nations Development Program, for example, funded a Gender Resource Center, which had a dedicated helpline for IDP women. But despite the fact that six women staffed the helpline full time, the number was never publicized to IDPs, and nobody ever quite defined just what a Gender Resource Center was or what help it might provide.

Aid came in the standard units of humanitarian planning, the project: pre-packaged short-term activities funded by international donors. From the IDPs' point of view, this resulted in aid that was not only topically obscure, as the Gender Resource Center was, but also temporally and spatially obscure. Projects seemed to begin and end without reason, popping into existence with a flurry of meetings and then blinking out of existence a few months later with no announcement. Mobile medical teams would arrive one day, for example, hand out strong prescription drugs, and then disappear without leaving so much as a medical record or a number to call if something went wrong. Psychologists, too, would drive in, start support groups, and then disappear a few weeks later. Nobody even knew for certain how long the World Food Programme would continue to deliver food. This temporal unpredictability was met with spatial variability: projects often covered one settlement but not another, which meant that just because Khurvaleti settlement got agricultural machinery or a free dentist visit, it didn't necessarily mean that Mtskheta settlement would get the same. With no knowledge of the donors' funding processes, how the NGOs divided the labor of aid, or any of the institutional constraints around aid and very little information about the aid process, IDPs were left completely unable to predict what would happen next and which resources would be available. In such a chaotic environment, rumors of backroom deals and covert political connections began to swirl. As far-fetched as some of these explanations were, they represented almost desperate attempts to impose some sort of principle of order on what appeared, at least to the IDPs, to be a completely arbitrary and unpredictable situation.

As conspiracy theories and rumors grew, they began to contribute not just to a sense of chaos but also to a profound sense of mystery and the belief that the real political decisions that affected people's lives were being made in secret. Mystery was enacted not only at the level of international politics but also at the scale of the nation-state. The president of Georgia, Mikheil Saakashvili, had presented the veneer of a democrat to his backers in the United States and Western Europe. But underneath the veil of democratic procedure, Misha—as he was known even among the general populace—was rumored to be acting in the same autocratic manner as had his predecessor, Eduard Shevardnadze. Sitting in the flapping cacophony of a UN canvas tent in the wind, my neighbor Nodar Gelashvili and the other men in Tsmindasqali would share tales of Misha pretending to do the work of state in front of the Americans in the afternoon, but then staying out in chic restaurants until 2 am, making decisions about matters as grave as whether to make a bid for NATO or how to respond to the Russians.[7] Government decisions, it seemed, were not openly debated in newspapers or carried out in open sessions of parliament, but made behind closed doors among a small group of people surrounding the president, and then announced as fiat. Nobody in the camps knew what interests, political or financial, drove these autocratic decisions, but they knew there had to be something.[8] The result was the odd sensation of knowing that a hidden world—one that the IDPs knew existed but couldn't see or access—controlled their fates (see also chapter 7).

Other decisions directly affecting the IDPs were also made abruptly, with little transparency or open discussion. In August hundreds of IDPs in Tbilisi, who were holed up in an old Soviet army hospital awaiting government-sponsored housing, were suddenly informed that they would be evicted in five days, forced either to move to provinces in the far western part of the country, far from jobs and relatives, or to go out onto the street alone. There was no consultation, no warning, no information, just a decision that came out of the blue in the same way the Russian bombers had, throwing the IDPs once again into the void. Even for the IDPs in the settlements, the eviction of their compatriots from the collective center in the hospital stood as a reminder about the mysterious and unseen forces around them that had the power to disrupt anything at any moment.

IDPs were held in a field of power between death and return, mystery and chaos. This placed them into a suspended temporality that renders the present incomprehensible and the future unforeseeable (Ramadan 2013, 72). And in the center, the place where people were held immobile by these conflicting forces, there is absolute zero, the point at which all energy is drained from the IDPs, leaving them absolutely paralyzed, incapable of envisioning the future or doing anything to create it. As Nodar Gelashvili said with an edge of frustration in his voice, "How can we make any plans for the future? We can't. All we can do is wait to return. We can't make any plans until there is peace." Stuck at absolute zero, he was frozen in both space and time, unable to return to the past, move forward into the future, or even go anywhere different in the present. He was left with nothing: nothing to own, nothing to do, and nowhere to go. So like the other IDPs, he sat in the camps, spending time talking aimlessly in knots of other men on the corners of the dusty roads in the settlement, getting drunk or watching endless hours of television, doing nothing more than waiting to see what catastrophic event might happen next to disrupt the situation and to force all of them to begin again.

Zones of Temporal and Spatial Indistinction

As anthropologists and geographers who work with displaced people have pointed out, camps for the displaced are spatially and temporally liminal. They are spaces of dislocation and exile that suspend their inhabitants on the geographic and social periphery. They also create a suspended temporality, a zone of temporal indistinction between permanence and transience that leaves displaced people in a state of waiting and stasis, pinned between the golden past (like the one the Georgian IDPs indexed with their jars of homemade food) and a future return (Ramadan 2013, 72). In this chapter, I have argued that this suspended state is not just the result of war or of an unresolved geopolitical problem, but is actively produced in the camp through humanitarian programs. When displaced people say they have nothing—as they do in camps around the world—they mean much more than that humanitarians have not delivered anything. They are pointing to the ways that life in the humanitarian condition evacuates meaning and presence from everyday objects, empties time and refills it with boredom, sucks away people's energy and will, and traps the displaced in-between competing political forces and futures. Nothingness is not a negative formation, defined merely by the absence of goods or homes or jobs, what people have when they don't have anything.[9] It is a state of being produced by humanitarianism, not just an empty bucket that can be refilled by the cheap stuff and manufactured activities of the humanitarian enterprise. The camps themselves—which are meant not as places of resettlement, but as places to facilitate the delivery of aid, to keep displaced people as a concentrated population that can be mobilized to reoccupy territory if it can be regained and to keep IDPs in a space where they can be governed—are engines that produce longing, inactivity, and anxiety, and that keep people frozen at the cusp of futures just out of reach. Nothingness is thus not merely the result of violence, but also the result of care; not merely the remnant of destruction, but also an effect of construction.

Because it constantly points to what has been lost, and because it creates an uncertain situation in which taking action is nearly impossible, nothingness leads to what Agier (2011) calls "the interminable insomnia of exile," the state of limbo in which people in protracted displacement live indefinitely. This is an existential problem, not a technical one, and it is an integral part of life in the humanitarian condition. The void that is created is why, after millions of dollars and countless man-hours spent by humanitarian agencies, more than 66% of the world's 65 million displaced people fail to "socially reintegrate" in the ways they are supposed to and instead end up in long-term relations of dependence with governments and international aid agencies (see Mitchneck et al. 2009; Milner and Loescher 2011, 3).

The effects of nothingness go beyond merely immiserating displaced people. As I will show in the next three chapters, nothingness seeps out of the camps to affect larger-scale politics. At the national level in Georgia, nothingness evoked not only what the IDPs themselves had lost, but also the territorial integrity lost by the nation as a whole (see also Kabachnik 2012, 47). As in many other countries, IDP camps in Georgia remain visible wounds, sites that bring failed politics and peripheral people into the center of the political landscape where they not only can, but must, be seen. For that reason the nothingness of the camps makes them into "anxiety-producing irruptions of politics that cannot be contained" (Manning 2008, 11). Constantly pointing not to a competent state or caring foreigners, but to a contingent state of being created by the humanitarian apparatus but beyond its control, the vacuity of existence in the camps becomes a symbol of the geopolitical impasse and the relations between a dependent state and his Western benefactors that produced it. At the level of everyday life, IDPs must come to understand these relationships, struggle against nothingness to find their own places within them, and to reforge shattered social relations within new national and international political contexts. As the next chapters show, displaced people often seek to overcome nothingness and reestablish their political roles as citizens in the national and international political orders by making ostensibly apolitical demands for care (see also Ramadan 2013; Feldman 2011). But the response they receive often comes in the highly politicized form of police or military action.

VOID

In the previous chapter I made the argument that *nothing is*. Rather than seeing nothing as an empty container, the condition that exists when people have nothing, or do nothing, or when what they are doing counts for nothing, I argued that nothingness is a way of existing in the world that has its own social reality. Following Sartre (1943, 110), who wrote that "there are many ways of not being," I tried to show three different forms in which nothingness is produced by humanitarian action: through the creation of antiartifacts, the constitution of black holes, and the suspended temporality of absolute zero. These are descriptive accounts of nothingness, meant mostly to establish that nothingness is something people experience and endure, something that keeps them trapped in the archipelago of camps and inhibits them from establishing new ways of being and doing after displacement. But the previous chapter left several key questions unraised and unanswered. If nothing exists, what is it? How is it constituted? What are its effects? What I am asking, at root, is: How is nothingness related to being? These questions—and especially the last one—are at the center of philosophical existentialism, which sees nothingness as the precondition for being, the ground on which being is constructed. But as I show in this second intertext, these abstract philosophical considerations cannot fully account for the forms of the nothingness that arise in the humanitarian encounter or explain the ways they transform the camp into a place where the purposiveness of life seems to be stopped dead in a temporal vacuum.

On the surface, nothing appears to be the negation of being. It's not just a question of absence—in any given situation, there are lots of things that aren't there, but they are mostly irrelevant. What creates nothingness is the negation of a positive expectation. In the humanitarian encounter—as I show in the next chapter on humanitarian abandonment—nothingness is created by negating expectation. Aid agencies promise grand visions but often leave having spent millions and achieved nothing. In Haiti, for example, the American Red Cross raised USD $500 million—half a billion dollars!—for post-earthquake reconstruction. Over $170 million of that was specifically earmarked for building durable housing. In the Port-au-Prince neighborhood of Campeche, for example, the Red Cross launched a $24 million project promising to build hundreds of new homes, a water and sanitation system, and a health clinic. Yet, despite the fact that the money was spent, only six houses were ever built (Sullivan 2015). Residents of the neighborhood thus contend not only with the shelter they have—mostly tents—but also with disappointment and the loss of the houses they were led to expect but don't have. "We still have tents," said one of the neighborhood's leaders. "I am going to show you that the Red Cross has not intervened here at all. If you're talking about change, people should not be living like this still" (Sullivan 2015).

But although the negation of positive expectations is the easiest place to spot nothingness in the humanitarian encounter, it is not the cause of the void. The deep and treacherous voids characteristic of the humanitarian condition are not brought on simply by disappointments, but by the destruction of state of the situation and the normal situation that it produces. Badiou's theory of the void, laid out early in the development of his theoretical structure in *Being and Event*, is a guide to this form of nothing. One might assume, following Badiou's use of Cantorian set theory, that the void is an empty set: a group that consists of zero elements. If that were true, then nothingness for Badiou would be the same as "nothing" in folk logic: the thing that there is when there isn't anything at all, the absence of things, an empty bucket. In that case nothingness would be pure negation, without reference to any affirmative notion of being. But this is not what Badiou argues at all. Rather, he argues (in his characteristically precise and paradoxically obscuring style) that "nothing is presentable in a situation otherwise than under the effect of structure, that is, under the form of the one and its composition in consistent multiplicities" (2006, 52).

That is to say, *nothingness is not the absence of elements, but a set of elements whose relations to one another have not yet been structured.* When a set of things-in-experience have been perceived, but not (yet) grouped into a count-as-one or placed into a structure that relates them to other elements of experience, what you end up with is the void. "By itself, the nothing is no more than the name of unpresentation in presentation," Badiou says (2006, 55). For that reason, Badiou says that the void is the "pure multiple upon which the count operates—which 'in-itself' as non-counted, is quite distinct from how it turns out in the count" (55). Were Badiou a Christian, he might say that nothing is the chaos from which God created the heavens and the Earth (see Genesis 1:1–2; Isaiah 45:18). Were he an astronomer, he might think of it as whatever existed before the big bang. Given that he is an atheist philosopher, though, he contents himself simply with the proposition that nothingness and chaos are one and the same: the unstructured multiplicity that is pure being is also the void.

The void thus stands as a chasm between the existence of a multiplicity and its structuration. It's a rift between perception and presentation, when sets appear as wholes, and a gulf between presentation and representation, when all the singular objects in experience are set into relation to one another in a situation. For Badiou this chasm gets leapt over all at once, instantaneously: there is no time between unstructured presentation and our perceiving things as wholes, nor is there any time between our perception of things as wholes and our experience of them related to other things we know and have experienced. With only two exceptions (the singularity, which I discuss below, and the excrescence, which I discuss in chapter 6 and in the meditation that follows it) what we see is immediately meaningful, immediately connected to other, familiar parts of our daily existences; there is no time in which we can experience the unstructured directly and without mediation. Thus, for Badiou, nothingness is not something that can be encountered: it's a purely theoretical figure that is not part of the situation. In a situation, normal or not, everything is counted. "A situation never proposes anything other than multiples woven from ones. . . . Naturally it would be pointless to set off in search of nothing" (2006, 54).

Yet the example of the Georgian IDPs suggests something quite different. The devastation of the war didn't destroy all structure. The IDPs still had a perfectly good command of language, for example, although life in the humanitarian condition introduced new terms that initially made no sense, like *arasamtavrobis organizatsia* (nongovernmental organization) and *shemosavlis momtani sakmianoba* (income-generating activity). They still perceived most objects in their experience as counts-as-one, although the physical destruction of houses and property sometimes showed just how easily the material world could be reduced to a disconnected multiplicity. An apple—to cite the example from the first intertext—was still an apple. What was ruptured was not the relationship between perception and presentation, but the relation between presentation and representation that had once been structured by the state of the situation. If (red) (round) (shiny) was still presented as (apple), that apple was no longer connected to (orchard), (ladder), (truck), (Roki Tunnel), or (Russian bazaar) in a structure of representation. That is, the apple no longer sat in space in the network of human experience where it used to, but at least in the present became free-floating in a disorganized array of other elements. New elements introduced by the humanitarians were similarly free-floating, present in everyday life but lacking a place in the structure of representation. Macaroni, for example, had no place in the grammar of everyday cuisine. The stools and tables the IDPs were given by the humanitarians presented themselves perfectly well—everyone of course knew what they were and what they should be used for—but because they were unmoored in everyday experience, when they encountered the damaged state of the situation or the "structuring structure," all they could do was point to the empty spot in the structured network of representation where people's own chairs and tables had once stood.

Elements that are presented but not represented are *singularities:* they are "a fundamental anomaly, something or someone strangely about of place, a violation of the way things should be" (Hallward 2003, 99; Badiou 2006, 93–94, 522). Antiartifacts like macaroni and stools are singularities because they exist in people's experience but are not transformed by the state of the situation into something that is represented. (As I will show in chapter 7 and in the final meditation, their failure to enter representation is precisely because they are without place, from nowhere and no one.) Black holes—those pits created by the humanitarian apparatus that swallow endless efforts in "participatory planning" meetings or devour energy in applications for microcredit programs that are later denied—are machines for creating singularities, since they disrupt IDPs' efforts to incorporate the new elements of their lives into a comprehensible network of elements that can be acted on or acted with. The result of these many singularities is that through its bureaucratic procedures, and because it treats displaced people as "universal victims," humanitarianism produces absolute zero: the sense that any attempt to alter the state of the situation and incorporate singularities into a meaningful structure of representation will ultimately be fruitless.

Badiou acknowledges that there can be elements that are "in the situation" but "are not counted" and thus violate the rule of the normal situation, which is that everything that is presented should also be represented (2006, 94). For him, this is what generates new truths or revolutionary ideas. But he fails to understand how frequently singularities are produced or what their implications are when people have to live with them over time. He argues that "the being of presentation is inconsistent multiplicity," that is, that there are unstructured elements, but that "despite this, it is never chaotic" (94). But as I showed in my discussion of how aid agencies operate and how IDPs experience their first months in the camp, the evidence suggests otherwise: that confronted with a large number of singularities, living in the midst of inconsistent multiplicity, people do experience existence as chaotic. Badiou writes,

> Any operation of the count-as-one ... is in some manner doubled by a count of the count, which guarantees, at every moment, that the gap between the consistent multiple ... and the inconsistent multiple ... is veritably null. It thus ensures that there is no possibility of that disaster of presentation ever occurring which would be the presentational occurrence, in tortion, of the structure's own void. (2006, 94)

For him, even though the void is an omnipresent possibility, situations are completely structured until they are dramatically decomposed in the Event, when a new truth demands their destructuration and compels the construction of an entirely new situation premised on a new structuring principle. In this, though, Badiou is hopelessly wrong. Because situations can be partially or incompletely structured, rather than only perfectly structured or completely unstructured— that is, because they can be characterized by *voidishness* rather than by either structure or its complete lack—the void can and does appear in extreme situations such as war and its aftermath. Humanitarians themselves can see this—they know that despite their best efforts to impose structure on the chaos of presentation by satisficing, using rules of thumb, or just guessing, a huge number of elements escape their structuring structures. Likewise, for IDPs the breach that Badiou sees as a latent theoretical possibility limited to the realm of pure being is in fact made absolutely apparent by the vast numbers of singularities presented, posing not the chance of revolutionary transformation but the constant threat of reducing lived experience to chaotic disjuncture.

The omnipresence of the void in the humanitarian situation would perhaps be insignificant if the leap across the chasm between presentation and representation were as instantaneous as Badiou portrays it. In his exposition this jump takes place timelessly, instantaneously, without any intervening lag. But what Badiou does not understand, at least insofar as presentation and representation are played out in concrete and specific situations,[1] is that the leap over the chasm can take a very long time, leaving people suspended in the void for days, months, or even years. In that case they must constantly encounter the disorganization and lack of structure that characterize nothingness. They have to contend with a wealth of things that are presented in their experience but not represented in any meaningful order, and live with the chaos that is constantly being produced. In the first place, of course, it is because war pushes them into nothingness and chaos, as it explodes the normal situation and renders much of what was once structured into pure chaos. But displaced people stay in that chasm for long periods of time because humanitarian action is constantly re-creating chaos, producing singularities, and creating disorder. The chasm becomes enduring because, as I explain in the next chapter, humanitarianism is constantly abandoning its "beneficiaries." In the humanitarian condition the aid that exists now may not exist tomorrow if it fails to arrive or disintegrates from lack of planning and maintenance or if it was intended to be temporary. The visions of the camp that are promised for tomorrow may or may not come to be, leaving half-implemented projects standing as ruins and half-fulfilled dreams cluttering the landscape. The frameworks that label some people as particular kinds of abjects—a member of a so-called vulnerable population, like an impoverished person or a victim of domestic violence—often fall to pieces as a new fashion in aid sweeps in, rendering those who were worthy of aid today unworthy of it tomorrow. Given the lack of information displaced people receive about the aid that is ostensibly for their benefit, it is always hard to tell what kind of aid will arrive and when, or—as I show in the next chapter—when aid will vanish altogether. The result is that with all its satisficing and rules of thumb and abstract frameworks that are badly fitted to real situations, the humanitarian apparatus attempts to impose order but ends up making it much more difficult not only for the humanitarians themselves to impose order on a highly disorganized context, but for displaced people to do it either.

PRESSURE

Eka Gelashvili woke up groggy, her short gray hair matted with sweat and sticking up off her head at odd angles. Her husband, Nodar, who had been sitting in the UN tent when I passed by, hustled me into the dark and stifling cottage just as she awoke, saying, "You should talk to her, she'll tell you how life in this settlement is affecting us!" One look at her, and I knew she was not right: usually she had bright eyes and a demeanor that combined gruff and bouncy in a strangely pleasing way. In the midst of so much unhappiness, Eka somehow managed to take things philosophically and to find some humor in the situation. But that day her skin was gray and pasty, and her right eye was swollen nearly shut. When she opened it I could see it was bloodshot, with tiny exploded veins leaking blood into the white of her eye. She looked like she was in excruciating pain. Closed into the small, bare main room of her cottage, she had been resting on a cot given to her by the United Nations High Commissioner for Refugees. "I feel horrible," she said. "*Tsneva makvs*, I have blood pressure."

Three streets away in the settlement, Anzor Kapanadze was gravely ill with complications of diabetes. His wife, Mariam Sabashvili, the former director of the village school, blamed it on the stress of being displaced from Tskhinvali during the first Ossetian war in 1991–1992. But now, in the wake of his second displacement, his kidneys had failed and he had been put on dialysis. Because there was no dialysis machine in Gori, and because Anzor was too sick to take public transportation, a private taxi came three times a week to take him on a 90-minute ride to the hospital in Tbilisi. The other IDPs on our street, who spent long evenings discussing the situation, believed that his kidneys had been killed by *tsneva* caused by living as a recipient of humanitarian aid.

Despite the violence of war, *tsneva*—not dramatic war wounds—was by far the most common health complaint among IDPs in the new settlements. Used to refer to both hypertension and hypotension, *tsneva* struck old and young, men and women. Although *tsneva* is a widespread ailment in Georgia, both IDPs and health care said they felt displaced people had more *tsneva* than the general population, and that many who had not had *tsneva* before the war got it during the war or in displacement. Like many of the IDPs, both Eka Gelashvili and Mariam Sabashvili used the "winterization" payments given by UNHCR to buy coats to instead buy a blood pressure monitoring device, and took readings five or six times a day. (In fact, during sixteen months of fieldwork, I rarely met an adult who could not immediately give a number to express their usual blood pressure, as well as any extremes of high or low pressure.) Despite the lack of any concrete epidemiological data, which nobody collected, the IDPs I knew believed that pressure was the leading cause of death for the people now buried in the makeshift graveyards on the edge of the camps, people who had died not during the war but in resettlement. *Tsneva* appeared as a brutal force, ripping through people's bodies and the settlement as a whole, killing people who would have lived if only they had been at home.

What was *tsneva*, though? In this chapter I argue that *tsneva* was not just a disease, but a part of living in the humanitarian situation. Medical anthropologists have long argued that diseases are as much social as they are biological, and that the body often encapsulates complex power relationships at the local, national, and international geopolitical scales (see, for example, Scheper-Hughes and Lock 1987). The anthropologist Paul Farmer, who both provides and studies humanitarian medical aid, has argued that many of the debilitating diseases faced by the world's poor and marginalized people are the result of "structural violence," or the damage caused by arrangements embedded in the political and economic organization of the social world (Farmer 2004a, 2004b). In this chapter I argue that "pressure" is not just an ailment, but a way of life caused by the political and economic organization of humanitarian aid that arises from the *flow* of aid to beneficiaries. Because of the ways that humanitarians organize aid temporally, a surge of goods and services inundates beneficiaries in the early days after displacement. But when this flow of aid is constricted suddenly and without notice, it creates enormous pressure in the lives, pocketbooks, and bodies of displaced people. This surge and constriction of aid arises from humanitarians' ideas about time: first, from the notion of "emergency" that governs contemporary humanitarian aid, and second, from humanitarians' conception of the "future anterior," or the way things will have been once the nation-state has once again assumed the burden of providing social services (see Frederiksen 2014). Pressure, a lethal force, is the result of relation between displaced people, the nation-state, and the humanitarian system that is mediated by time.

Tsneva as Cultural Category

In Georgia, *tsneva* is a catch-all disease, much like the German "weak blood" or the French *crise de foie*. It's an ailment that many Georgians believe they suffer from on an occasional or regular basis. Unlike American biomedicine, which holds that hypertension is usually asymptomatic and hence a "silent killer" (Schoenberg and Drew 2002), Georgians believe that *tsneva* varies continuously during the day and can be easily felt if too high or too low. According to Lia Maisuradze, an IDP and a physician who treats IDPs at an ambulatory clinic, symptoms of *magari tsneva*, high pressure, include a dull ache at the back of the head, pain in one eye or both, and vomiting. Symptoms of *dabali tsneva*, low pressure, include dizziness, cold hands and feet, a feeling of laziness, and the desire to sleep. Many IDPs told us that *tsneva* fluctuates in response to the weather, with hot, humid conditions or rain being particularly productive of hypertension.

Tsneva is more than the concrete state of high or low blood pressure, however. It translates more broadly as problems or difficulties, restrictions and blockages in daily life that give one the feeling of being under pressure. *Tsneva makvs*, "I have pressure," can often mean "I have a lot of stress" or "I'm under pressure," rather than literally meaning that one has hypertension. Although the words for hydraulic pressure (*tsneva*) and oppression (*chagvra* or *zetsola*) are not the same, the concepts of "pressure" from daily life and vascular pressure overlap considerably. *Tsneva* thus functions as a prime mediator among the physical environment, social relations, and the psyche. It is a way in which the world impinges on the body and it acts as a corporeal index of the individual's problematic relationship to others and to the material world.

Georgian and Ossetian IDPs do not see the cause of *tsneva* in the terms often laid out in liberal or neoliberal states, where health problems are deemed to be the result of personal failings or individual choice (cf. Povinelli 2008). They do not see it as being related to an individual's decision to exercise, for example, or to a person's choice of diet or the amount of sodium somebody elects to consume. Rather, *tsneva* is seen as a collective problem, one that can be caused by the structural forces that cause "nervousness," or *nerviuloba*. The dramatic violence of the war, of course, is a primary reason that people were *nerviuli*. Being in their homes as Russian aerial bombs and Ossetian artillery hit, being showered with broken glass as they tried to make it out on the main road as tanks and artillery moved in on Tskhinvali, and seeing the corpses and bloodied clothing of wounded soldiers and fleeing civilians as they passed certainly caused them to be *nerviuli*. As the biophysical manifestation of trauma or anxiety, *tsneva* could be the result of acute, catastrophic violence, of crisis and emergency. But for the people in the camp, *tsneva* was not just the result of war. As horrific as some IDPs' war experiences were, by the time they had been in the settlements for nearly two years, they no longer linked *nerviuloba* or *tsneva* only to the spectacular violence of the war or their adrenaline-fueled flight. Rather, they saw the cause of their *tsneva* as the daily, noneventful conditions of life constructed by humanitarian aid, which they saw as degrading, frustrating, nerve-racking, and most of all, as constricting and obstructive. To the displaced, pressure arises in the dusty streets of the settlements as much as in bombed-out villages, in the constrictions of forced migration and the frustrations of being the beneficiaries of humanitarian aid as much as in the sublime violence of war. Pressure is a symptom of life in the humanitarian condition.

The Hydraulics of Aid

Why is *tsneva* caused by humanitarian aid rather than being relieved by it? One way to understand is by examining the key metaphor that both international aid workers and IDPs use to understand forced migration: *flow*. On the one hand, workers very often see forced migration through hydraulic metaphors, using images of flowing water to conceptualize the movement of large numbers of people forced from their homes. In the talk of donors, aid agencies, and the national and local governments who are supposed to host the newly unsettled, displaced people are referred to as a deluge, a human tide, or a torrent that streams out of danger zones, washes up in host nations, and pours into refugee camps in ways that threaten to overflow the channels that contain them (Turton 2003, 4). Yet, on the other hand, in the eyes of many displaced people themselves, once they are enclosed in camps and settlements after the first traumatic migration, they are not the ones who move. From their perspective it is the humanitarians and the enormous sums of money they are following that flow at enormous speed and volume and then, almost as suddenly, dry up.

In Georgia there was good reason to think of the arrival and withdrawal of aid as a tide that came and went in a cyclical process. Many international NGOs focused on humanitarianism and development had come into the country in the late 1990s to aid the IDPs from Abkhazia and from the First Ossetian War, who had been ignored during the period of state collapse and then mostly neglected by the Shevardnadze government. After the 2003 Rose Revolution the tide reversed. Once the NGOs were assured that the new Saakashvili government was restoring the economy, providing more services, and taking greater responsibility for its citizens, most of them left the country (Frederikson 2013). But in the wake of the 2008 war, the tidal wave of aid returned when international donors meeting in Brussels pledged over $4.5 billion in aid to deal with "the state of emergency." Humanitarian agencies streamed back into Tbilisi with a flood of money, goods, new workers, and new institutional structures.

Flow, of course, is not just the movement of matter across space. It is the movement of matter across space and through time—a fundamentally temporal process that has to do not only with geographical dispersal but also with the rate at which matter moves. Like other kinds of flows, the aid stream is predicated on an implicit notion of time that governs its rate, duration, and course. That notion of temporality, for contemporary humanitarianism, is *crisis*. Because the humanitarian imperative to "do something" to alleviate suffering demands that something be done *now*, humanitarianism operates in a near-constant temporality of emergency (Calhoun 2008, 76; Redfield 2005; Redfield 2013, 32). Although humanitarianism may have arisen as a more general and long-term attempt to "remake the world so that it better serves the interests of humanity," the fact that the industry today is overwhelmingly based on donor-funded projects has made the emergency the fundamental unit of humanitarianism, a short-but-intense slice of time in which action must be taken quickly and within which goods and people must move rapidly across space (Calhoun 2008, 76).

The temporality of "emergency," as an exceptional state counterposed to the norms and laws of action found in ordinary time, means that humanitarian action tends to be overwhelming and fast, but also fleeting (Pandolfi 2003, 376). Humanitarian agencies are dependent on donors entranced by spectacular violence and suffering. For this reason most contemporary humanitarians focus on the acute, not the chronic. Medical humanitarians focus on machete wounds and bullet wounds, not hypertension or diabetes. Humanitarians occupied with shelter focus on getting people under roofs, not on building spaces where they can live for decades. Food aid is mostly used to provide deliveries for immediate consumption, not on rebuilding agriculture.[1] They operate in temporal bursts defined by ad hoc projects, but then must radically slow or stop operations when project funding ends.

The Russo-Georgian War did not meet the template for emergency used by most aid agencies because its acute phase was so short and its chronic phase was so long. The war only lasted five days, and despite Georgia's early claims that "most" ethnic Georgians in South Ossetia had been executed, it appeared that in fact very few Georgians had been killed[2] (Bahrampour 2008; BBC 2009). There were none of the gruesome injuries that conflicts in Rwanda or Congo engendered: no limbs hacked off, no piles of corpses. There had been no chemical warfare, as there would be later in Syria, and no epidemics of contagious diseases, as there would be the next year in Haiti. The scale of the displacement was even somewhat underwhelming: although 158,000 people were displaced during the war itself, almost 130,000 of them were back home by October. But because Georgia was of strategic value to both the United States and the EU countries, and because the success of Saakashvili had become so important to the Bush administration's democratization projects, the US and Western European donors provided vastly more funding that it would for similar emergencies in places of less geopolitical interest, and this drew Western aid agencies. As in many other emergencies, there was a flash flood of aid that overwhelmed the capacity of both the government and the IDPs to absorb it.

As emergency funding ends, though, and as one war fades into memory, it is replaced by new catastrophes to chase elsewhere. The tide of humanitarians rolls out, and the channels carrying aid begin to constrict. Redfield (2013, chapter 6) has written about "triage," or the sorting of people into those more and less deserving of aid, those who can be helped and those who must be sacrificed, those who have the greatest potential for recovery and those who have the greatest need, as an integral part of humanitarian aid. This happens not only at the level of individuals but of entire emergencies as well. Faced with the prospect of fresh emergencies, more temporally urgent crises and new project funding, donor support dwindles and the aid agencies depart. In Georgia, finding no acute wounds to heal and seemingly uninterested in the IDPs' chronic diseases, Médecins Sans Frontières stopped working with the IDPs in mid-2009 and focused on preparations to hand off its long-term project on tuberculosis to the Georgian government (Koch 2013). By the end of 2009 many of the international employees of aid agencies began to leave the country. In 2010 two new emergencies called many of the remaining humanitarians away: in January, the massive Haitian earthquake (which called forth more than $3.8 billion in aid by March), and in June, the ethnic clashes in Osh, Kyrgyzstan. As donors and agencies withdrew funding, pared down to a skeleton staff, and then left, the IDPs in the camp were no longer carried along by a wave of humanitarian aid. Instead they now found themselves in the drought of humanitarian abandonment.

Abandonment is an integral part of the cycle of humanitarian aid, but it is rarely discussed in the aid world. Western liberal democracies have explicitly used the notions of "sovereignty as responsibility" and "the responsibility to protect" as pretexts for entering other nations at will and taking over many of the functions of government (Pandolfi 2003). But along with that prerogative, they have also assumed a sovereign prerogative they do not discuss, name with catchy slogans, or write books about: the right to leave when they wish, no matter what conditions they leave their beneficiaries in. It is the end of the project, not the end of the need, that defines the terms under which the recipients of aid will be abandoned, and so the constant cycles of emergency and crisis, care and abandonment, create a flow of aid that is almost never a constant stream, but instead a flood followed by a quick constriction of the pipeline that puts displaced people under tremendous pressure. The effects of this flood-and-drought cycle are rarely captured in the postproject evaluations that aid agencies conduct, which seem to capture mainly the gratitude that recipients feel and only sometimes the long-term effects of the aid. But what about the effects of withdrawing aid and of abandoning beneficiaries? These are not planned for, recorded, or evaluated by the aid agencies, most of whom are long gone. What the humanitarian flood-and-drought cycle does to local economies or social structures, and what it does to individual lives, seems to go without notice.

Future Anterior and Past Perfect

How is it that donor countries and aid agencies, which are genuinely concerned with the welfare of the people they have come to help, can leave with such impunity? They do not callously abandon their beneficiaries to their fates. Indeed many of the aid workers I interviewed—particularly at UNHCR, which was the international agency most intensely involved with the IDPs—showed enormous concern for what would happen to the people from South Ossetia after the international community had moved on.[3] What international agencies do, instead, is to look to the idea that states create sovereignty by taking responsibility for human welfare. Very often they believe that continuity of care is assured by handing the project over to the national government to continue. But, as much of the research on humanitarian aid, development aid, and democratization projects shows, the assumption that the government can or will continue providing needed services is deeply problematic.

In Georgia one of the reasons that the humanitarians could withdraw without making plans for the IDPs' futures was that—with a strong push from USAID and UNHCR—the Georgian government seemed to have come up with plans of its own. Healthcare reform was underway, and the government said it would have insurance policies that would cover the IDPs at the low cost of 5 GEL (about $2.50) per year. Alongside that, the government promised that it would soon have programs for psychosocial aid to help those emotionally traumatized by war (Frederiksen 2013). The social welfare system was also in the midst of being reformed, and the government promised that it would have means-tested social-support payments for the poorest of the IDP families. And, in concert with the remaining skeleton staff at UNHCR, the Ministry of Refugees and Accommodation was making plans to build even more settlements for those remaining in temporary housing after the 2008 war, and for the IDPs from the early

1990s still lingering in hotels and old hospitals. It seemed as if—now that what they called the "emergency phase" was over—many of the international NGOs could safely transfer their programs and responsibilities to the Georgian government and move on to a fresh crisis, one that was acute rather than chronic. The "development phase," as the United Nations agencies labeled it, was to be led and coordinated by the nation-state, whose ability to govern had ostensibly been "strengthened" by a multitude of donor-funded "capacity building" projects.

The act of making plans and promises was the defining characteristic of the Saakashvili government, not just in relationship to IDPs but as a general principle of political action. Like many developing states, Georgia was a "will-be" state, one that "gains its legitimacy by promising a better tomorrow" and by contrasting itself with an imperfect past (Frederiksen 2013, 2). Saakashvili always contrasted his administration with the pre–Rose Revolution Shevardnadze regime, which had left the country mired in poverty and corruption. Before 2003 apartment buildings had dark and crumbling staircases and elevators that almost never worked, factories had been pillaged for bricks and scrap metal, and public buildings such as schools and libraries were characterized by torn-up flooring, broken windows, and weed-choked courtyards. The power grid did not reliably provide power, unemployment was staggeringly high, and manufacturing had almost completely disappeared (see chapter 2; also Dunn 2008). Saakashvili's promises to regain the disputed territories of South Ossetia and Abkhazia, to promote economic development resulting in improved living standards, and to create a democratic and uncorrupted political environment promised to change all that. He made these promises and visions of the future material and demonstrated what widespread social and economic change might look like by taking carefully bounded spaces that were rundown and poor and transforming them into showplaces full of upscale comforts and amusements. Tbilisi's Shardeni Street, a restored bit of the old city now full of expensive boutiques and restaurants, was one example, as was the Iveria Hotel, the vertical refugee camp transformed into a Radisson Hotel with a rooftop bar and swimming pool. Batumi, a run-down seaside resort, was transformed into a hip destination for wealthy young people (Pelkmans 2006, 182; Frederiksen 2013).

Alongside these visible indicators of what might be possible, Saakashvili floated big dreams. He promised to build an international ski resort in the remote Svaneti district, and broadcast plans to build an entirely new port city on the Black Sea, Lazika, that would be second in size only to the capitol. A telling video about Lazika posted to Saakashvili's YouTube account shows just how important the notion of a radiant future was to his political project (see Saakashvili n.d.). In it, Saakashvili's Dutch wife sits on the front porch of a wooden cottage reading dusty books as his son, dressed in the traditional Georgian *chokha*, first sits on a grandfather figure's knee while learning to play the stringed *panduri* typically used in Georgian folk music. Then the little boy builds a skyscraper out of transparent blocks, puts it on a cart, and hauls it across a bridge to a beach, where he announces "We will build a new city" (*chven vashenebt akhal kalaks*). Other children begin drawing pictures of what Lazika, the city of the future, will look like.

In compact form the video offered *temporal folding:* a vision that brought two different "slices of time" together at once (Cole and Durham 2008, 12). On the one hand, the video invokes a *past perfect*, a romanticized past full of Georgian warriors and musicians, quaint rural cottages, and strong ties to past generations. On the other hand—across the metaphorical bridge—it invoked a *future anterior*, the hypermodern city and a transparent political order that *will have been* once the planning and building have been done and the dream has been realized (see Frederiksen 2014). Tbilisi and Lazika evidenced this temporal folding in different ways. In Tbilisi the restoration of historic facades in the center city was accompanied by the destruction or complete renovation of Soviet-era buildings, and their replacement with glittering glass skyscrapers. Temporal folding in Tbilisi brought the past perfect up against the future anterior in ways that were deliberately aimed at effacing the Soviet period, while, at the very same moment, reproducing the Soviet Union's emphasis on monumental architecture, which the anthropologist Bruce Grant has called "the edifice complex" (Grant 2014). In plans for Lazika, built *ad novo* on a swamp, the skyscrapers were not meant to indicate that the city was in the same class as Paris or New York, as the rebuilt environment in Tbilisi did. Rather, the dream of Lazika, which was to be a Special Economic Zone (SEZ) for manufacturing and transshipment, was to signal membership in a class of global cities based on an Asian model: Singapore, Shanghai, Kuala Lumpur (see Easterling 2014). Implicit in the video of Lazika, but always present as a comparison, was the dystopian recent past full of derelict buildings, economic collapse, and government corruption that was still in plain sight all over the country and that, the Saakashvili regime implied, could return if the current administration were not there to implement its plans. In the symbolic argument launched both by urban renovation in Tbilisi and in the Lazika video, the state itself had become "the necessary present ground" for moving toward the future (Frederiksen 2014).

The same political principle applies to IDPs. Because states often promise that IDPs "will have been" taken care of when governmental reform has been completed and the "capacity" built by NGOs in state structures is put to use, international humanitarian NGOs feel confident in declaring that "the emergency phase" is over and in leaving the "development phase" to the government and the NGOs that remain behind. In Georgia the American and European donor nations and international humanitarians were thoroughly seduced by Saakash-vili's vision of the future, happy to believe that the future promised by Saakash-vili was already coming into reality, and willing to trust that the utopian camp of their dreams, Karaleti, was being built on the terrain of the dystopian camp that existed, Tsmindatsqali. But in fact no plans were made to ensure that the government enacted all the programs and plans it had promised, not even the much-vaunted but terribly vague IDP Action Plan written by the government in 2007 and revised in 2009 at the behest of international donors and aid agencies. Indeed there were almost no mechanisms in place to ensure any form of account-ability from the Georgian government to donor nations, much less the NGOs that had temporarily taken over its functions. Nor had any plans been made or budgets allocated for meeting the IDPs' needs *while* the IDP Action Plan or welfare reform or healthcare reform were between being planned and being fully implemented (see Frederiksen 2014, 8).

The central dilemma of the humanitarian condition, then, isn't just spatial but also temporal. Where there are multiple spaces in the camp—topolgangers that appear as both utopias and dystopias—multiple temporalities appear with them. IDPs are abandoned in the state of being permanently temporary, stuck between the past perfect of their now-idealized lives in the village, the past imperfect of a still-incomplete war, and the future anterior of governments that seem strong on ideas but weak on implementation. The camp becomes not just an island in space but in time as well, a place that is not only the site of aid delivery but, even-tually, also a site where IDPs are cut off from flows of aid and marooned. This is the source of much of the debilitating pressure that IDPs experience not only financially and socially but also bodily, in the form of *tsneva*.

The Chronic Present: The Emergency Ends but the Crisis Endures

If IDPs are stranded in time between past and future, how should their present be characterized? What are the distinctive features of the temporal bind created in the humanitarian condition? In the heterochronia of the camps, there is a third time beyond both the past imperfect and the future anterior. Rather than living in the future anterior that characterizes the utopic vision of the camps held by both the humanitarians and the government, or in the past perfect of their vil-lage lives, IDPs more often live in the *chronic present*. The chronic present has no defined horizon: it endures without any preordained end. But it is not a static time where nothing changes. Rather, it is characterized by a slow, grinding decline.

To explain the chronic present, it might help to adopt the distinction one humanitarian NGO, Médecins Sans Frontières, draws between *crisis*, by which it means a critical condition or conjuncture of social and political forces, and *emergency*, by which it means a more specific set of immediate problems requiring rapid medical response (Redfield 2013, 14). At the geopolitical level wars are emergencies, flare-ups of radical violence. But the conflicts and standoffs that underlie them can endure for decades, making wars that are years apart episodes in the same crisis. What happens when the emergency ends but the crisis continues? This was the situation with the South Ossetian conflict, but it is not unique to it. Around the world there are many "frozen conflicts"—Abkhazia, Cyprus, Israel and Palestine, Congo, Transnistria—that endure for decades through cycles of standoff and open conflict without ever being resolved. These long-standing crises frame the chronic present.

In South Ossetia the crisis intensified even as the humanitarians declared the emergency over and began leaving. After pulling back into South Ossetia proper in late 2008[4] the Russian Army intensified its occupation, using the pretext of protecting the Ossetians to establish a forward base on the south slope of the Caucasus that could be used for other military adventures. In a symbolic move Russians built an air base on the ashes of Kurta, the alternative capital established by pro-Georgian residents of South Ossetia and funded by the Georgian government. The FSB, the post-Soviet descendant of the KGB, took over border control from the disorganized Ossetian forces and began patrolling the border with guard dogs.[5] For the Georgian IDPs, who were still trying to secretly enter South Ossetia to pick through the ruins of their homes, to visit friends and relatives, to smuggle goods from Russia, or even to just chase straying livestock or pick *jonjoli* and other wild foods to supplement their diets, the intensification of the occupation meant losing yet more of their social worlds and livelihoods.

For IDPs stuck in the chronic present, then, the problem of displacement isn't just *flow*, as it is for humanitarians or the nation-state, but *blockage*: the closed borders and checkpoints that prevent them from returning, their inability to get the material goods needed for daily life, and their stymied attempts to get water, find jobs, obtain NGO grants or material aid, grow food, or find markets for trade. Blockages are chronic. They intensify at the same moment that the humanitarians begin to abandon the IDPs and the flow of aid starts to become significantly constricted. Just as a blocked or constricted channel increases the pressure of the water that flows through it, then, the dams created by ongoing political tensions, combined with constrictions in the channels of aid available to help deal with them, create chronically escalating worry and pressure.

In the Georgian IDP camps in the second year of displacement, the aid pipeline became narrower and narrower as the acute state of emergency was transformed into unspectacular chronic suffering in the present. Although residents of the camps were perfectly free to come and go as they pleased, and as citizens had the right to work, unemployment remained extremely high. In my small sample in Tsmindatsqali, which was near Gori's urban center, unemployment was 80%. In the rural settlements like Shavshvebi and Khurvaleti, unemployment was nearly universal: there were no large workplaces nearby and it was unaffordable to commute by *marshrutka*, leaving people with few streams of income outside of aid.[6] But aid was quickly being reduced. In October 2009 donated clothing and household goods stopped coming. In rural settlements firewood was no longer delivered. Gas and electricity stopped being free of charge, and IDPs were presented with large power bills they had to pay or face having the power cut. In March 2010 the World Food Programme stopped delivering food packages, leaving the IDPs reliant on what they could grow in their small plots or what they could afford to buy in the Gori market. In May the Ministry of Education announced that university education would no longer be free for IDPs, and that university students who failed to earn merit scholarships would have to pay fees of more than 2,000 GEL ($1,000) per year. Both the intensification of the geopolitical standoff and the withdrawal of aid provoked a huge constriction of household budgets and an enormous financial crisis for IDPs in the settlements. Where before the war they could provide for most of their needs by growing food and selling surplus crops to Russia via Ossetian traders, now they were largely locked down in space, no longer able to access their orchards or move agricultural goods across the border to Russian markets. They were reliant mainly on cash to purchase the basics of daily life, but were blocked from the spaces that had traditionally allowed them to generate cash.

There were a few ways to alleviate the pressure, and so some settlements and some families felt it less than others. In Tsmindatsqali and the other periurban settlements near Gori, the regional center, some women found part-time work as substitute teachers or nurses, usually at a fraction of their former salaries. The enormous postwar growth in the military and security apparatus provided some employment opportunities for a few of the men, who joined the army, the Ushishroeba (state security service) or the Spetsnaz (special military forces). Mariam and Anzor's family, for example, began patching together government jobs. While their two youngest sons remained unemployed, and Anzor was too sick to work, Mariam found part-time work in a preschool. Their oldest son, who lived near the camp, had been involved in the Georgian State Security Service. He profited from the diversion of humanitarian funds to the security apparatus and began rising in the ranks. These state salaries became lifelines for families with somebody lucky enough to have one: one person's salary of 400 or 500 GEL a month ($200–$250) often supported an extended family of six or eight unemployed people. As I show in chapter 6, dependence on these jobs created another kind of pressure: intense political pressure to support the Saakashvili regime.

But government jobs were few and far between, even for supporters of Saakashvili and the United National Movement.

A few people, especially in the rural settlements, made enormous efforts to alleviate the pressure by following the NGOs' prescription to become agricultural entrepreneurs. Aleko Mentashvili, the bee guy, was one of the first people to seriously attempt farming for the market while living in the settlement. Initially he took the "winterization payment" each IDP received, and instead of buying coats and boots, had his wife and three children make do all winter in layers of donated sweaters and sodden carpet slippers. With the money he bought chickens and a piglet and began raising them in makeshift pens in the small yard around his cottage. He could not afford commercial animal feed, so he fed the livestock on table scraps and macaroni, emptying the bags of pasta that had piled up under beds to throw to the animals. Soon he was selling eggs and piglets in the local market. But his economic situation was still precarious: crops can be damaged by hail and piglets can die. So he too began to search for a government job—a search that would, very soon, lead to an enormous crisis for his family and the destruction of his marriage.

NGO projects offered alternative sources of income in some (but not all) of the settlements, in the form of microcredit loans that were offered to the select few IDPs who completed a "business training course" given by the NGO and submitted a winning business plan.[7] For the few who succeeded—like the family that won a grant from CARE International to open a machine tractor station, or the musician who was given a keyboard and speakers by a French NGO so he could play at weddings—the new businesses were the possibility of enough income to raise the standard of living to what they considered "normal" and to add comforts like real sofas to replace the UNHCR cots or linoleum to cover the gaping floorboards. But far more often the new businesses started with NGO support quickly failed. Eka Gelashvili's husband, Nodar, was given a grant to open a barber shop, which he built in a metal shipping container outside their home. With few people in the settlement having much disposable income, though, it closed for lack of customers only a few months after it opened.

For most of the families in the settlements, then, the only source of cash income in the chronic, enduring economic crisis was government welfare payments, including IDP status payments, old-age pensions, and disability payments from the government. But the withdrawal of aid affects aid that flows through the national government as well as aid that flows through NGOs. In Georgia, as in most "humanitarian spaces," this abandonment is dressed up with the decidedly neoliberal rhetoric of Western liberal development, which emphasizes the virtues of economic self-reliance for "integration" of the IDPs in the same way the public health messages given to displaced people emphasize individual choice and responsibility and ignore the larger political and social factors that disable them. Neoliberal approaches to development tell displaced people, like other poor people around the world, that they must meet their needs for income, employment, food, health care, and other goods on the open market rather than relying on the government (see Li 2007; Povinelli 2008). Echoing these neoliberal messages about virtue, the Georgian government explicitly stated that "reduction of the IDPs' dependence on the state" was its "main goal" (Government of Georgia 2010). To that end the government began planning to withdraw the small payments of between 24 and 30 GEL (about $13–$16) given to each IDP on the basis of their being displaced. In its place means-tested "social assistance," for which not every IDP would qualify, would be offered. When in the future this change might occur was unclear, but the uncertainty it generated added more pressure to the already stressed IDPs.

Lethal Humanitarianism

What happens to displaced people when the emergency ends but the crisis endures? When the channels of aid narrow and the flow of people and money becomes increasingly blocked, how does the increasing pressure shape daily life? For many IDPs the financial and physical effects of the constriction of aid are first felt in the domain of health, as the effects of humanitarian abandonment and the temporality of the chronic present are made manifest on the scale of the body. In the Georgian IDP camps the ripple effect from international policy to national budgets and then down to the scale of the body happened largely in the domain of medicine. Although constriction of the aid pipeline limited people's access to jobs and money, doctors' visits, laboratory tests, and medications all had to be paid for in cash. Like other Georgians, the new IDPs had suffered the endemic poverty and the collapse of the Soviet health system common to all of Georgia between the end of the USSR and the Rose Revolution of 2004. But as a group they were older and sicker than the general Georgian population because many of the youngest and healthiest members of their villages in South Ossetia had migrated in search of work before the war. In almost every household there was a person with a serious health condition—*tsneva*, most frequently, but also bleeding ulcers, epilepsy, postmeningitis paralysis, thrombosis, and other disorders.

Pharmaceuticals quickly became a mainstay of life in the new settlements. Georgia has a weak health infrastructure, but such a well-developed pharmaceutical sector that it is one of the only prosperous parts of the economy (Koch 2013). The country has what might be termed a "pharmaceutical culture": both doctors and patients see pharmaceuticals as a first line of treatment, patients seek prescriptions in order to hoard drugs, and it is common to see four, five, or more drugs prescribed during a single doctors' visit. In the first year of displacement, mobile medical teams met the IDPs' demands for pharmaceutical treatment by holding chaotic consultations in crowded rooms in cottages and apartment blocks. In a largely ad hoc manner, without creating a medical record system or relying on laboratory work, medical teams set up pharmacies on tables in empty cottages or in plastic bags brought by the doctors themselves, and dispensed pharmaceuticals liberally and without cost. Antibiotics, antidepressants, and antihypertensives were given out freely, but with no records kept of what was prescribed and no plans for how to refill the prescription.

Once funding for "emergency health" ended and the mobile medical teams vanished, the IDPs were largely on their own to provide medicine. IDP doctors, who had set up a clinic in Tserovani with the help of the Czech government, did their best to provide aid to their fellow IDPs, who otherwise had no health infrastructure in the settlements and who, even with the weak government-provided health insurance, had difficulty affording access to either state or private clinics. Unemployed nurses in the settlements offered blood pressure checks and advice. But with limited equipment and no ability to provide lab tests, the help they could offer was severely limited. Pharmaceuticals were extremely expensive and had to be paid for immediately.

Although the government had made a gesture at providing insurance to the population by promoting insurance policies that could be purchased for 5 GEL, insurance proved to be mostly useless: pharmaceuticals were rarely covered except when they were administered by ambulance crews or in a hospital. There were exceptions: insulin was free, as was chemotherapy and some other drugs administered in an inpatient setting. But most people were in the same predicament as Eka Gelashvili, who showed me not only a shoebox full of medications but also a sheaf of prescriptions she could not afford to fill. "You can just read the prescriptions three times a day," her husband said, sardonically, as if in the absence of the drugs themselves, the papers representing them would have to serve as a healing talisman.[8] Like many other people in the settlement, Eka took medication when she could afford it but stopped when she couldn't. IDP patients took three or four days of a course of antibiotics and then stopped, or took oral diabetes medications for a few days and then economized by skipping a few days. Eka herself had antihypertensives meant to be taken daily, but only bought five tablets at a time rather than a month's worth because that was all she could afford. Because of the expense, she took them only when she felt she had *maghali tsneva*, which could be understood either as "high blood pressure" or "major stress." As the months wore on her blood pressure continued to rise, and she developed the symptoms of acute

hypertension: increasingly painful headaches and a pain behind the eye that suggested her optic disk was being degraded. Twice already, Nodar had called the ambulance for Eka, and the paramedics had confirmed that she was experiencing a life-threatening hypertensive emergency, one that threatened stroke or long-term organ damage. None of us knew when her hypertension might become a stroke that could kill or disable her.

Other people in the settlements experienced the same erratic mix of care and abandonment as the humanitarian NGOs transferred the responsibility for the well-being of the displaced population to the Georgian government. One woman in Tsmindatsqali had a six-year-old daughter with a seizure disorder. In the early days after the war the mobile humanitarian medical teams provided the little girl with Convulex,[9] the drug she needed. But once they had left the insurance no longer covered the drug, which cost roughly half of the family's monthly income, unless it was administered in a hospital. So the family waited for the girl to start convulsing and then called an ambulance and had her admitted to the hospital, where she could stay for days. A diabetic in the settlement was in a similar predicament. Although the state Ministry of Health covered the cost of insulin and provided a blood sugar monitor, it did not cover the cost of needles and test strips. To economize, the diabetic man tested infrequently and waited until his blood sugar was dangerously high to use a needle to administer insulin.

The erratic mix of care and abandonment, flow and blockage, was hardest on Anzor Kapanadze. The state provided the very expensive dialysis treatment he needed for free—it was seen as an emergency measure. But it did not cover transportation, which was deemed a chronic problem outside the domain of healthcare. At 40 lari per trip, and with three trips a week, the cost of transportation placed an enormous financial strain on his wife and sons, who struggled just to get him to the hospital. Even as some of the IDPs got government jobs or used NGO grants to begin improving their cottages and their living standards, I watched as the Kapanadzes' cottage became even poorer and more run-down than when they moved in. Between the cost of transporting Anzor and the cost of purchasing the Convulex, which had been prescribed for their hydrocephalic infant grandson,[10] every spare penny was going to pay for medical care. *Tsneva* came in multiple forms: pressure on the veins, pressure on the pancreas, pressure on the pocketbook, pressure from government bureaucrats demanding more paperwork, pressure from doctors demanding another test that the Kapanadzes couldn't afford and the government wouldn't pay for.

Many aspects of life in the settlements contributed to giving people chronic and potentially lethal *tsneva*. The food packages from the World Food Programme gave people bread, salt, sugar, and macaroni, all of which shot enormous amounts of sodium and sugar into the IDPs' bloodstreams. The sugar essentially caramelized their veins, bonding with proteins and other carbohydrates on cell surfaces and damaging small blood vessels. The damage was worsened even more by the cortisol released into their systems by constant emotional stress.[11] People who were already suffering from years of poor health care began to decline:

between December 2009 and June 2010, on our side of the settlement alone, four people got diabetes or found their diabetes worsening precipitously. Three more developed kidney damage from high blood pressure, and two died of heart attacks. The effects of pressure are multiplicative: poverty causes hypertension and diabetes, diabetes causes kidney disease, kidney disease causes more hypertension, and it all causes more poverty, as people struggle to medicate themselves. By 2010, when I was back teaching in Colorado and returning to Georgia on university breaks, there seemed to be a new roster of the ill and the dead each time I arrived back in the settlements.

Among them was a death clearly attributable to the effects of *tsneva*, both in its physical and emotional senses. Temo Javakhishvili, the man whose son had died in the bombing of Gori, faced intense pressure. Unemployed and unable to find even daily labor jobs, living on a meager disability pension that he got for being legally blind, he coped by using what we jokingly referred to as "Georgian Prozac"—recycled plastic bottles full of wine or *chacha* that were sold for a few lari from the windows of people's cottages in the settlement. Temo had been an alcoholic long before the war. He had dealt with the constant shooting in his home village, Eredvi, for years by drinking alone. But now, in Tsmindatsqali, his alcoholism had gotten much worse and much more public. Although he wasn't divorced, his wife had left years before, and had now taken his surviving grandchild to live in another city. With his son Zviadi dead and his other son, Zura, drifting in and out, Temo spent most of his time alone in his cottage, which was quickly becoming run-down and filthy, his dishes encrusted with dried-on food and his walls covered in cracks and mold. When he was sober, he was a quiet, even shy man whose shoulders curled in toward his body and whose eyes peeped out from behind thick glasses. I had come to see an enormous sweetness in Temo. But liquored up, he was loud and obnoxious. When I went to see him one day in 2009, he offered me a shot of *chacha* in a glass smeared with fingerprints and crusty with tomato sauce, and asked me to sleep with him. At night we could often hear him roaming around the settlement, yelling and singing. Within a few months I almost never saw him sober at all.

When I returned to the settlement in 2010 Temo was nowhere to be found. Finally I found Zura, sitting on the makeshift patio of their cottage behind a sunshade made of blue plastic tarpaulin. "Temo is dead," he told me, his own voice slurred and his breath potent with alcohol. "He just fell over one day, and that was the end." Temo's enormous consumption of alcohol had finally led to a clot in the blood vessels in his brain, Zura told me, and with the pressure mounting inside his head, he had died of a stroke. But even in death Temo couldn't go home. As we sat and talked, and as Zura drank, he told me about Temo's funeral. "We couldn't bury him in our village, Eredvi—but that is where he should be, in the soil along with his ancestors! Instead we had to bury him in the Gori cemetery, so far away from everybody." Zura had done the best he could for his father: he buried him near his son Zviadi, at the top of the cemetery, with his head pointed toward the green rolling hills of Eredvi.

Humanitarian abandonment was even more deadly than war. For those with jobs or functioning microbusinesses, life-threatening chronic conditions like *tsneva* were treatable. But others, people like Eka Gelashvili or Temo Javakhish-vili, were subject to a new form of biopolitical lethality. Just as the humanitarians appropriated the right to intervene and the right to withdraw, they also appropriated the means to make the IDPs live and the right to allow them to die. Elizabeth Povinelli argues that the misery brought about by these neoliberal principles of aid and abandonment result in

> a quieter form of abjection [and] despair. . . . There is nothing spectacular to report. Nothing happens that rises to the level of an event. Life drifts into a form of death that can be certified as due to "natural causes." As a result, any ethical impulse dependent on a certain kind of event flounders. . . . An agentless slow death characterizes their lethality: quiet deaths, slow deaths, rotten worlds. The everyday drifts towards death; one more drink, one more sore; a bad cold, bad food; a small pain in the chest. These kinds of deaths only periodically fix the gaze of national and international publics. (2008, 175)

Mundane suffering in the chronic present hardly competes with war or terrorist attack as the focus of ethical attention, precisely because of its uneventful and chronic temporality. Whereas spectacular violence "seems to create the ontological necessity to respond ethically," the grubby, slow deaths from poverty and disease do not call down the same floods of humanitarian action.

Humanitarians' decisions to believe in the national government's vision of the future anterior, and thus to abandon displaced people in order to pursue other emergencies, fresh catastrophes, and suffering that is more sublime, is a decision to let die. Cancelling the support for life—no matter how ineffective—is as much a form of authorized state killing as war itself is. And yet withdrawing this life support is seen as a moral good, a necessary push toward virtuous self-sufficiency (Povinelli 2009). Slow suffering and death in the chronic present is therefore authorized within the framework of humanitarian action, as chronic disease is deemed to be "not war related" or "not unique to the displaced," and hence not within the purview of humanitarian agencies, even as it is caused by humanitarian abandonment.[12] Although an exploding vessel in Eka's brain would kill her just as dead as an exploding bomb in her house, a stroke brought on by displacement and poverty would not count as war related, and so was not seen

as a death to be prevented within the framework of humanitarian aid. Likewise, Temo's alcoholism, surely exacerbated by war death and displacement, was seen as a failure of individual responsibility, not a war-related disease, and so neither noticed nor treated by either the government nor any of the international NGOs.

While the NGOs lined up to provide art classes and soccer matches to children, Temo died and Eka struggled.

Like the squeezing of blood vessels and the narrowing of the aid pipeline, the decision to place disease linked to protracted displacement outside the realm of humanitarian concern constricts the temporality of crisis itself. Is a crisis only something that happens fast? Is life in slow, enduring crisis not in enough crisis to matter? Like the decision to move aid to another emergency altogether, the decision to place the chronic health effects of displacement outside the purview of humanitarian concern is a form of triage integral to the humanitarian mission. It is a decision about who is weak enough to save and who is strong enough to struggle alone, whose life is worth saving and who should be allowed to suffer. Such decisions are based not only on the characteristics of the individual patient, but also on constructs of time and event and the difference between "emergency" and "crisis." Most of all they are made on the difference between the sublime suffering of immediate catastrophe that offers a burst of adrenalin and terrific pictures for a website, and a dusty, boring, long-term suffering that seems to never end.

The Temporality of the Lesser Evil

In *The Least of All Possible Evils* (2011), Eyal Weizman traces the history of a profound philosophical split that has riven the humanitarian community since the 1970s. On the one hand, Weizman argues, there are the activist humanitarians, people inspired by the call of Médecins Sans Frontières to not only provide the short-term aid that would keep people alive in the midst of catastrophe but to also take a longer view and to intervene in the political conditions that are the root of conflict in the first place. This standpoint, which arose out of MSF founder Bernard Kouchner's split from the International Red Cross during the Biafra War in Nigeria, is obviously the genesis of the Responsibility to Protect policy that makes military intervention an option when states are committing human rights violations against their own populations (Weizman 2011, 49; see also Redfield 2013, 12). But it is also at the root of ostensibly milder interventions: humanitarian and development aid aimed at rewarding states for becoming more democratic, for example, or at building the state's capacity to care for its own population (This, perhaps, was the reason for MSF abandoning aid to IDPs and returning to the project of building the Georgian government's program to treat TB.) Those who believe in transforming states—with violence or bureaucracy or both—believe that successful humanitarianism requires the creation of security: not just the immediate security offered by food and shelter, but also long-term security constituted at larger scales through the creation of a democratic nation-state and stable geopolitical relations (see Weizman 2011, 52–53; James 2010, 13–17).

On the other hand, however, there are those who subscribe to the humanitarian ethos set out by the International Committee of the Red Cross in 1965: the notion that humanitarian action should be impartial and politically neutral, aimed at saving biological life but not at intervening into the social and political lives of those they save or the countries they inhabit (ICRC n.d.). Here Weizman cites the philosophy of Rony Brauman, a founding member of MSF who split with Kouchner after watching aid to Ethiopia turn into a tool used by the government to forcibly deport its opponents. Brauman came to believe that humanitarians should eschew any involvement in politics. This, Weizman says, is the "lesser evil," a practice that doesn't seek to create the utopian or even the good, but only to mitigate harm. The "lesser evil" is a humanitarianism aimed at preserving biological life without trying to govern or manage the people it treats. It presents itself as politically neutral and does not aim at solving the underlying problems that cause violent conflict. In Brauman's view this kind of humanitarianism is and should be "temporary autonomous act of solicitude that is about little more than caring for bodies" (see Weizman 2011, 54).

Weizman himself comes to subscribe to Brauman's argument that humanitarianism should be both temporary and minimal. He endorses Brauman's argument for a humanitarianism that "takes no political stand, makes no claim to transform society, and doesn't come to make war or peace, promote economic development, help administer justice, or export democracy or human rights values" (Brauman, cited in Weizman 2011, 55). He writes, "Humanitarianism should indeed aim to provide no more than the bare minimum to support the revival of life after violence and destruction" (61). Summarizing the views of humanitarians who take Weizman's side of the argument, Mariella Pandolfi writes:

> The purpose of the complex apparatus of humanitarian intervention is not to implement the long-term agenda of economic development; it is not the promotion of democracy; it is not advocacy for human rights. Its purpose is to provide an immediate response as dictated by the emergency imaginary with its emphasis on apparently sudden, unpredictable, and short-term explosions of suffering. (2010, 228)

But here's the problem: short-term crisis-driven humanitarian aid cannot substantially alleviate the suffering of the displaced or "support the revival of life." The experiences of Eka Gelashvili and Temo Javakhishvili, along with the other people who suffered and died in Tsmindatsqali, force us to look at the implicit assumption in the first part of Weizman's argument. Perhaps, in the short time scale of the emergency, humanitarianism can reduce mortality. But in many cases humanitarian aid doesn't support the long-term revival of life. Instead, by shutting down the flow of aid, abandoning displaced people to the unfulfilled visions and plans of the nation-state, and making them dependent on the very government that routinely fails to provide the services they need, the temporality of aid forces displaced people into a precarious form of citizenship that places them under severe economic pressure and creates lethal forms of disease. Modulating the flow of aid, as Weizman himself points out, is a form of control that not only keeps people alive in some minimal state. It also kills them through a "slower, more cumulative process in which deaths that might have been averted are actively not prevented" (Weizman 2011, 86). Humanitarianism often just transforms the spectacularly and acutely lethal into a cruddy, chronic pressure that is equally—although more slowly—lethal. As long as it is organized into short-term temporal units called "projects," as long as there is a financial premium to chase disasters and to move to the next emergency, as long as people are pushed into camps because that's where it is efficient and convenient for humanitarians to deliver aid to a central location, the short-term support of life will create long-term poverty and ill health. The humanitarian condition thus doesn't revive life, but only forestalls death, making it take place in the creeping temporality of the chronic. Is that a lesser evil, or merely an evil that attracts less attention?

THE DEVIL AND THE AUTHORITARIAN STATE

In late August 2010, almost two years after the war, I sat in the kitchen of Manana Abaeva's small cinderblock cottage in Tsmindatsqali, canning fruit with her on a day that reached 106 degrees Fahrenheit. As we sweltered over the boiling jars, Manana told me a startling story: in Tsmindatsqali, Khurvaleti, and Tserovani settlements, IDPs had been finding large snakes curled up in their beds and coiled on their kitchen tables. Apparently the snakes had been entering through cracks in the floorboards and walls of the hastily built and badly constructed cottages in search of shelter from the blazing heat. "See that?" said Manana in her thick Ossetian accent, pointing to a nearly 2-inch gap between the floor and the wall. "No wonder we are being besieged with snakes!"

Incursion by all sorts of pests had become routine in the settlements. Sleeping at Manana's one night, I woke up to find ants crawling through my hair. Mice and bugs were regular presences in the cottages, and even tall stalks of grass pushed up from the bare earth underneath the cottages and through the gaps between the raw-pine planks on the floor to emerge in the middle of living rooms all over the settlements. But it was the snakes that were the most unsettling to the IDPs in Tserovani and Tsmindatsqali. The problem was not the physical danger they posed, since they were mostly nonvenomous species. Rather, they posed an enormous spiritual danger. In Georgian Orthodox Christianity, snakes are *eshmakebi*, "that which cannot be mentioned," fetishes or incarnations of the devil (see Barry 2011). The snakes marked life under the humanitarian regime with a demonic aspect that seemed to pervade the camps with evil and danger.

Soon the demonic became a key trope in the camps, a symbol that began to reappear in new contexts. When I told Manana that I planned on interviewing a former neighbor of hers, she hissed at me, "Watch out for that one, he's an *eshmaki*," a devil. Not an hour later, the man's sister-in-law told me, "Watch out for Manana. She's Ossetian, so she's an *eshmaki*. You should watch out for Elena Chochieva too, the other Ossetian woman." I found this hard to believe: Elena, a roly-poly red-haired woman who seemed to chortle her way through all our conversations, seemed to be the soul of joviality. But sure enough, not more than a day later, I heard Elena Chochieva had been telling anybody who would listen that I was an *eshmaki*.

Why did devils, whether real, imaginary, or metaphoric, seem to infest not only the physical spaces of the camp but its social spaces as well? Why did the diabolic become a recurring motif? In this chapter I argue that the increase in talk about the devil marks a dramatic rise in mistrust caused by humanitarian statebuilding. By tracing the figure of the devil through the camp and the state apparatus, I show how suspicion and distrust are not only effects of the statebuilding project but also come to transform the nature of humanitarian sovereignty itself, suffusing it with a distinctly post-Soviet logic of power. As the Georgian state became hypervigilant in the search for hidden enemies, aid dollars meant to improve the state's capacity to care for its population soon resulted in covert authoritarianism and a revival of repressive state action.

In the previous chapter I engaged with the debate over whether humanitarian action should focus only on providing emergency aid to sustain life in the short term or whether it should seek to eliminate the root causes of suffering by transforming states, fostering democracy, upholding human rights, and preventing political violence (Barnett 2011, 39). I argued that temporary emergency aid could not do the good it claims to do. In this chapter I make a similar claim about the attempt to provide long-term aid by improving the state's capacity to care for its citizens. I argue that humanitarian statebuilding cannot create long-term political stability, economic growth, or better living conditions for the impoverished displaced. Rather, when millions of dollars in aid are aimed at increasing the state's institutional capacity, aid can lead to brutal authoritarianism, the rise of the secret police, widespread denunciation, and politically motivated incarcerations. Aid can contribute to the erosion of trust and the revival of suspicion as a fundamental principle of sovereignty and a way of living. Thus if the work of the displaced is to make their new situation comprehensible, they must also work against the shortage of information, political chaos, outright secrecy, and pervasive mistrust produced when statebuilding is a form of aid. This problem is marked by the figure of the devil, which I argue is a framing device or a model that takes fragmentary information about half-sensed political forces and makes sense of them. In doing so, the figure of the devil offers IDPs a way to make sense of the erosion of democratic sovereignty and the covert damage wrought by authoritarianism inadvertently bought and paid for by the humanitarian statebuilding project.

Eshmakebi: **The Return of the Devil**

In Tsmindatsqali, the boundary between the natural and supernatural worlds was as unmarked, fragile, and volatile as the boundary between South Ossetia and Georgia proper.[1] All of the players in the 2008 war, including the Georgian IDPs, most of the Ossetians who ousted them from their homes,[2] and the Russian soldiers who fought in South Ossetia, shared a single religion: Orthodox Christianity. Orthodoxy was not just nominal either. Although Orthodox Christianity had been largely banned during the Soviet period, the end of Communism had been accompanied by a robust religious revival throughout the former Eastern Bloc (see Rogers 2009; Steinberg and Wanner 2008). Fervent religiosity was evident in all three groups, and even though the Georgians looked to one patriarch, Ilia II in Tbilisi, whereas the Russians and the Ossetians looked to Patriarch Kirill I in Moscow, many IDPs appealed to a shared religious heritage during the war by holding up icons or crosses to ask for mercy from enemy forces. For years after the war the IDPs often mentioned that although their houses had been destroyed, the village churches had never been damaged or looted because the Russians and Ossetians were too afraid of divine retribution to harm the icons within. But nationalistic tensions as well as cross-cutting religious ties manifested themselves supernaturally. Mariam Sabashvili's niece, for example, told me that a black cloud had hung over Tskhinvali and stayed for more than two weeks. Within the cloud, she said, people saw inexplicable things at night. Sometimes it was just bright lights flying around, but other times people saw angels or an apparition of the weeping Virgin. "It's God rebuking the Ossetians," Megi said. "They know what they did to us."

The battle between the divine and the demonic was a trope within which many of the IDPs came to understand the enormous pressure caused by humanitarianism. Rather than understanding the steep drop in available resources as a problem of limited resources and bureaucratic roadblocks, as the donor community did, or in geopolitical terms, as a result of the Obama administration's increasing unwillingness to confront Putin, many of the IDPs saw their own struggles in theological terms and began to appeal to God, Jesus, and local saints as a means to exercise agency while understanding powerlessness. As Mariam Sabashvili's husband became sicker and sicker, for example, family members and neighbors pooled scarce cash to buy a goat, which Mariam and her sons led three times around the church at Goris Jvari, on the bluff overlooking the town. Once the goat, who dragged its heels and fought the entire way, had completed its circumambulations, Mariam's son slit its throat, skinned it, and hung its head and blood-smeared hide next to tens of others on the pikes outside the church walls. Even Manana, whose natural skepticism had been strongly reinforced by Soviet atheism, began to pray once her husband began passing secretly through South Ossetia, through the Roki Tunnel, and up into Russia, where members of the local mafia, local Russian nationalists, and the police in equal measures had been harassing migrants from the Caucasus. God was close to people in Tsmindatsqali, and his presence was routinely felt in prayers, omens, and visions. But if God was close in the camp, so too was the devil, who appeared to cause accidents, job losses, money woes, and other forms of intense pressure. The snakes were fetishes that merely confirmed what other forms of ill-fortune had suggested.

Devilry, as a symbol, takes the chaos of humanitarianism and the dramatic shifts in power caused by the statebuilding project and frames them in a narrative that makes them comprehensible to those who experience their effects. For the IDPs the devil is both a very literal being and a figure that identifies an unseen space in which unknown agents plotted the vagaries of life in the humanitarian condition. The devil functioned as a framing device—a symbol embedded in a narrative that allows the people subject to humanitarian power relations to identify the largely hidden agents of power shaping their new lives and thus to bring at least some order and comprehensibility to life in the settlements.

For more than thirty years anthropologists have looked at the ways people use devil imagery to understand macrolevel political and economic forces and to conceptualize new forms of sovereign power. In his classic work *The Devil and Commodity Fetishism* (1980), Michael Taussig argued that among Colombian plantation workers, the devil was a symbol of the alienation of labor by capitalism and the estrangement produced by their immersion into a regime of repression and terror. Forced into hard labor, beaten and sometimes killed while working, the Colombian peasants Taussig describes used the devil as a means of representing capital, the unseen and hostile force that could not be controlled at the local level. Gaston Gordillo, looking at the claims the Toba people make about the presence of the devil at plantations and sugar processing factories in the Argentinian Chaco, concurs. "The power of the diablos . . . was a historically and spatially specific type of power: one produced by capitalist conditions of exploitation" (2004, 137). In these explorations the devil is an artifact of new systems of sovereignty and domination made logical by capitalism, spread around the world by colonialism, and experienced locally in the form of appalling labor conditions (see Gordillo 2002, 34). This view is echoed by other anthropologists, who argue that visions of the diabolical (among Christian populations) or possession by other evil spirits (among non-Christians) come from the brutal exploitation of workers, the alienation of their labor, and their wrenching separation from their communities of origin and prior ways of life (see Ong 1987; Nash 1979).

The figure of the devil condenses the experience of terror into a potent symbol. Terror is not just the sharp, temporally acute experience of systematic torture or mass murder, or war. It is "a fear of death embedded in appalling . . . conditions, high mortality rates linked to rampant diseases, and political repression. The routine nature of this sustained fear does not make it less sharp than other, more violent forms of terror" (Gordillo 2002, 35). Long-term chronic fear, like the fear of death experienced as "cruddy suffering" (Povinelli 2008) in the Georgian camps, is a form of slow-motion terror caused by new structures of sovereign authority. As Turner (1986) suggests, the devil is a symbol of power, whatever its form. The figure of the devil expresses terror, labels it as evil, and points the finger at *somebody* acting behind the scenes to cause it. The generalized experience of terror, then, is transformed into mistrust, or fear of specific agents with the potential to cause harm. As I show in the next sections, this deep mistrust originates in two kinds of power characteristic of the humanitarian encounter: first, in the micropolitics of the camp, and second, in the macropolitics of the postwar humanitarian state.

The Micropolitics of the Devil: *Eshmakebi,* Distrust, and the Rupture of Social Relations

To understand the critique of the humanitarian condition that the serpent presents, and to grasp the ways in which the sense of the diabolical reflected a profound transformation in the social relations of the IDPs to one another, the state, and the international humanitarian community, it helps to return to the most embodied, most inchoate sense of terror that the IDPs could label: *nerviuloba,* or nervousness. *Nerviuloba* is itself caused by a profound mistrust endemic to the humanitarian encounter and the drastic destruction of social relations it entails. Devilry is not a sign of evil or of sin, but of pervasive suspicion, the affective state caused by both the micro- and macropolitical relations of humanitarianism.

The Georgian term *nerviuloba* pointed to the hypervigilance common to almost all people in refugee camps and IDP settlements, a condition in which people must constantly watch, wait, and worry. Many humanitarian workers conceptualize this hypervigilance as part of posttraumatic stress disorder (PTSD), a mass psychological disorder that affects populations subjected to the violence and trauma of war (see Pupavac 2004, 491; see also Fassin and Rechtman 2009, 163–83). Explained in the psychological literature as a biological medical problem caused by the overstimulation of the amygdala, the part of the brain responsible for the "fight or flight" response, PTSD is both immediately medicalized and individualized (Pupavac 2004, 493). Stephen Jones argues that "PTSD has come to signify all the moral, social and political evils of war. To say that people did not have PTSD appeared, to some, to be saying that they had not suffered" (2014, 6). But as Bracken (2002, 187) writes, the diagnosis of PTSD reduces the very collective experience of war and the damage wrought to the socially constituted fabric of meaning to individual biologies and feelings of anxiety (see also Pupavac 2004, 494; Fassin and Rechtman 2009; Walters and Cortina 2007). Nervousness and suspicion are not necessarily individual responses to the war, but rather collective responses to life in the humanitarian condition, where displaced people do not just wait passively for aid but must constantly contend with different groups in the immediate present (in Georgia, the Russians, the Ossetians, neighbors, government officials, aid workers) who seek control of them and who therefore might harm them. As Valentine Daniel and John Knudsen say baldly, "The refugee mistrusts and is mistrusted" (1995, 2). This constant state of vigilance and suspicion is not just a conscious state for refugees but an ontological one as well, an unsettled and unsettling form of being in the world that stems from the radical uncertainty and lack of control endemic to camp life.

Although identifying the constant sense of unease and mistrust is easy for displaced people to do, finding the source of it is a much more complicated problem. Whom to suspect? What quarters might harm come from? In the Georgian camps it was not always evident who might harm the IDPs or their families. There was little information about the military situation, the kinds of aid that might be forthcoming or withdrawn, or shifts in the government's policy, and no way of predicting how the situation might change in the future. With only rumors and odd snippets of information gleaned from television, the IDPs came to believe that a shadowy, half-seen world existed apart from the settlements, where deals were struck and decisions made that affected their very ability to survive. With no clear idea about whom the agents of this power were, the IDPs began to suspect the people around them of being *eshmakebi*, or demons. The IDPs did not believe that the *eshmakebi* among them were literally demonically possessed. But a neighbor (or a visiting anthropologist) deemed to be an *eshmaki* was a person following demonic counsel, willingly violating deeply held norms of Christian principles of solidarity and charity in order to take advantage of those around him or her.[3]

The individualistic, self-interested search for leverage and advantage is a direct effect of humanitarian abandonment. As humanitarians move on to other emergencies and withdraw aid, IDPs must begin calculating and strategizing frantically to obtain resources—jobs, contract work, grants, cash assistance, and access to the remaining NGO projects—for their own families. At the same time they condemn others for calculating and strategizing in similar ways. This creates webs of suspicion that drive wedges among neighbors, often isolating people who, before conflict and displacement, were engaged in webs of mutual assistance, entertainment, and even affection. The figure of the devil embodies the ways mistrust tears at social relations already damaged by war and exodus.

The irony is that it is bureaucratic attempts to distribute the remaining aid fairly, and therefore to ward off jealousy, that render the recipients of aid into *eshmakebi* who strategize and scheme to gain scraps of donated help. In Georgia as the NGOs declared the end of the period of emergency aid and began what they called "postconflict recovery," they no longer wanted to hand the same package of aid out to every family or individual. Instead they sought to introduce market logic by searching out those IDPs who could be transformed into entrepreneurs, the ideal recipients of neoliberal development aid. For example, under the Stabilization and Integration of IDPs into Mainstream Georgian Society (SIIMS) project, CARE international began holding competitions for aid, in which IDPs had to compete to participate in various business-related trainings, and then compete again to write the best business plan in order to gain funding. The awards were sometimes small microcredit loans, as they were to twenty-five IDP women who were funded to start handicrafts businesses and kiosks, but on some occasions were significant sums. In Skra, Berbuki, and Akhalsopeli settlements, small groups of IDPs were given agricultural machinery worth USD $135,000, including gigantic tractors, plows, disk harrows, and more (CARE International 2011).

CARE officials subscribed to the common belief among development agencies that creating a quasi-market for aid by holding open competitions among potential beneficiaries made the process open and transparent and eliminated any suspicion of corruption or injustice. During the Soviet period when the economy was characterized by endemic shortage, citizens' access to everything from vegetables to health care to university educations was largely dependent on their social connections and on their ability to cultivate patron-client relationships (Verdery 1996). In the post-Soviet era, when personal connections still very often structure people's access to opportunity (see, for example, Ledeneva 2006; Dunn 2004), Western donors use competitions for bids, tenders, and services to create the illusion that competition itself creates justice and fairness even though it also creates inequality. But although replicating the market logic that had taken over the humanitarian industry among the beneficiaries of aid was self-evident for CARE's donors and officials, it was not at all self-evident in the camps, where these competitions and the unequal delivery of resources they engendered felt deeply corrupt and unfair. Winners of the grants were accused of being *eshmakebi* who had unfairly used their connections to people working at CARE to influence the outcome of the decision. Meanwhile the same people calling others *eshmakebi* often went to great lengths to build connections and get resources. For example, an IDP who was a *mamasakhlisi*, a settlement official, once sidled up to me and whispered, "You know the director of CARE, don't you? I want a grant to build a supermarket. Call him and tell him to give the grant to me."

Humanitarian aid allocated by competition erodes trust throughout the community, making the IDPs not only distrusted by outsiders but also distrustful of the aid agencies and of one another. In the Georgian settlements the combination of intense economic and social pressure and the competition for aid began to erode the trust that people had formed as neighbors of long standing in the South Ossetian villages, where mutual aid had become essential after the USSR collapsed and the Georgian state failed. Manana Abaeva and Elena Chochieva, for example, both ethnically Ossetian women, lived as neighbors in an ethnically Georgian village for decades. They knew each other's histories, families, and situations in intimate detail, and had asked for cottages near each other and the other villagers from Ksuisi. Yet within a year of their arrival in the camps they were deeply suspicious of each other and had nearly severed relations among themselves, their husbands, and children. The same erosion of trust was even more pronounced among IDPs from different villages, who had less shared history and less knowledge of one another. Where, in the first year after the war, they had begun by acting out of the solidarity created by their same plight, by the end of that year members of different villages were so distrustful of one another that they often refused to participate together in the NGO-sponsored community mobilization programs aimed precisely at creating a sense of shared purpose among them.

Material comforts, virtually anything beyond the things that had been handed out to everyone, became the traces by which *eshmakebi* could be identified. New tools for production were a clear sign of illicit dealings: one of the gigantic new tractors, new saws given to a woodworker, the new mixer and speakers given to a wedding singer, or a new kiosk made of a metal shipping container set up outside someone's house were all signs of scheming self-interest. Consumption goods too were signs of the diabolical: a cellular telephone, a new dress, or even a chicken for dinner might be seen as evidence of one's scheming. So while donor governments and aid agencies dutifully subscribed to the notion that these small luxuries would motivate people to compete in a capitalist market, and thus put forward all sorts of small business development and microlending projects, the IDPs themselves saw these objects as both alluring and potentially dangerous, and hid as much as they could to avoid becoming the targets of envy and jealousy. It may be, as Taussig (1980, 427) argues, that the devil has a special affinity with the social disruptions caused by capitalism. This is not unheard of in the

former Communist bloc, where Marxist ideals of economic and political equality were often upheld even as the Communist Party was roundly criticized for
failing to live up to them, and where the move to a market economy has caused
new forms of inequality. The figure of the devil, then, was a comment on the ways

that humanitarian aid created unequal access to capital itself under conditions of dramatic scarcity. Accusations of devilry stood as a sharp critique of humanitarianism's drive to instill the habits and values of the market and to create the social relations of capitalist production among a population already dispossessed and unlikely to resist.

In a larger sense, the figure of the devil was also a comment on the inherently moralizing tendency of contemporary humanitarianism. If humanitarianism is not just about restoring the world to its precatastrophe state, but, as Michael Barnett writes, about "making the world a better place" by creating the social relations of the world as it should be, then the figure of the devil reveals that humanitarianism not only promotes virtues like altruism and selflessness but also fosters selfishness, secretiveness, corruption, and vice. The devil became a symbol not only of one's neighbors' strategies but also of the morally repugnant behavior that each of the IDPs was forced to engage in to survive. The bureaucratic rituals that were meant to constitute transparency, trust, and moral probity (Power 1997) that would lead to cohesion in the camps in fact created an entire domain of covert action premised on secrecy and suspicion. The devil thus became, as Ware (1979) says, "not an existent being or substance" but a marker of communal moral decay.

The Macropolitics of the Devil: Conspirativity and Statebuilding

The sign of the devil was not just an artifact of the IDPs' struggle for resources. Because humanitarian aid in Georgia was so deeply entwined with statebuilding, the appearance of the devil also marked a profound transformation in the relations of citizenship that linked the IDPs to the Georgian nation-state. Here devilry was transformed from mere scheming into spying, or a secretive relationship that forged new connections (or re-created old ones) between IDPs who denounced their fellows and the shady, hidden parts of the Georgian state. Many of the IDPs in Tsmindatsqali believed that their fellow IDPs were reporting on them and conspiring against them as a means of gaining political and economic advantage. As I show here, conspiracy theories—which are one of the central means people use to make sense of state structures and actions they can sense but cannot see or know—are an especially potent framework among displaced people, who must contend with both the overt and covert effects of the humanitarian statebuilding project.

My first exposure to the collective paranoia that swept the camp came from Manana Abaeva, who focused especially intently on her neighbor Elena Chochieva's daughter, Tamta, who worked for the Georgian-backed South Ossetian government in exile. Her job was particularly political. She was an appointee of the National Movement, the political party led by President Mikheil Saakashvili, which had attempted to win the hearts and minds of ethnic Ossetians before the war by plying them with social services and economic development projects. What precisely Tamta did, I never found out. She carefully evaded the question every time I asked, offering only a plastic smile and saying in a condescending tone, "I help the *gamgebeli* (the mayor) of our old village." But Manana Abaeva believed that Tamta's job entailed reporting on the activities and political sentiments of the IDPs in Tsmindatsqali, and that this affected the ways that aid projects, government assistance, and most especially government jobs were distributed. "She's worse than her mother when it comes to gossip," Manana said. "Everything you tell her goes to the *gamgebeli*, and from there who knows where." Like many of her neighbors in the camp, Manana also believed that the government was paying people—even those who had no formal employment in the government—to spy and report. She said, "Those poor devils. They'll turn you in for the price of a pack of cigarettes. Really! The government is only paying 10 lari (about USD \$5) for a denunciation, but they will do it. They will turn in their neighbors and their friends to get a liter of *chacha*." Who precisely was doing all this spying, conspiring, and denouncing other than political operatives like Tamta, Manana would not say. But she firmly believed that even when there was nobody in sight, eyes were on her, reporting everything she said and did, providing information to the unknown forces in the state who decided whether aid would arrive, whether her daughter would be admitted to the university, and whether her husband, who was working unofficially in South Ossetia and Russia, would be able to travel safely.

It was no accident that these theories of diabolical behavior arose in post-Soviet Georgia and in the context of a war with Russia. Although conspiracy theories exist around the world,[4] they have particular resonance in the former socialist bloc. There is, of course, a long history of well-elaborated conspiracy theories in this part of the world: the infamous, fabricated text *Elders of the Protocols of Zion*, which posited a secret cabal of Jews that ran the world, originated in tsarist Russia. Joseph Stalin, born in the town of Gori, made conspiracy theories the hallmark of Soviet power in the 1930s and early 1940s, as he used the NKVD, the notorious secret police, to identify "enemies," publicly reveal them at show trials, and then eliminate them in spectacular purges. Under Stalin conspiracy became a machine for consolidating sovereignty. It gave the state "the power to designate arbitrary social facts of the world as matters of security" (Borenstein 2014a) and to regulate or expunge not only elite political opponents but also people engaged in banal activities, from saving seeds to working on railways.

Conspiracy theory as a mode of governance might have originated with Stalin, but it found an amazingly hospitable ecosystem in the Brezhnev era, where the Soviet state became a "reliable provider of conspiratorial narratives, overfilling any conceivable paranoid plan with Stakhanovite zeal" (Borenstein 2014a). In the domain of producing material goods, state socialism was vastly hampered by its economy of shortage, which made getting the necessary inputs to production constantly problematic (Verdery 1996; Kornai 1992). Information too was in constant shortage during the Brezhnev era (Borenstein 2014a). The more the Communist Party believed there were secret conspiracies among class enemies to defeat the revolution, the more it guarded its own secrets about everything from military installations to scientific research to Five Year production plans. The role of the state security services, especially the KGB, was critical to making the economy of information supply-constrained: they were especially zealous about restricting the flow of information, keeping not only their suspicions about conspiracies led by outside enemies a secret but also carefully guarding their own work methods and associations—everything from the names of informers to the placement of hidden microphones—from public view (Verdery 2014, 83). The KGB itself was plagued by an information shortage, one in which the need-to-know principle restricted the flow of information inside the organization as much as it outside it, leaving everyone in the organization well aware of the presence of hidden information they did not have access to.

Unlike shortages in the realm of material goods, though, shortages of information were endlessly productive. The more the socialist state zealously guarded its own secrets, the more it came to suspect that others outside the state—from hostile Western countries to its own citizens—were involved in secret conspiracies. Soviet Bloc citizens outside the security services, constantly aware of the presence of state secrets and of state-sanctioned conspiracies that affected their daily lives—but unable to see them clearly—soon came to see the state itself as a conspiracy, as an actor that kept itself in the shadows and forced its citizens to join the conspiracy by informing on relatives and friends, even as it relentlessly sought to expose the secrets of its citizens by spying on them. The anthropologist Katherine Verdery, reflecting on her own secret police file compiled by the Romanian Securitate, writes that this self-reinforcing cycle spilled out from the secret police into socialist-era society at large, making the entire socialist society responsible for both producing and protecting secrets:

> In this way, the secrecy first dictated by the persecution of the Bolsheviks under the Tsar's secret police gradually expanded to take over the life of all Romanians . . . now *everybody* was supposed to keep and

discover secrets, making vigilance a constant frame of mind and emergent aspect of subjectivities. The population as a whole would become its own surveillance instrument, and the domain of the secret would become boundless (2014:131).

Verdery defines "conspirativity" as the compartmentalization of information within the secret police, in such a way that one officer of the secret police did not know what the others were doing. But conspirativity is more than a principle of management that came from inside the secret police. It is a central political logic that suffused the USSR and that continues to suffuse both Russia and some of the post-Soviet successors, such as Georgia. The result during the Soviet period was an entire society—not just the secret police—that operated on the principle of conspirativity (see Verdery 2014, 32). By making everyone constantly on the lookout for conspiracy, and by suffusing society with mistrust that bordered on collective paranoia, the Soviet state made conspirativity into a fundamental principle that animated socialist governance as a whole. In the interests of providing for the welfare of the people, and of building a better society, the Soviet state sought to know everything so that it could plan and control everything, destroying all foci outside itself while partitioning knowledge into silos within itself (see Verdery 2014, 21; see also Szakolczai and Horvath 1991; and Gross 1998). The fact that this totalitarian impulse could never be fully realized didn't mean that the principle didn't apply. Rather, the impulse to bring all aspects of society under the control of the state by making society completely visible in its most minute elements while at the same time concealing the operations of the state itself was the key to eradicating not only current enemies but also all potential opposition.

Given this history it's no surprise that conspiracy theories became a widespread template in Georgian society used to make sense of the apparently inexplicable workings of power. Over the six years I spent going back and forth to Georgia doing research on the aftermath of the war, I heard many entirely plausible but largely unsubstantiated rumors: that Saakashvili had started the war in order to get humanitarian aid and prop up the Georgian economy, that the Ossetian separatists were backed by Putin even before the war, and that the Russian Army was prepared to invade Georgia for weeks before Saakashvili attacked Tskhinvali. I also heard many rumors that were wilder and seemingly less plausible, many of them starring Saakashvili, Putin, or both. There was a rumor that Zurab Zhvania, Mikheil Saakashvili's closest partner in the Rose Revolution, had not died in a kerosene heater accident, as was officially declared, but instead had been assassinated because he was involved in a homosexual affair. There was a rumor that the Russians had installed an earthquake machine under Tbilisi (which is, not coincidentally, on a geological fault) and were using it to periodically shake the city in order to destabilize the political situation.[5] There were persistent rumors that the Saakashvili government was spying on opposition political figures and then blackmailing them with videotapes of their sexual peccadilloes.[6]

But conspiracy theories had a special utility in the camp. Conspiracy was not simply a just-so story but a real theory: that is, like all theories, a streamlined and simplified model that represents reality in ways that are easier to grasp (see Lampland 2016). After a year of adhocracy and epistemological chaos, conspiracy theories offered a cognitive template that allowed the IDPs to account for both the influx and the subsequent withdrawal of aid. These narratives of bedevilment and suspicion were a kind of *bricolage*, an assemblage that worked to pattern half-understood facts and seemingly random events, linking them together in chains of explanation that, while they led to an embittered and unsavory view of the world that kept the community atomized, at least gave some plausible explanation for what was going on. If the IDPs' highly partial viewpoint on the aid system was akin to the view that a person at the bottom of a river would have of a ship passing overhead, then conspiracy narratives offered a theory about the boat and the rigging above the narrow oval they could see. As Eliot Borenstein writes, "Conspiracy is a disease of information, and a communicable disease at that. A better word than disease, though, would be disorder, if it weren't for the fact that conspiracy's relation to information is to take what is dis-ordered and express it as a surfeit of order. It is a disorder of signal to noise, in which all noise is construed as signal" (2014a, 8).

It wasn't just that lack of reliable information in the camp created a "knowledge vacuum easily filled by speculation and rumor" (Borenstein 2014a). Rather, it was that even as humanitarianism's temporality of emergency, fragmented institutional structure, and lack of planning and coordination created the characteristic chaos of humanitarian aid, conspiracy theories worked as antientropy devices that, in the face of the enormous disorder created by the rupture in the normal situation, placed new information into an increasingly orderly system. Conspiracy theories allowed the Georgian IDPs to make what Badiou (2006) says is the essential move in reforging a new normal situation: They committed to a truth and followed its consequences, which produced a new structure of meaning and order, even though the truth they committed to was not necessarily true at all. Conspiracy theories demonstrated that the "truths" that seed new normal situations can be *false* but *reasonable*. In the midst of an enormous void of meaning caused by the war, and in the middle of humanitarianism's constant tendency to prevent the production of new meaning, it is the reasonableness of the conspiracy theories—the way they appear to fit the fragmentary bits of information that beneficiaries have—that allows them to function as an architecture with which to structure information. They allow camp residents to make sense of what happens in the camp, among the foreign aid workers, in the national government, and at the level of international geopolitics, even if the story they tell is not entirely or even partially true.

Theories of devilry, scheming, illicit behavior, and other forms of covert skullduggery had two important virtues that made them particularly potent as explanatory frames. First, they explained the tremendous inequality of aid—why, under the quasi-market conditions imposed by the aid agencies, some people received large grants or expensive machinery while others received nothing at all. In that sense they revealed that although aid agencies attempt to use particular bureaucratic methods to make aid transparent and accountable, those methods do very little to create a sense of trust or fairness for the putative beneficiaries of that aid. However much the aid workers protested that their methods prevented corruption and handed out aid in an impersonal-and-just-but-still-unequal manner, the uneven division of the spoils of humanitarianism can still be explained by reference to social relations that were both covert and corrupt.

More important, though, the notion of devilry as a form of corruption assigns agency. Conspiracy theories are part of a much larger genre of ideas concerned with the attribution, misattribution, and distribution of agency in the world (Rogers 2014). Like Christianity, which endeavors to persuade animist converts to stop believing that the spirits of the trees or rocks or ancestors have agency and to believe instead that a single God is the animating force in the world, or like neoliberal economics, which seeks to persuade people that the market itself is an actor that can decide the value of goods and people, conspiracy theories seek to identify and understand exactly who is responsible for actions that profoundly impact people's lives in contexts where power is unclear (Rogers 2014). When power is obscure, conspiracy theories imagine actors in power, imagine the conditions under which they make decisions, assign them capacities for action, and weave narratives that appear to make their decisions and actions rational. Whether the devil comes to be seen literally as the agent of power, or whether those who invoke him use him knowingly as a metaphor for unseen actors whose presence can only be felt through the effects of their actions, theories of diabolical or conspiratorial action are attempts to assign agency in a situation where large-scale changes appear to be the product of agentless forces. In doing so they make it possible for those envisioning the conspiracy to act themselves: once those who push the levers of power can be identified and their methods described, it becomes possible to organize against them, to combat them, or to strategize around them. For Georgian IDPs the role conspiracy theories played in identifying power and enabling them to plan and strategize within its defined structures made the world actionable again. Despite the fact that these theories identified immense and seemingly insuperable power, they made mistrust into the central principle of social relations in the humanitarian encounter (at least from their perspective) and thus allowed them to plan and act. In that sense conspiracy theories were empowering in ways that the humanitarians' programming was not.

The Unseen World of the Georgian State

It would be easy to dismiss the IDPs' constant state of suspicion as a paranoid fantasy and a complete misreading of the way the newly democratized Saakashvili government actually worked. Yet, although Saakashvili publicly proclaimed his commitment to democracy, transparency, and accountability, many of the IDPs' conspiracy theories and accusations of devilry were rooted in factual, although partially observed and dimly sensed, changes in the way the Georgian state was consolidating and constituting power. They identified the fact that the Saakashvili government, still rebuilding after the twenty years of state collapse and civil war under Eduard Shevardnadze, operated as much on conspirativity as on humanitarianism, and as much on the desire to root out enemies as on the responsibility to protect the citizenry. This was exacerbated by one of the fundamental paradoxes of humanitarian statebuilding: the fact that building a state strong enough to uphold the responsibility to protect human rights seems also to require building a state strong enough to engage in authoritarianism and the violation of those same rights.

In Tsmindatsqali we knew we were watched by the Ushishroeba, the Georgian National Security Council,[7] part of the Ministry of Internal Affairs that succeeded the KGB in Georgia after the breakup of the USSR. One day as I sat with the women from Ksuisi outside a cottage chatting and eating sunflower seeds, a large black SUV pulled up and the driver inside signaled to Manana. She obviously knew the man. But rather than shout to him, as she would usually do rather than getting up on her bad hip, she rose and went to the car's window to whisper with him. When she returned she was white and shaken. He was one of the men from Disevi, she explained, and his brother was a high-ranking official in the secret police. He had come to tell Manana that her conversations with her husband, who was in Russia, were being tapped. Soon more and more people in the camp came to believe they were being watched, and collective paranoia increased. The settlement leaders, or *mamasakhlisebi*, in particular no longer appeared to be the benevolent "community elders" the NGOs believed them to be, but instead highly dangerous informers and state enforcers whose intimate knowledge of the camp community gave them the power to put their fellow IDPs in danger of arrest or harassment (see also Jones 2013, 135). Once one of the NGOs built small but well-appointed community centers in the camp and fitted them out with computers, IDPs began to suspect that the government was monitoring their electronic communications as well. In fact it was highly likely that the government was spying on IDPs' electronic communications, since the government had set up a massive "black box" network that allowed it to intercept not only phone conversations but also Internet traffic (Walker and Hartley 2013). The fact that spying could now be accomplished so remotely, by people unseen and far away, led to the feeling of constant surveillance.

At the end of 2009 a seemingly innocuous but strangely ominous form of surveillance appeared. Workers arrived in each of the camps and began placing power meters outside each cottage. Why the meters, nobody knew: electricity and gas were free, paid by the government as part of the humanitarian aid package. When I asked Aleko the bee guy what he thought they were for, he shrugged, "I don't know what they mean, or why they put them in. Probably in the future they'll tell us," he said, with a resigned voice. But a few months later, in the middle of a freezing February, the IDPs in the camp suddenly found the heat and electricity cut off. The unnamed Western donors who had been paying the bills were no longer paying, and the IDPs now had to repay monstrous sums before power would be turned back on—four hundred, five hundred, or even a thousand lari when the average family was receiving less than 50 lari in aid per month. Some families managed to find the cash to have the heat turned back on: in families where the grandparents had a state pension, where a sick family member was receiving government welfare benefits, or where one of the adults had a government job or was in the military, they reluctantly parted with whatever cash they had to pay the arrears and have the gas and electricity reinstated. But the poorer families in the settlement went without. As Dato Khutsishvili said,

> How could they cut off the electricity and the gas in the middle of winter? They made us these terrible gas heaters, they hardly work, and now they cut off the gas? What is this government doing? When the electricity was cut, we all had bills of 600–800 GEL. Nobody was told we would have to pay for gas and electricity after January, so when we got the bills it was a shock. Some people still don't have power. What was worse, they cut the power right on the old New Year! We could see the streetlights burning outside, but inside we had no light. It was so humiliating, so belittling to us! We aren't Megrelebi [the first wave IDPs from Abkhazia— ECD], we aren't aggressive people, and we have some culture. We have doctors and lawyers and engineers among us. But this was a provocation, cutting off the power. It's oppressive.

What could they do, though? In Tsmindatsqali a small group of IDPs decided to respond to what they saw as government provocation and to take political action to alleviate the pressure of the cold and the damp. Gathering together, they went to the East-West highway, which passed the far end of the settlement. The highway was Georgia's single artery: as the Russians had demonstrated during the war, blockading the highway cut the country in two, isolating the capital from the rest of the country. For the IDPs to block the highway, then, was no mere attempt to "have their voices heard," no mere symbolic demonstration of fear or ire. It was an intense political threat, one that threatened to cut Tbilisi off from the entire western half of Georgia.

Shoulder to shoulder, the IDPs blocked the road with their bodies. Traffic was stopped, and the buses and *marshrutkas* (minivans) that were the main form of transport between the regions and the capital began to pile up behind the blockade. The IDPs did not have long to wait for a response from the government: within an hour, police and militia came to break up the protests. Soon an official from the local *gamgeoba* (the regional government) came. "Come on, go home, and we'll talk to the power company for you," the official said, trying to disperse the protesters. "Let's go to the electricity company ourselves," somebody shouted from the crowd. "Let them come to us!" shouted somebody else. Surrounded by armed soldiers and police officers, the IDPs held firm, waiting for the power company to come and negotiate. But when the power company official came, it was to bring hard news. As Dato Khutsishvili recalls, the man from the power company refused to be swayed by the protest. "Your power was being paid for by a foreign donor," Dato recalled the man saying. "But now the donor is gone, and you'll have to pay for this yourselves. You have to pay what you owe, or we're not turning the heat on."

The Saakashvili government later justified cutting off power subsidies to IDPs in a typically neoliberal way, based on the notion that continuing subsidies to the IDPs would make them dependent on the state—something that was increasingly anathema to the Saakashvili administration, which believed that the best solution to the IDP crisis was to force them to become fiscally responsible for themselves. Worse yet, aid to the victims of ethnic cleansing was seen as something that might introduce distortions in the power market, an economic sector that had only recently been privatized and that was held up as a model of capitalist progress in this formerly Soviet state. As Valeri Khopeliashvili, the deputy minister for refugees and accommodation, put it in an e-mail in response to a query by Transparency International, which had inquired about the electricity shut-offs:

> In the new settlements, the Government of Georgia paid unlimited electricity bills until October 2009. From October settlements officially became collective centers [government-supported housing for

IDPs—ECD] and [were] provided support through ordinary schema [which did not include unlimited electricity—ECD]. In October this information has been shared with IDPs. But as always the IDPs thought that the Government of Georgia would give them an exemption. This is regulated by law. MRA cannot pay more than 13 GEL per person. A household with 6 persons will receive about 80 GEL. My family consists by 7 persons and my expenses in winter time are about 90 GEL per month (I heat water using electricity). They overspent their limit. . . . The only instrument to avoid it is a good management of expenditure. We would like to provide electricity to all IDPs without limitation but it is impossible because the electricity is a marketable product and it can spoil all supply and whole Georgia could be one day without it. We have huge experience of this issue. There is no room to make exemption (only in particular specific cases) because it will just increase pressure on market and spoil it. (pers. comm.)

Of course, despite the deputy minister's assertions, heating a poorly constructed, uninsulated, leaking cottage was remarkably more difficult and expensive than heating a well-built Tbilisi apartment. Yet the blame for high energy bills was firmly rooted in the failures of individual IDPs, whom Khopeliashvili portrayed as failing to manage their own household economies. He blamed the IDPs too for potentially despoiling the free market for energy by gorging on the largesse of the state, potentially depriving other Georgians of heat and light, despite the fact that power companies in Georgia were routinely selling energy abroad, most notably to Turkey, where the Georgian government planned spend over 240 million euros to increase electricity exports from 100 megawatts to 1,100 megawatts.

At the protest on the Gori highway, the discouraged IDPs, who were unarmed, outside in the below-freezing weather, and surrounded by the threat of armed violence, began to break up and go back to their dark, uninsulated cottages. Some hoped to plan another action to demand that the government pay the arrears and turn the power back on. Late that night, though, spies revealed themselves and the state became manifest, as unnamed agents from the Ushishroeba began going house to house in the settlement. As one of my neighbors in the camp told me, "We didn't know them. But they knew us. [They] came to each house, and they knew what each one of us had. If we were getting humanitarian aid or social welfare payments or IDP status payments, they knew it. If one of us had a government job, they knew."

The reasons for such intense surveillance soon became clear. Refugee camps are notorious sources of political unrest, and the ostensibly democratic Saakashvili regime had no intention of allowing displaced people to become an oppositional political force. At each house the secret police made it clear: if anyone in the family joined another protest, the state would cut off humanitarian aid and welfare payments, and fire anyone in the family with a state job. Authoritarian political pressure was applied individually, in a calculated manner, in the form of concrete threats to the reproduction of physical life. But there was no need to send anyone to the gulag, as the secret police had done in the Stalin era. The state had only to turn off the tap of humanitarian aid—the very money that was a reward for transparency and democratization—and the IDPs would suffer.

In Skra settlement the real shock came when Aleko Mentashvili, the veterinarian and bee farmer, was arrested by the Ushishroeba and taken away. Of all the IDPs I knew, Aleko had come the furthest in making a new life for himself. He'd bought not only new beehives but had also scraped up the money for pigs and a cow, and he was beginning to make money selling piglets and milk. But the animals needed more feed than just the macaroni he had gotten from USAID, and so he looked for a job with the only employer of significance in Shida Kartli province: the government. He found a job as a forester and was put in charge of a small forest near Skra. Forestry was less about agriculture than about guarding, however: with so many IDPs and poor villagers nearby, and with fuel so expensive once the foreign donors stopped paying, the pressure for fuelwood on forests was intense, and the forester's job was to prevent the locals from chopping down trees to burn for fuel. There was a line for permits to collect wood, not everybody could get one, and there was limit on the amount of wood anyone could take, so being able to jump the line and cut trees unrestrictedly would have been a huge boon. One day two men came to Aleko and offered him 50 lari—about USD $25—in exchange for turning the other way while they collected firewood. Calculating how much animal feed he could buy with the sum, he acquiesced—upon which they revealed themselves to be agents of the Ushisroeba. The bee guy had been caught in one of Mikheil Saakashvili's notorious anticorruption stings, which had been very frequent during his first years in office, but had diminished greatly from 2007 to 2009. Now they were back with intensifying frequency and force.

I found all this out only when I came to Skra looking for Aleko. Running into his elderly father on the gravel road, I asked how he was. "In prison," Chichiko told me, pushing me in the cottage to talk to Aleko's wife, Mariko, who looked completely beaten down. "They got the whole thing on camera," Mariko told me. Oli, my field assistant, nodded. "I saw the whole thing on television. They held him up as an example of their anticorruption program." Aleko took the bribe (*krtami*)—and then it turned out they were from the Ushishroeba, and they'd recorded the entire transaction as evidence for his trial. "He was sentenced to four years in Gldani prison for taking a 50 lari bribe," she said. When I asked how they were surviving without him, she just shook her head. Outside the cottage, I saw Aleko's father feeding a weak slop of milk and bread to a piglet. "I bought two pigs a week ago," he said. "They cost 250 GEL. But one has already died. I don't know why it died—Aleko is gone, so we have no veterinarian. It just died. We're hoping this one will live."

So the devil in the camp, appearing in the form of spying neighbors and secret police, was not entirely fantasy. The figure of the devil revealed that despite constant declarations of democratic principles, mistrust, as much as compassion or altruism, was a driving force behind humanitarian government. The figure of the devil thus signaled the tension between opposed forces within the humanitarian state: violence and care, mercy and oppression, abandonment and strict rule. But although mistrust was fed by humanitarian action—especially, as I show below, by particular funding mechanisms for humanitarian aid—its effects were not limited to those deemed "beneficiaries" of humanitarian aid. Instead mistrust came to structure relations between state and society that extended far beyond the camp to all of Georgia. It shaped the growth and development of the Georgian state and presaged the fall of Mikheil Saakashvili. Most crucially, pervasive mistrust soon jeopardized the entire attempt by the United States and the European Union to draw the Caucasus into its sphere of influence, throwing the high-stakes political game between Russia and the West into a tense and highly dangerous state.

The Devil and Misha Saakashvili

Democracy is not a technical exercise, but a living experience. Daily encounters with the police, court officials, bureaucrats, local representatives—all are central elements in evaluating democracy. For citizens, these encounters determine the quality of democracy, their understanding of it, and their willingness to participate in it.

(Jones 2013, 107–8)

In 2009 and 2010 the lived experience of democracy throughout Georgia was flavored by suspicions of spying, surveillance, and other forms of covert political action that swirled through the entire country as Saakashvili began to eliminate his political opponents. Initially police action had been overt. In 2007 Saakashvili had come under intense political criticism after he used the military to break up an antigovernment rally with over one hundred thousand protestors (Jones 2013, 112). In 2009 another political rally had erupted after the son of Sulkhan Molashvili, a member of the Shevardnadze administration and a critic whom

Saakashvili had sent to prison on charges of corruption, was arrested for hooliganism.[8] After Saakashvili ordered the police to break up the rally by shooting rubber bullets, opposition forces blockaded Tbilisi's main street, Rustaveli Avenue, for nearly three months in protest. In the wake of these protests, it seemed that Saakashvili was not only concerned about eliminating his current opposition, but any sources of future opposition as well. This was done through much more covert means. In Gori a group of ex-athletes meeting at a sportsmen's cafe to criticize the government were broken up when the cafe was raided and then shut down. As one of the group's members told me, the group had initially been supportive of Saakashvili's National Movement Party. But as soon as they became a proto-opposition, they were pursued by the tax authorities, had their power turned off for alleged nonpayment of bills, and were subjected to other forms of harassment. Throughout Georgia, citizens were increasingly experiencing the state not as a democratic entity based on the free exchange of knowledge—as it still claimed to be—but as an entity shrouded in secrecy whose actions could not be seen directly but only by the shadows they cast.

How can a police state coexist with a government publicly committed to transparency and the rule of law? How can an authoritarian regime arise out of a humanitarian project? Is one state true and the other somehow false, a facade that masks an underlying reality? What brings these two apparently opposed tendencies together is the notion of "statebuilding"—and that is what, in the end, is strongly supported by the donor governments who attempt to provide humanitarian relief by routing aid dollars through the nation-state and by "building its capacity" to uphold the responsibility to protect. This is not a new phenomenon. In his discussion of the 1984 Ethiopian famine, Weizman discusses the West's uncritical support of "totalitarian regimes disguised as utopian liberation movements in the 'promised land' of the third world" (Bruckner 1986, cited in Weizman 2011, 28). In Ethiopia humanitarian aid ended up being used by the government to fight a Marxist insurgency by luring rebels from famine-stricken areas into places from which they could be forcibly deported. Romy Brauman, then the head of Médecins Sans Frontières, said that the realization that aid could be used as fuel for a totalitarian regime forced a dramatic rethinking of MSF's role as a humanitarian actor: "We began to reflect more seriously . . . upon the fact that we could inadvertently play into the hands of agencies whose objectives had nothing to do with humanitarianism" (Brauman, quoted in Weizman 2011, 48). What MSF had learned is that when "building capacity" in a state it is impossible to dictate how that capacity will be used. Money meant to develop government structures for administering aid can be used to build the security service, and practices of knowledge collection installed by international agencies in government ministries to manage development more effectively can also be used to devastating effect by intelligence agencies, who deploy their own means of seeing and governing. In short, in the humanitarian state the capacity for repression is co-constructed with the capacity for protection at every moment. While humanitarians hope recipient states will use increased capacity to protect the citizenry, it is equally likely to be used to oppress the citizenry, to eliminate political enemies, and to consolidate the power of an autocratic regime.

In Georgia Western donors tried to circumscribe the ways that funds routed through the Georgian government were used. In a document dated October 22, 2008, USAID agreed to transfer USD \$250 million to the government of Georgia with the express purpose of providing budget support to "rapidly adjust and recover from the crisis created by the [August 2008] invasion and to meet additional needs of the Georgian government generated by the crisis." This transfer, the first tranche of the eventual \$1 billion in aid provided by the United States, was enormous even by the standards of US aid to its allies: historically the United States has provided this level of support only to strategic partners such as Egypt and Jordan (Piccio 2013). As Vice President Joe Biden remarked, "Even where I come from, a billion dollars for five million people is a lot of money" (cited in Piccio 2013). The stated goal of this very large transfer was to improve the Georgian government's capacity to care for the population by propping up the Georgian economy and economically supporting the war-affected population, and in doing so to keep the Saakashvili government in power even though it was already facing political opposition and widespread discontent because of the economic effects of the war.

As USAID claimed, the government of Georgia "used the Cash Transfer Assistance (CTA) primarily for the reimbursement of pensions, allowances for refugees and internally displaced people (IDPs), student stipends, financing secondary schools, health care programs and salaries and compensations for government organizations and municipalities at the national level" (USAID 2010). The cash transfer agreement explicitly stated that "grant proceeds may not be used for any military or paramilitary purposes," to finance "the purchase of surveillance equipment," or "assistance for police or prisons or any other law enforcement forces" (USAID 2008). This clearly ruled out using any of the aid money to support the Ushishroeba. Yet there is no rule in US-sponsored cash transfer agreements that prevents a recipient state from using donor money to replace budget items that the state would have previously paid for, and repurposing its own money to spy on its own population, to undermine political opposition, or to jail political opponents. There is no way to know how much the Georgian government increased its financial support of the Ushishroeba, whose budget is a state secret. But after 2009 evidence of the Ushishroeba's increased surveillance of the Georgian population began to appear. First, in 2010 the Ministry of Internal

Affairs claimed that by using surveillance and a double agent it had broken a ring of Russian spies (Barry 2010). Then it was revealed that the State Security Service had demanded that the country's largest cellphone providers, including Geocell, install equipment developed by the Swedish telecommunications giant Ericsson that gave the government a real-time feed of up to twenty-one thousand telephone lines and Internet connections at a time (Lomsadze 2013; *Tabula* 2013; Transparency International 2013a and 2013b; Mchedlishvili 2013). In 2013 a trove of over seventeen thousand covertly recorded audio and video files, recorded between 2006 and 2013, was found at the Ministry of Interior Affairs. Ninety-four of the files were covert recordings of illicit sexual affairs, including extramarital sex and gay sex, apparently made for the purpose of blackmail. Some of the other recordings were of politicians, journalists, and civil-society figures conducting political conversations, made to document their political leanings for the purpose of applying pressure (Transparency International 2013b; Hammarberg 2013). But many of the recordings were of "persons unknown," apparently Georgian citizens, whose activities and political beliefs were being documented (Hammarberg 2013).

But the worst proof of rising authoritarianism came from video secretly recorded by Vladimir Bedukadze, the warden of Gldani prison, the prison where people protesting against the government in 2009 and 2011 had been incarcerated. The video showed prisoners being savagely beaten and one prisoner being sodomized with a broom handle. Aleko the bee guy had been sent to Gldani prison after his arrest. We had no idea what happened to him there, whether he had been just subject to the horrible overcrowded conditions of the prison, beaten, or worse. His wife, Mariko, told us that she did not know either.

What was clear from these revelations was that humanitarian statebuilding had resulted in a state built on conspirativity, the pervasive belief in the existence of unseen conspiracy. The tensions between the transparent and the covert and between autocracy and democracy were, of course, latent in the Georgian political system before the 2008 war. Saakashvili, hailed in the West as an advocate of liberal democracy, in fact had a much stronger interest in building a strong state than a democratic one. He alluded to this when he said, "People compare my style with that of J.F.K., but in terms of substance, I feel much closer to Ataturk or Ben-Gurion or General de Gaulle—people who had to build nation states" (T. de Waal 2010, 194). But Saakashvili built this state on the basis of mistrust: he designed a state premised on the notion of hidden enemies that itself became a hidden enemy. In his attempt to build a state powerful enough to combat entrenched corruption and to avoid being hamstrung by his opposition, Saakashvili increasingly engaged in actions that were not only illegal but that also partook of the same authoritarian practices of the Soviet state he claimed to be radically different from. The result was a government that alternately concealed and revealed in unpredictable ways. It was strong enough to persecute people it saw as potential threats but weak enough to fear them. It was powerful enough to act outside the law but weak enough that it could not simply disregard the law. Using humanitarian funding the Georgian state leveraged its newfound institutional capacity to act duplicitously toward both its foreign donors and the citizens who were supposed to be the recipients of its aid. But while it was savvy enough to tell international donors what they wanted to hear and to keep the money flowing, it was also naive enough to think its tactics could be hidden indefinitely.

The use of humanitarian donor money to fund rising authoritarianism is not in any sense unique to Georgia, although Georgia's Christian Orthodoxy and Soviet past put a unique spin on the ways the population perceived the government's actions. Rather, this link between humanitarian statebuilding and authoritarianism is intrinsic to any project that seeks to build state capacity by routing large sums through the national government. In March 2016 the European Union signed a deal to provide the government of Turkey EUR 6 billion in exchange for holding Syrian refugees, millions of whom had been streaming into the European Union. It is not coincidental that in July 2016 the government of President Recep Tayyip Erdogan, which had become increasingly authoritarian, cracked down militarily on a coup attempt led by a former ally. Flush with cash and knowing that the European Union was powerless to object for fear he would release millions of migrants into Europe, Erdogan incarcerated journalists and academics on the grounds they were conspiring against him, threatened writers, and crushed even incipient political opposition.

The Evasiveness of Humanitarian Politics

Katrine Gotfredsen (2013, 21) argues that in Georgia the political assumes a "dual form, oscillating between presence and absence, visibility and invisibility, articulation and silence." It is the tension between these opposites, a constant veering between what is seen and what is unseen, that creates an "evasive" politics that leaves citizens with the sense that power is opaque and constantly uncertain (Gotfredsen 2013, 196). Evasive politics, which are by no means unique to Georgia, stem from both the legacy of state socialist conspirativity and the aftermath of war. They entwine humanitarian action so deeply in a thicket of the covert and the deceptive that humanitarian politics becomes premised on the idea of duplicity.

One of the most unexpected outcomes of end of the Soviet Union has been that although Soviet institutions have largely collapsed or been transformed, and although most of the political players have changed in the last twenty-five years, the general principles that animate the political sphere across the region have remained resolutely based on the notion of conspirativity. Whatever the party, whatever the ideology, whatever the issue at stake, all of the parties involved are convinced that enemies in the shadows are taking action secretly. This creates a cyclical problem: those paranoid about secrecy must then themselves act secretly, screening their own attempts to discover the secrets of others. And when actions taken in secret are revealed—as Saakashvili's spying was, for example—it does not create the sense that "sunshine" has disinfected politics, but instead confirms the prevalence of secrecy and validates suspicions of even more conspiracy (Borenstein 2014b). The only reaction to the revelation of specific secrets is to wonder what else has been concealed—and that is what makes conspirativity into a self-reinforcing cycle. The more that information is withheld, the more conspiracy theories rush to fill the information vacuum. The fact that some of these theories turn out to be true merely makes conspirativity, as an operating principle, even more powerful.

Duplicity is fostered not only by Soviet legacies but by war itself. As Diane Nelson writes, "Duplicity—the sense that the world available to our senses hides another face behind it—is a site of intense affective and hermeneutic investment in the aftermaths and ongoing experiences of war and violence" (2009, xv). Duplicity marks, in the first place, the epistemic turmoil of the postwar environment. But it does more than signal confusion, meaninglessness, or the rupture of the normal situation. By communicating the commonsense notion that it is impossible to *really* know how the world works, the idea of duplicity enters into the postwar environment as a hermeneutic device for confronting, ordering, and making sense of epistemic turmoil. Duplicity and conspirativity are mills that grind out possible explanation after possible explanation, endlessly seeking to supplement the known facts with enough suppositions to glue them together into a narrative that, however tentative or preposterous, has the possibility of making sense.

The people who spin these stories are engaging in the work of remaking a Badiouian normal situation, one in which things and facts and people are linked together in predictable ways. But the conspiracy theories that arise out of the pervasive sense of the duplicitous or the covert in a postwar environment are necessarily deformed. They are not explanations but pseudoexplanations, narratives that don't really explain how things happen but instead, by virtue of their outlandishness and unproveability, draw attention to how much cannot be effectively explained. The figure of the devil, which comes to sum up or represent these conspiratorial narratives, marks the deformation. The devil reveals the untrustworthiness of not only neighbors, friends, and politicians, but also of explanations, hermeneutic devices, and narratives that purport to make sense of anything. The devil shows how suspicious narratives about potential falsification themselves generate suspicion that they are falsified, and in doing so send everyone who attempts to make sense of them spinning down the rabbit hole.

The two-faced state that emerges from the chaos of the postwar environment is itself diabolical, and this is also marked by the sign of the devil. It constantly generates the sense that it is false, lying, and contradicting its own stated principles. It is more than it reveals itself to be and less than it claims to be. Both legitimate and criminal, it purges corruption and engages in it. It simultaneously represents its citizens' political interests and represses their political speech. It creates rules and insists on normalizing while at the same time becoming a "freak show, functioning precisely through its abnormality, its awesomeness, its massive differentiation from the every day . . . it simultaneously manages the mechanisms of horror and is accountable for them" (Nelson 2009, 234). It generates political power by keeping everyone—its donors, its citizens, and its enemies—constantly off-balance, wondering what is true and what is not. It fabricates itself, both in the sense of making itself and of lying about itself, in and through its duplicity. In this sense what humanitarian statebuilding results in is an uncanny puppet state, one that crosses and recrosses the boundary between the true and the false as it claims to be independent while in fact doing the bidding of donors, while at the same time probably doing something else entirely in secret. It was this very unreliability that, in the end, compromised attempts by the United States and Europe to carve out a sphere of influence in post-Soviet space.

THE STATE AND THE STATE

What is the relationship between liberal humanitarianism and illiberal forms of state sovereignty? How do the "caring state," which is supposed to be the outcome of humanitarian "capacity-building" projects, and the authoritarian state, which is also fueled by those projects, come together to both support and dominate the ostensible beneficiaries of humanitarian action? In the previous chapter I argued that the figure of the devil highlights the link between the humanitarian statebuilding project and authoritarian states, as well as the illiberal political outcomes that political and financial relationship creates. In this intertext I want to continue that line of thinking to explore what the figure of the devil and the marriage between humanitarianism and authoritarianism might reveal about what the state is and how it works. I begin from Badiou's own notion of "the state," which is underdeveloped and trapped in its own ideological premises, but which offers a provocative link between the state—that is, an institutional structure of governance—and the state of the situation, or the structure that defines the relationships among elements in a situation. This lets me think more carefully about link between sovereign power and lived experience in the humanitarian encounter. In the end, I argue, the humanitarian statebuilding project contains within it not only the potential for care but also for "pastoral hunting," a brew of violence and care in which the state searches for enemies in the name of protection.

The State and the State: Badiou's Notion of "Governance"

Badiou's theory of the state is slippery and ambivalent, which makes it difficult to explain or to use theoretically. On the one hand, he often uses the term "the state" to mean the state of the situation, but on the other hand, he uses the same term to refer to the institutionalized political state. Even more confusingly, he sometimes uses the term "the state" to refer to an ideological figure through which power is legitimized, and he sometimes uses it to think about techniques of governing. This means that despite Badiou's focus on revolutionary moments, it's often quite hard to see what he believes should be overthrown, or if it is possible to overthrow it. The slippage is intentional, I think: it reflects the expansive notion of "the state" introduced by his teacher, Louis Althusser, whose notion of the "ideological state apparatus" asserted that the parts of the state that overtly ruled—the police, the courts, the prison system—were not the only social institutions that upheld the political order. Rather, Althusser argued, because ostensibly nonpolitical institutions like churches, schools, and families reinforced political domination by creating social norms and instilling particular forms of practice, they too should be thought of as adjuncts of the state (Robinson 2014; Althusser 1970; see also Allison 1991). Badiou seems to uphold Althusser's blurring of the boundary between state and society. He argues that the institutional state, which appears as the form of legitimate power, covertly governs not only via institutions but also via the construction of reality itself. The nation-state, for Badiou, is the institution that builds the state of the situation and therefore structures the elements of experience for everyone else.

Badiou's argument is that the political state (which, for the sake of clarity, I'll refer to as the capital-S State) is an *excrescence*. An excrescence is something that is represented but not presented, something that has a place in the state of the situation but does not appear in experience (Badiou 2007, 99). These are the opposite of the ontological "nothings" discussed in chapter 3, which were objects, people, ideas, and so on that existed in the real world but that couldn't be represented in any structure of meaning. Rather than standing for a lack of representation, an excrescence marks a surplus of representation, the excess of structure over the elements that it has to order (2007, 108). Since the devil too is something represented but not presented, it makes sense that it comes to indicate the presence of the half-hidden state in the camp: the devil marks not only the appearance of the state but its excrescent nature as well.

In Badiou's ontology there is only one state of the situation (which, for clarity, I'll refer to as a small-s state), and therefore only one political State (the capital-S State). The State has the job of classifying or naming other elements and specifying the nature of their relationship to one another, and maintaining through law, violence, and mythmaking the set of rules that create a stable, predictable social world. So, for example, in a capitalist society the State is the entity that uses laws, courts, police, and so on to uphold the principle of equivalent value, or the notion that commodities are transferrable properties that can be exchanged as equal values based on the amount of labor they embody (Robinson 2014). Yet the State/state does not fully organize reality: in Badiou's theory, there are always elements outside the situation that threaten to spark an Event, tear apart the state of the situation, and impose new ordering principles. Badiou sees the fundamental goal of the State as protecting its own order by preventing the eruption of these revolutionary Events: "The State is not founded on the social bond, which it would express, but rather upon un-binding, which it prohibits" (Badiou 2006, 109; cf. Bosteels 2011, 39). Thus the primary goal of the State is to ensure that nobody corrodes the social order it establishes by either disconnecting elements in experience currently connected by the state of the situation or by rebinding elements in a new state of the situation. Put simply, for Badiou the goal of the State is to prevent the ontological revolutions posed by an Event.

There are three problems with this understanding of the State. First, true to his Marxist/Maoist origins, Badiou sees the state in the singular: as a unified entity that has no competitors for the ordering function. But as a wave of anthropological research has argued, what we think of as "the state" is in fact fragmented and multiple: in any given situation there are different actors or agencies claiming the right to define the social order and structure the situation (see Das and Poole 2004; Roitman 2004). In Georgia there were clearly at least three different actors vying to structure the situation: the Russian military state, the Western humanitarian system coordinated by the United Nations, and the government of the Republic of Georgia. As chapter 3 showed, the humanitarian system, which claimed a certain form of mobile sovereignty, was composed of multiple and often competing entities. Likewise the Russian military state and the Georgian government were also composed of institutions and parts that didn't always act as one, which led to both organizational chaos and internal tensions.

Second, contrary to Badiou's view of the state as authoritarian, the State is clearly not only repressive but rather both productive and repressive at the same time. Certainly any state based on liberalism in some form—as both the humanitarian system and the Georgian government were—is compelled to engage in what Foucault (2004) called "pastoral power," or the duty of the State to structure the situation in ways that facilitate the economic, social, and political wellbeing of the population. Pastoral power places the State in the role of the shepherd, providing for the flock but also guarding it from external harm and protecting it from outside threats. In chapter 3 I argued that one of the central goals of contemporary humanitarianism was not only to provide this kind of care when the state cannot—that is, to enact a mobile pastoral sovereignty to replace that of a weak or failed state—but to also "build capacity" in the states where it operates so that these states can assume the burden of pastoral care themselves. Humanitarianism is centered not only on managing resources and populations in aggregate in order to create "human security," nor solely on deciding which individual lives are worth saving and which must be sacrificed to serve the greater good, but also on teaching recipient States like the government of Georgia how to make these calculations themselves.

But States can also be centered on what Chamayou (2012) calls "cynegetic power," or power based on the sovereign's right to hunt and kill excluded subjects. This is the Agambenian sovereign: a State that is not worried about caring for the flock or obsessing over the question of whether the one should be sacrificed to benefit the many, as pastoral states are, but that is entirely concerned with establishing and maintaining its own power (see Fassin 2007; Chamayou 2012, chap. 2). Cynegetic power is not troubled by the logics of sacrifice because as far as it is concerned the entire population can die as long as those deaths serve the goal of increasing the State's power (Chamayou 2012, 17–18). Interestingly, this form of power is also not fully grasped by Badiou, the former apologist for Stalinism, who still believes that the creative force of revolution may justify violence. As he says,

> My problem is not principally the use of violence or not the use of violence. It is dependent on circumstances. You cannot say anything about that. In some cases violence is a necessity; everyone knows that (Ashville Global Review 2005).

He acknowledges that sometimes the pursuit of power for its own sake can overtake fidelity to the central Truth of a revolution and, in doing so, corrupt that Truth. But he still cannot look this form of power in the eye and, within the confines of his own philosophical system, account for why "forcing" a new Truth into being so often leads to brutality (see Johnson 2012).[1]

Third, Badiou's theory of the State presents the state as a done deal, the ordering that the State carries out as complete and totalizing except for the odd singularity, which on rare occasions might create a revolution. As I showed in chapter 3, for humanitarian attempts at sovereignty, any notion of a form of governance as totalizing massively overstates the ability of states to impose their ordering principles across their subject populations. First, neither of these forms of the State is a completed project. Rather, these models of the State refer to tendencies, or imperfectly realized goal states. We can classify the kind of power a given State or State-like apparatus is engaging in as a project of rule, an effort at a desired outcome, without seeing that project as being totalizing or that form of rule as being absolute. Thus when the international humanitarian order takes over the functions of the state, it is not a pastoral sovereign but a "pastoral-ish" one. It is always trying to create a carefully managed social order to improve wellbeing, but, as I showed in chapter 3, mostly falls short. Likewise the Saakashvili administration had well-documented authoritarian leanings, but, as I show in chapter 8, mostly failed to transform the chaotic, adhoc-ish Georgian state into a strong authoritarian government. The very presence of other, competing States on the same terrain shows that the structuring principles put forward by States are not finished orders to be defended but intentions, wishes, or projects that are always incomplete and forever in the process of falling apart even as the State struggles to shore them up (see Dunn 2012b; Dunn and Cons 2014).

So how do we conceive of these multiple, partial, and incomplete states? How can we think about the forms of power that their interaction presents? How do we conceptualize the effects of their coexistence, their oppositions, and their accommodations of one another? The figure of the devil, I argue, marks not just the presence of the State-qua-excrescence, but also the necessary multiplicity, partiality, and ambivalence of the State, or more accurately, of Statist projects. The appearance of the devil in the camp shows this because it marks the existence of a hybrid form known as "pastoral hunting" that results from the copresence of multiple States on the same terrain.

Pastoral Hunting

The relationship between authoritarian states and the international humanitarian apparatus, two Statist projects, is symbiotic, despite the fact that on the surface they often have opposing ideologies, values, goals, and political practices. They exist side-by-side, sometimes conflicting with one another but often reinforcing or supporting one another's ambitions, intentionally or not. The pastoral State enforces a definition of "order" centered on the responsibility to care for the flock benevolently, protectively, and nonviolently; the cynegetic state enforces a definition of "order" centered on the need to hunt prey. The result of this intersection is a state engaged in "pastoral hunting," or the protection of the flock not by promoting life and wellbeing but by hunting and killing members of the flock deemed threatening or corrupted:

> What fundamentally distinguished the pastoral model from the cynegetic model, and what radically forbade the former to entertain any predatory relationship, was the imperative of caring and protecting. A protective power versus a predatory power: that was the line of opposition. But pastoral hunting took place precisely in the name of protecting

the flock. To protect the flock sometimes one has to hunt down certain sheep, to sacrifice a few to save all the others. Here we are no longer in a logic of predatory appropriation but rather in a rationality of salutary ablation and beneficent exclusion (Chamayou 2012, 20).

In the idea of "pastoral hunting," we find a State centered on the protection of its own state of the situation. A State that protects its population not by opposing enemies outside but by seeking out the cancer within. A State constantly searching for people inside the polity that it deems dangerous, and needing to find them so badly that if they don't exist the State will construct them. What is this, other than the operations of the secret police that were made visible by the sign of the devil? What is it, other than the notion of "security" that operates in the camps, nestled alongside the Foucauldian notion of "security" as managed wellbeing? What is it, other than conspirativity as a principle of political life and its reflection in suspicion as a principle of social life? As I showed in the previous chapter when I focused on the operations of the secret police in the Georgian camps, conspirativity takes the possibility that hidden agents are engaged in unauthorized unbindings and rebindings and are therefore corroding the existing social order, and makes it into a general principle of governance. Since the prime job of the State is to prevent this corrosion, a State that sits at the nexus of humanitarian pastoral power and authoritarian cynegetic power must make conspirativity, or pastoral hunting, its fundamental principle of governance.

Rethinking the Badiouian State

Badiou's concept of "the State," unitary and almost totalitarian, cannot account for the rise of pastoral hunting or the forms of conspirativity that emerged in the camp. So if we are to remain centered on the problem of how the state of the situation is rebuilt and how it structures reality, and more specifically, to understand how the state of the situation is rebuilt in the humanitarian encounter, it is essential to revise the notion of "the State."

First, of course, it is imperative to acknowledge that the State itself is not one, but inherently multiple: There are competing Statist institutions that themselves are made from multiple and competing parts. This is particularly true in the wake of an Event or an event when, contra Badiou's understanding, a new totalizing state of the situation is not necessarily immediately on offer. Rather, in the chaotic time after an event, there are often multiple potential states of the situation on offer from different political and social institutions.

Second, this inevitable multiplicity means that the relations between competing Statist projects, whether cooperative or conflicted, can result in unplanned outcomes and undesirable forms of governance (see Dunn and Cons 2013, where we label this form of governance "aleatory sovereignty," or rule by chance). The outbreak of pastoral hunting, which arises from a mixture of the humanist conception of the value of human life, the humanitarian mandate to protect it, and the authoritarian drive to repel enemies, is a case in point. So it is not true, as Badiou argues, that the only form of State/state transformation is revolution, when one fully formed State/state replaces another. Rather, the building of a new state of the situation unspools over time and in unpredictable ways. The State promised by a revolution—for example, Saakashvili's supposedly democratic revolution—is not always the State that emerges over time, especially when a State permeated by conspirativity and engaged in pastoral hunting begins to eliminate its enemies in the name of protecting the citizenry.

Third, whereas Badiou argues that the political State and the state of the situation are theoretically identical, I argue that we should split them and keep them separate. If we agree that no one State is fully capable of determining the state of the situation (that is, if we argue that even if a State has totalitarian impulses, it cannot actually create a totalizing state of the situation), we open the door to the notion that the state of the situation may be created not only by competing Statist institutions and hybrid forms of power but by other actors as well. As I show in the next chapter, non-State actors (here, the IDPs of Tsmindatsqali) can produce alternate forms of representation that are not revolutionary but nonetheless are not fully controlled by the State. As Andrew Robinson (2014) writes,

> We don't live in a single, locked-down reality—or if we do, it's for contingent reasons, not ontological reasons. That means a lot more political actions are available to alter the balance of power and create other worlds than Badiou's model allows.

There are a lot more actions available to create other worlds than Badiou's model allows—this is the argument of the next chapter, which looks at actions that are not marked explicitly as political, and are not aimed at competing for power, but that are aimed at building an inhabitable world outside the sterile confines of either the humanitarian project or the authoritarian one. Whether that project too has political effects remains to be seen.

DEATH

In the fall of 2009, a little more than a year after the war, Anzor Kapanadze lay dying. As he neared death, his two sons left the camp and headed for the border of South Ossetia, the province from which the family had been ethnically cleansed a year earlier. They dodged Russian and Ossetian soldiers, guard dogs, and snipers as they stole across the border, knowing that if they were caught they would be sentenced to a five-year term in a South Ossetian prison or, worse, shot on sight (see Jomarjidze 2011). Once across, they walked to their destroyed home in the village of Disevi to collect two items: a jar of water from the village's spring and a bag of soil from the village graveyard.

Why was recuperating these two objects meaningful enough to take such terrible risks? In the opening pages of this book, I argued that the central work of displaced people is not just to suffer and endure but to remake a meaningful world. Their task, if they are to resettle rather than remain permanently temporary, is to knit together the fragments of their old lives, the often disconnected and strange things presented by the international humanitarian agencies, and the violence and care of the nation-state into the "normal situation," or an integrated network of objects and ideas that creates an environment stable enough to act in. But in the face of the powerful forces unleashed by the humanitarian system, which I have detailed in the previous chapters, and the ways they disrupt the production of a normal situation, how do displaced people make a lifeworld that is coherent, or at least coherent enough to make sense of the world and take action?

In this chapter I argue that the process of worldmaking is not just a question of discourse or of symbolic action, but a process of remaking the blank and desolate *space* produced by humanitarian action into a socially and spiritually meaningful *place*. Here I follow the work of Adam Ramadan, who argues that the fates of displaced people rest significantly on the places they inhabit (Ramadan 2013), and Michel Agier (2002, 2011), who demonstrates the ways in which the camp is often transformed from a standardized space of humanitarian intervention into a novel sociospatial form where displaced people create historical, political, and social identities (see also Feldman 2014). Whether a camp remains the abstract space of humanitarian action or becomes a place where people can not only exist but also live, whether it remains a geographical island or is instead connected to the surrounding community, and whether it contributes to social reintegration or, conversely, creates enduring forms of social isolation for displaced people are all open questions of enormous magnitude for the rapidly increasing population of the world's archipelago of camps.

I explore how IDPs make abstract space into meaningful place by returning to the notion of the *topolganger*, or the juxtaposition of one place on top of another place within the same space or terrain. Humanitarians, of course, often superimposed the camp of their imaginations—one full of busy, cooperative, and grateful IDPs engaged in productive economic and psychosocial activity—onto the terrain of the camp. The camp as *technicity*, as an urban space amenable to technocratic control, existed on top of the *space of being* in which displaced people were mostly paralyzed by fear and uncertainty. But as displaced people came to inhabit the space of the camp rather than merely wait in it, another topolganger was called into being: that of the camp-village. In this chapter I show how the IDPs in Georgia began to use death to reconstruct life as a coherent "normal situation." By insisting on proper burial for those who succumbed to life in the humanitarian condition, the IDPs engaged in a cosmic reordering that partially rebuilt the village in the camp and connected the world of the living to the world of the dead. In struggling to prevent their dead from becoming displaced again, the IDPs mapped their current existences, which were liminal and temporary, to the historically and spiritually deep world of the village. In doing so they fought against the spatial and temporal limbo of the camp to reemplace themselves in the world of the living.

Eternally Displaced People

Anzor Kapanadze's *shakari* ("sugar," or diabetes) had been a problem long before the war. "The first war killed his pancreas," his wife, Mariam Sabashvili, told me, telling me how Anzor had been expelled from Tskhinvali during the 1991–1992 war between Georgian and Ossetian paramilitaries and displaced to Disevi, one of the Georgian villages surrounding Tskhinvali. "The stress and worry, being back to live in the village of Disevi, it was just too much for him, and his pancreas died. That is what gave him diabetes: the war." By the time pain in Anzor's joints drove him to the doctor in 2000, he had been suffering from unchecked diabetes for eight or nine years, and it was breaking his body down. By 2006 he was almost completely blind, despite a US$5,000 operation in Turkey paid for by his wife's Ossetian cousins in Moscow. Yet, as Mariam insisted, until the second war broke out, he was fine—or at least surviving. Mariam attentively supervised his treatment and carefully wrote everything—his blood pressure, his diet, his lab results—in a notebook she took to each medical appointment, while Anzor, who was one of the most well-liked men in Disevi, spent time with friends at the corner *birzha* or at *supras* in his own home.

By the time Anzor got to Tsmindatsqali, though, his kidneys had failed and he was on dialysis. Displacement made his insulin treatments erratic, and being forced to live on the high-carbohydrate bread and macaroni handed out in the World Food Programme's aid packages played havoc with his blood sugar. He had spent weeks sleeping on a cardboard box on the floor of a school building in Tbilisi. Yet it wasn't the physical privations of wartime that made Mariam say that the second war had killed his kidneys, much as the first war had killed his pancreas. "It's the *tsneva*. All the worry and pressure has overwhelmed his kidneys," she said, blending the notions of emotional pressure and vascular tension. Anzor was soon on dialysis three days a week. In early October, ten months after they entered Tsmindatsqali, Anzor Kapanadze had a massive stroke and fell into a coma. He was rushed to Gori hospital for *reanimatsia*, a Soviet-era life-support technique meant to revive organs in a state of clinical death (see Swain 2013), but it was too late. On October 20 Anzor Kapanadze died. He was a victim of the Russo-Georgian War—one who died more than a year after the shooting ended, but a casualty of war nonetheless.

For five days after his death the women in his family and I sat by his corpse, laid out on the table in the small cottage, as it grew steadily greener. Mariam began the wrenching wailing characteristic of Georgian funerals. But her lament was different from the other speeches I had heard given over corpses: hers centered not around the problem of death but on the problem of displacement. She began by crying about the fact that he would be buried in Gori, a strange place that seemed at that moment incomprehensibly far from his village, Disevi, and from the graves of his ancestors. "*Ai, bicho,* if only we could bury you in Disevi! If only I had some water from Disevi, to give you a drink. . . . The water here has a strange taste, it's foreign (*utskho*), not good like our water in Disevi!" She worried what would happen to him in what she called "the Other Country" if he were buried in the cemetery near the camp rather than in the soil of Disevi. "How will it be for you, in the place where you're going?" she asked. "If you're buried here, you'll go to a place in the Other Country where nobody knows you, where you don't know anybody. It's a foreign place, where you're going. How will it be for you, alone there?" As she spoke, Mariam tried to wave the flies, which were swarming on that uncharacteristically warm October day, away from Anzor's decaying corpse. Finally she sat down across from the cadaver and began waving the flies away with a branch covered with small leaves. The smell coming from the body was intense, and it mixed with the sweetness of the incense and the flowers arrayed in cellophane wrappers around the body. Mariam sat with her head enshrouded in a black veil, keening over and over that death was Anzor's third displacement: after his forced migration from Tskhinvali and then from Disevi, he was now being forced to migrate alone from the camp to the land of the dead. Twice an IDP and about to be buried in the wrong soil, Anzor seemed to be destined to be not just internally displaced but eternally displaced, condemned to wander unmoored from his village community after death and into eternity.

Anzor's postmortem predicament expressed the deepest existential dilemma of displacement: the severing of people from familiar places and thus from a social world. Indeed the image of his wandering corpse showed how significant the loss of place inherent in displacement is to one's continued existence as a coherent human person. As Hannah Arendt, herself a displaced person, wrote,

> The first loss which the rightless suffered was the loss of their homes, and this meant the loss of the entire social texture into which they were born and in which they established for themselves a distinct place in the world. (Arendt 1951, 372)

Displacement marks the loss of symbolic meaning, everyday practice, and a sense of self. Much of this loss is connected to a loss not just of property, but of place: the sites where laws and other rules are enacted, where daily routines are carried out, and where people's memories are attached and constantly brought forth. Particular places strongly condition what the world is like and what it means to be in the world because they constitute and are constituted by personal, political, or religious meaning (see Delaney 2010). It is no wonder that the loss of place prompts an existential crisis: existence itself requires, in the first instance, emplacement. Place is "how the world presents itself; that is to say, being inevitably requires a place, a situation, for its disclosure" (Larsen and Johnson 2012, 633). To exist is to exist in a place, to be bound by its rules or to challenge them, to be socialized into its routines and habits, to move through it and to experience oneself within it. The spaces people are thrown into, and the daily tasks and practice that those spaces condition, are to a large part what shapes both identity and agency, who a person is and what he or she is capable of doing in the world (see Malpas 2012; Ingold 2003). In this sense place is an existential topography, one that doesn't just create the ground for existing or act as a container for it, but that creates fundamental experiences of inside and outside, of origin and horizon, of possibility and limit, and of the cocreation of the world with other people and with God (see Malpas 2012, 2; John Paul II 1981). The set of spatially related features around people so profoundly shape the ways they exist within those features that to lose a familiar place is to lose one's fundamental ontological structure (see Malpas 2012, 4). The IDPs' struggle in the first years of displacement to learn about the camp as a place—its social structure and terrain, its capacities and resources for security or comfort, its local and macrogeopolitical dangers, the ways it shaped both daily routine and a place in the geopolitical order—were thus a struggle to regain not just their physical welfare but their ontological footing as well.[1]

Place shapes identity and action in both predictable and unpredictable ways. Although the indeterminacy of place has been most often explored in cities, villages have much in common with the teeming urban environment described by Michel de Certeau in *The Practice of Everyday Life* (1984, 129). Despite many attempts to create planned "model" villages in the twentieth century, the village has remained a setting where multiple ways of operating and acting, unaccounted for by planners and unnoticed by governments, take place (Scott 1998; Cloke 1988). Messy and makeshift, built in historical layers rather than according to a master plan, the village is other to and more than rationalized spatial planning. It is a place where practices of everyday life, far from being homogenized, regulated, and sterilized, instead "reinforce themselves in a proliferating illegitimacy" and combine "in accord with unreadable but stable tactics to the point of constituting everyday regulations and surreptitious creativities that are merely concealed by the frantic mechanisms and discourses of the observational organization" (de Certeau 1984, 130). Village life spills over the confines of state planning in unplanned and unforeseeable ways. This was nowhere more true than in the rural villages of the USSR, which grew in the interstices of Russian imperial governance and Soviet urban planning. Dissolved into private peasant landholdings by the Stolypin reforms of 1905 and then violently collectivized by the Soviets in 1924, the Soviet village, as a sociospatial form, nonetheless evaded most of the rationalized spatial planning of Soviet urban development, which was focused more on governing urban centers, building industrial enterprises, and constructing huge apartment blocks (*mikroraioni*) for urban workers (see Scott 1998). Although there were occasional attempts to "modernize" some villages, the Soviet village was both a remainder, something left behind by ambitious plans to transform the economy and to create an urban industrialized *homo sovieticus*, and something completely alien and profoundly resistant to those plans (see Dudoignan and Noack 2014).

In Tsmindatsqali the people ethnically cleansed from Disevi described the village as "paradise on earth," mentioning key features such as the church on the top of the hill, the apple orchards that provided most of people's legitimate incomes, the picnic grounds by the hornbeam trees, and the spring blessed with healing powers by St. Nino. Although these sounded like disconnected elements, to the IDPs these were not isolated sites but a coherent whole, a set of elements linked by movement and inhabitation together into a single entity, the village. The messy "plurality of the real," as de Certeau (1984, 129) calls it, was made into a coherent whole through the daily practices of working in gardens, shopping, going to church, cooking, and so on. Most of all the village was made into a coherent whole through motion, as people walked from point to point along well-worn trajectories within the village. The network of sites in a village, constantly traversed, creates paths that link people and places in an order that appears mostly seamless. The village is thus not just abstract space or a bunch of disconnected sites, but a meaningful place where history, family ties, and the embodied experience of daily habit combines to form a sense of deep attachment between people and their environment (see Cresswell 2004; Tuan 1974). Although chronically buffeted by conflict, the village was, to the people who lived in it, a "normal situation" that presented a sense of mundane, and largely expected, order. As Delaney writes, the very spatialization of daily life creates a lived sense of stability:

> Ordinary spatialities and legalities contribute to the lived texture of our mundane orderings and give form and expression to what is taken to be remarkable and unremarkable, expected or unexpected, in *lived situations.* In doing so, they commonly confer the appearance of stability and order of a certain kind. The spatiality of everyday life is lived vis-à-vis the ordinary separations, partitions exclusions and confinements of social life: the affected, psycho-social-spatial arrangements of homes, workplaces, public and institutional spaces . . . that we continually encounter and inhabit. This, for us, is simply how the world is put together (Delaney 2010, 44).

The village was likely not as idyllic as the IDPs remembered it. Like their counterparts across the border in Shida Kartli, almost all[2] the villages in South Ossetia were poor and had decaying infrastructure, and they were plagued by semiregular outbursts of violence when young Ossetian men and their Georgian counterparts would begin firing at one another. But after the dissolution of the USSR poverty and violence were not exceptional, but were integrated into the habits and place-based practices of village life. When the shooting would start villagers would routinely depart for a few days and return once the situation calmed down. It was dangerous and unpleasant, and it generated a great deal of anxiety. But it was also a normalized experience, part of a way of life. After nearly twenty years of frozen conflict, dealing with endemic poverty and intermittent violence had become part of the normal situation in the village (see de Certeau 1984, xv).

The deep connection between people in the rural South Caucasus and their villages formed by practice extended from the material world to the supernatural one (see Grant 2004). In the villages of South Ossetia, the terrain of the village formed an important connection to the Other Country, the land of the dead where loved relatives and unknown ancestors awaited. For those villagers properly buried, the location of the grave in the village cemetery in close proximity to the graves of other family members ensured that the newly dead would be properly received into a posthumously enduring community. The experience of place constituted by the village, then, was not only physical but also spiritual, not only about the practice of everyday life but also about the practice of the everyday in the afterlife. As a repetitive social practice, burial not only helped turn the village into a particular place (that is, "our" place, for the villagers who inhabited it), but also brought the village into a defined spatial relation with a particular location in the terrain of the Other Country, the place where ancestors awaited the newly dead.

The displacement caused by war, then—as opposed to the temporary relocations occasioned by low-level interethnic violence that had become more or less normal in South Ossetia—is enormously significant because it entails not only the loss of property or land or buildings, but also the loss of an entire social and metaphysical order based on place. Displacement means a loss of a sense of self that is not only embodied but also spatially oriented, and the destruction of a phenomenological experience of the individual and collective subject as it is constructed through dwelling or inhabiting a specific place. If being in place is what creates the boundary "between known and unknown, the world and the all-encompassing void, life and thought from mortality and nothingness" (Larsen and Johnson 2012, 633), then the loss of place threatened to throw the IDPs into the void.

Anzor's corpse, the first among the people of Disevi after their exodus from South Ossetia, posed a vexing problem that became the immediately present symbol of both the loss of place and the threat of the void. How should the body be interred, given that Disevi was occupied by the Russian Army? What to do if he was buried in the wrong soil? In her work on postcommunist burials, Katherine Verdery has documented the many ways that the problem of being buried in the "wrong" place has been resolved by reinterment—that is, by digging up physical remains and moving them to the "right" place.[3] Reburial, she says, is an essential part of resignifying a place as "ours"—as the right and proper territory of a particular community. This place is "ours" because our dead are buried in its soil. But for Anzor's family, the problem was different: the camp was very markedly not their proper place, as they had been militarily forced into it, and signifying the soil of their village in South Ossetia as the territory of Georgians by burying the Georgian dead in it was clearly not going to be permitted. The body was on hand, but the place was not. What to do? The dangerous journey past the militarized border and back to the village of Disevi embarked on by Anzor's two sons in order to return with water and soil offered a creative solution to both the immediate problem of burial and the larger existential questions common to all displaced people.

The Curious Properties of Corpses

Displacement demands grappling with the incoherent multiplicity of rubble, the destruction of space, and the loss of a structuring spatialized network of materiality that undergirds meaningful action (see Gordillo 2014). More than just a makeshift solution or the temporary preservation of aid for biological survival, displacement demands the reordering of the entire lifeworld of those who are displaced. It poses what Verdery calls "a problem of reorganization on a cosmic scale," which requires redefining virtually everything, including daily practices, ethical and spiritual beliefs, and fundamental meanings that before had been taken for granted.

> Reordering worlds can consist of almost anything—that's what a "world" means. To reorder worlds of meaning implicates all realms of activity: social relations, political ideas and behavior, worldviews, economic action . . . and dead bodies can serve as loci for struggling over new meanings in any of them. (Verdery 1999, 35, 36)

Corpses are indeed particularly fecund material for reordering worlds. Like living bodies, they connect the individual, the community, and the place they inhabit (Hammond 2004, 145). But corpses are uniquely interstitial: they bridge the worlds of the living and the dead, function as both subjects and objects, and tap into profound affect. Verdery argues that their value is symbolic rather than material, "less to do with their concreteness than with how people think about them." But I suggest that the reason that corpses are so efficacious in reordering chaotic social worlds is precisely because of their materiality, which necessarily invokes their spatiality. As things that come from dust and that will return to dust, corpses have an intimate tie to soil and thus to the particularities of place. Verdery writes that corpses are "indisputably *there*," and says "their corporality makes them important means of *localizing* a claim. They state unequivocally . . . *hic locus est*" (1999, 28). Tied to the living by kinship or routine interaction, rooted in the soil of a particular location yet free to wander the afterlife, the corpse creates a spatial order that ties living people to concrete sites saturated with social meaning and gives them both origin and final destination. Properly buried, the corpse is a map that defines not only people's right places in the world but also the spatial and temporal contours of the world itself. What makes dead bodies powerful is that they are highly skilled at making places. They demand that the living attend to the particularities of topography, location, and belonging, and territorially anchor the community of both ancestors and their descendants. The place-making skills of corpses are in the first instance topographic, in that they divide the plain of Cartesian space, create boundaries between "our" space and "not ours," mark places as sacred or secular, and link specific practices to defined social practices, including burial. But they are most importantly topologic. Just as time could be folded (see chapter 5), so too can space. Corpses can fold space so that one place exists on the terrain of another, twist terrain to bring the world of the dead into the world of the living, and suture together places blown apart by violence.

Anzor's body lay in state on the dining room table in the small cottage in Tsmindatsqali for five days. Then, Saturday morning, a crowd began to arrive for the funeral procession. While people living in Tsmindatsqali had come earlier to sit with the body during the wake, the funeral procession brought more than five hundred people, mostly people from Disevi, who had been scattered into other camps. At neighboring cottages—Manana Abaeva's and Elena Chochieva's among them—friends not seen since the war broke out arrived for the funeral. Up and down the row of cottages inhabited by the people from Disevi, people hugged and smiled and caught up, making the occasion as joyful as it was sad. The socializing was almost completely gender segregated, as most public occasions are—the women stood together in knots, the men stood separately, smoking. Inside the *kazino* (the "casino," an open cottage owned by Elena Chochieva's brother-in-law but not lived in, where men sometimes went to play cards), men and women sat at two tables pushed together, eating small meals (not a full-blown *supra*) and talking together. As the time for the funeral neared, one table in the "casino" was devoted to a small group of men taking money from each of the visitors. The money was meant to cover the costs of the coffin, the burial, and the large funeral banquet that was to follow, and each donor's name and the exact amount he or she gave was carefully written down in a book that would be given to the widow.[4]

At the appointed hour rented buses pulled up to the camp, and all the mourners loaded up for the short journey to the cemetery in Gori. At Anzor's grave, in front of the more than five hundred people that came, his sons poured the water onto the ground and sprinkled the dirt from Disevi onto his coffin, while other mourners prevented his wife, who was carrying out the traditional display of wailing and grief, from throwing herself in the grave along with it. What Anzor's sons had done was to rework the cartographically literal topography that separated the village from the camp by acting topologically, by folding space so that the graves of their ancestors now lay squarely on top of the soil of the camp. Rather than moving the body, as in a reinterment, they had moved the village, creating a second topolganger on the terrain of the camp. The village topolganger created by Anzor's sons was another place in the exact same terrain as the "place of experience" presented by the camp and the technicity created by the humanitarians (see chapter 1), utterly distinct yet existing in the identical space.

The very notion of being able to properly bury the dead in the soil of the village was a huge change from the fate that had befallen people who had died in the other camps in the early days after the war. In Skra, for example, IDPs were forced to bury an elderly man named Misha in unconsecrated ground, since the nearby "host village" refused to let the IDPs bury their dead in its cemetery. His grave, stuck in a field just outside the camp's residential area, left without the traditional headstone and photographic image of the deceased, and lacking a table for his relatives to come and feast with him, was essentially nowhere at all. Because it connected him with neither his living descendants in the camp nor his ancestors buried in the village, it became the site of the void, the place of meaninglessness that condemned him to eternal displacement. Anzor's grave was the opposite. The spring water and the soil symbolically re-created the graveyard of Disevi in the graveyard of Gori, and in doing so transformed Tsmindatsqali from camp to village.

The IDPs thus used the corpse not just as a mediator or a link that brought the village and the camp into proximity, but as an *onto-topological device*, an object that laid out a theory of space and being far different from the one proposed by the international humanitarian system. The humanitarian topolganger is what Henri LeFebvre (1992) labeled *abstract space* or *l'espace conçu*, space as it is conceived through representation or theory. Driven by NGOs that operate as multinational corporations, it operates on the logic of capitalism and creates the hyperhomogenized space characteristic of capitalist places. Thinking of IDPs as identical units of consumption with identical needs, humanitarians pay no attention to kinship, although this is often the most important form of identity for displaced people, and largely ignore their preexisting ties to the places from which they came in order to keep them at least minimally existent, if not truly alive.

The village remade at Anzor's funeral was a topolganger of a profoundly different order. Rather than being abstract space, *l'espace conçu*, the topolganger created by the reemplacement of the village in the camp was *l'espace perçu*, space as it is perceived through everyday practices and perceptions. The burial was the first event that had reunited the people of Disevi explicitly as a village since they had been dispersed by the government and the humanitarian agencies. The soil and water that resurrected the village in the camp symbolically thus also served to resurrect it socially, as the spatial mirroring of the funeral ritual in a new place served to reestablish the social ties among members of the village, who had been scattered among distant camps. By virtue of the movement of soil, water, people, relics, and symbols, the corpse's declaration of *hic locus est*, this is the place, expressed the notion that one could dwell in two places simultaneously: in the world of the camp, structured by the humanitarians and their programs and policed by the nation-state, while at the same time living back in the world of the village, with its meanings, habits, regularized hardships, and social connections. The routines of the village, beginning with burial and all its attendant rituals, were transplanted onto the ground of the camp. The corpse thus stood for the resurrection of social space, and therefore the remaking of social communities formed and enacted in spatialized actions. Disevi lived, to be sure. But it did not live in its own space in South Ossetia, where the village square had been transformed into a military outpost and the hillsides transformed into sites for sniper nests. It was resurrected in the Gori cemetery and in the dusty graveled streets and stark white cottages of Tsmindatsqali. The creation of *l'espace perçu* was the linchpin of what Hammond (2004, 3) calls emplacement, or the transformation of space into "personalized, socialized place." Through the difficult process of emplacement, IDPs worked to create a basis for organized sociality, of meaningful work, and of community identity far richer than the prefabricated abstractions of humanitarian aid could provide (Hammond 2004, 9)

The *Supra* of the Displaced

Corpses are nodal objects, things that proliferate connections among objects, emplacing them in topographic or topological relation, and thus integrating them in a more stable order. But what makes them particularly important in the context of forced migration is that they not only help create spatial structure and order in the material world of daily experience but also help create spatialized order in the spiritual domain. In Tsmindatsqali Anzor's corpse generated relations among ever more objects, and in doing so created a third topologanger that brought the specific geographies of the Other Country into topological relation with the concrete terrain of the living.

Although this is not Orthodox theology, many Georgians believe that the dead live in a mirror world richly populated with social and geographic features that parallels our own and that comes into topological alignment with the world of the living at particular ritual moments when the actions of the living and the dead are identical. This is especially true at the funeral banquet, the *kelekhi*, which inverts the signs of the more joyous and life-affirming *supra* ritual banquet regularly practiced across Georgia. When a corpse is buried, the dead welcome him to the afterlife with a festive *supra*. But it is the living who must move food and wine to the table of the dead by holding their own ritual banquet, the mournful *kelekhi*. In moving these material objects to the spirit world, the living reemplace both the newly dead and themselves in the community of the ancestors.

After Anzor's burial, nearly all of the five hundred guests drove back into the center of Gori and came to Anzor's *kelekhi*. Because there was no place in Tsmindatsquali (or indeed, in any of the camps) large enough for life-cycle events like weddings and funerals, the *kelekhi* was held at a local banquet hall. Men and women were seated separately, and the feast was led by the *tamada*, the toastmaster, who proffered long and elegant speeches at regular intervals. Usually the order and theme of the toasts is fixed and proceeds in expanding scale, from the family to the nation to relations with foreign guests, and finally to God (see Tuite 2010; Mühlfried 2015; Manning 2012).[5] At Anzor's *kelekhi*, however, the toastmaster focused not on social relations but on geography. In toast after toast he called out the names of each of the Georgian villages lost during the war. He traced the places Anzor had lived, from Tskhinvali to Disevi to the IDP camp. "Long live Disevi!" he shouted, invoking the village and Anzor's connection to it, detailing the fields and orchards Anzor had worked in, and talking about the hills and the groves where he and the other villagers had hiked and picnicked. Over and over he constantly reinforced the links between Anzor's corpse, the village, and the site near the camp where he was buried. It was as if he were leading the participants along Anzor's own path across space, creating an integrated trajectory from city to village to camp to the Other Country.

What was happening was the creation of a third topolganger, a third place on the terrain of the single camp. Folding space with his words, the *tamada* first laid the inaccessible village over the space of the camp, and then folded the Other Country beneath it. As in other cases where the spiritual intersects with political violence, the summoning of the Other Country helps to create a domain of social order and action that exceeds both the secular governmentality of the humanitarians and the hybrid authoritarian democracy carried out by the nation-state (see Dunn 2014; Frederiksen 2014). It is a spectral space that, on the one hand, stands for death as the most radical form of abjection (see Navaro-Yashin 2012, 149). Yet, at the same time, it is part of the attempt to create a new spatio-temporal ordering of the world in the aftermath of war. In contrast to the chronic present of the humanitarian order, in which surviving until the next day is the only goal (see chapter 5), or to the future anterior of the nation-state, in which a brilliant future is always "that which will have been" when continually postponed measures will have finally have been taken (Frederiksen 2014), the Other Country offers a connection to the immediate past when the newly dead were still alive, as well as to a longer historical past inhabited by distant ancestors. If the topolganger of the village offered the IDPs a spatial transformation in the form of a reconnection to the spaces they were cut off from, the topolganger of the Other Country offered a similar temporal transformation in the form of a reconnection to both historical and mythical time, from which they had also been severed by the war. It is no wonder, then, that rather than talking about dying (*kvdeba*, a term also used for animals), the IDPs mobilized the Georgian euphemism *gardatsvaleba*, which loosely means "transformation (to another life) by moving across boundaries."[6] With the Other Country brought into close proximity to the camp, and the path to the correct places and correct people carefully laid out, death seemed less a final stop than a transition to another way and place of being.

The grave served as a conduit between the three layers of the village, the camp, and the Other Country. It was a borehole through space that allowed people and things—especially food—to move between them. Sitting in front of a truly massive quantity of food, the mourners would pour some of the wine onto torn pieces of bread (which stood in for bare earth) with each toast, ritually offering

the wine and food to the dead having their *supra* in the mirror world. This was an abbreviated version of the more elaborate rites for the dead I had seen in gravesite banquets, where people poured wine into the earth and buried pieces of food in the soil. The food, acting as a mediator, sutures the spatially distant places of village, camp, and afterworld together, and so is yet another catalyst for the spatial reconstruction of the normal situation.

This use of food is clearly about a regenerative cycle: Like bodies or corpses, food springs from the soil and returns to it. Water sinks beneath the earth to reappear in springs used to irrigate the grapes, which are made into the wine that is poured back into the ground. In a universe properly arranged in space, both material objects and people transit back and forth between this world and the Other Country on well-worn circular paths of death and resurrection. But displacement can prevent people from tending their land and producing food to permanently resettle the dead in their new abodes. Just before Anzor died Mariam had a dream about this possibility. In her dream Anzor stood in their gardens in Disevi, sad and angry because the garden was terribly overgrown with tall grass clotting old furrows and new plants growing in unruly tangles. "His soul has gone to Disevi, but there's no place for it to rest there," Mariam told me. "He's wandering around in the fields, but his grave is not there, so he can't lay down anywhere." Her dream alluded to the fact that when space and place are disarranged by violence this essential movement is disrupted and the reproductive capacity of corpses and soil and water are all blocked.

Kevin Tuite has argued that the Georgian *supra* came into being in its current form in the nineteenth century as a response to lost sovereignty, as a means of reconstituting horizontal solidarity among members of the newly defined Georgian nation and of simultaneously rejecting traditions and values imposed by the tsarist regime (2010, 7). At the Georgian IDP camp the funeral *supra* of the displaced not only reconstituted damaged solidarities among covillagers, but also remade the solidarities among objects by linking together elements from village, camp, and afterworld. The corpse summons the soil, which summons the food, which summons the iron pot from the house in the village and the plastic basin given out by CARE International and so on, each piece being progressively anchored in the structured spatial order of place, each contributing to the restoration of the normal situation and an orderly world. Sartre, paraphrasing Heidegger, says "the world is a synthetic complex of instrumental realities inasmuch as they point to one another in ever-widening circles" (Sartre 1943, 41). It is the reemplacement of these objects, the making of spatial relationships between them, that makes them point to one another and thus transforms them into the opposite of the "antiartifacts" handed out by the humanitarian aid agencies (see chapter 4). Objects become representable by being emplaced, if we take

"representation" in the sense of not only appearing in human experience but also being made meaningful by virtue of being spatially, and therefore semantically, organized in a system of meaning (see also Hammond 2004, 9). But reemplacement makes not only an epistemic system but an ontologic one as well. It not only makes the world, or makes it thinkable, but because it is rooted in place it also makes it habitable in ways that the spatially rootless and essentially cosmopolitan humanitarian project, with its antiartifacts and voids, can never do.

No wonder, then, that the feasting and feeding of the dead continues beyond the day of burial. After Anzor's death and Mariam's dream of him, there was a feast in Tsmindatsqali for the *meore dghe*, the second day after the funeral. Forty days after the funeral, there was again a feast, again in the camp, in which toasts were pronounced and food and wine cast into the soil and Anzor's spirit gently encouraged to depart. That night Mariam dreamed of Anzor again. He stood silently at the foot of her bed and then turned and walked away, headed toward his friends and ancestors in the Other Country. Right relations of people, things, and places had begun to be restored.

Making Difference: Navigating Topolgangers

In the months that followed it seemed that the funeral had unleashed a process of emplacement in which a proliferation of spatial, social, and temporal connections linked village, camp, and afterworld together. By the time I returned a year and a half after Anzor's death, Tsmindatsqali had changed dramatically: Where once there were lines of bare white cottages sitting on bare dirt along straight, dusty streets, now there were gardens and grapevines and fruit trees. People had built onto cottages to accommodate new brides and new children, built awnings to shield the front doors from the rain, and poured concrete patios in front of the cottages to make space for sitting outside. Inside the cottages people began to make homes out of what had been bare shelter. When the terrible quality of the original building became evident, the Gori municipality funded a "renovation" of many of the cottages in Tsmindatsqali, which gave people fresh paint to replace the cracked and peeling original paint and vinyl flooring to lay over the gaping pine floorboards. In Tserovani and Tsmindatsqali some of the IDPs began to acquire chairs with backs to replace the flimsy stools they had been given by the humanitarians, or bought small sofas to replace the beds that had been in the main rooms. Slowly people began to hang decorations—often cheap toys or plastic clocks—on the walls, or to put up wallpaper over the mold-covered plaster on the cottage walls.

Over the next few years some people's occupations began to return, if hesitantly and partially. When last I saw Manana Abaeva she was wearing a new gold necklace and had an old Mercedes parked in her yard: her husband's business, which involved selling tomatoes and cucumbers in Russia, had taken off. Sopo Tsuladze, who had been a nurse in South Ossetia, found a job as a nurse in one of the settlements three afternoons a week, doing blood pressure checks and handling minor illnesses in a walk-in clinic. Aleko Mentashvili, the bee guy, was released from prison after two years, and although Mariko, his wife, had left him, he returned to Skra to tend the farm he had built in the tiny spaces and unused corners of the camp. Even Mariam Sabashvili, Anzor's widow, found work: although she never found a job as a school principal again, she worked part time in a daycare center for a few months, and then—with her great love of history—landed a position in the museum at Joseph Stalin's birthplace, in the center of Gori. Their lives were not as they were before: although each of them was somehow "socially reintegrated," it was always in a degraded form that was less than they had before. But it seemed like a beginning, a move away from nothingness and paralysis toward reconstructing a life.

Social life, with its small joys, also began to sprout in the camp. At the end of the first year in insile, the first IDP wedding among the former residents of Ksuisi village took place. This, like Anzor's funeral, was a chance for a village to reunite and to link camp to village, and they came together over an enormous *supra*. Manana Abaeva, sitting next to me at the wedding banquet, looked at the tables piled high with food and sighed contentedly. "It's a good wedding, a *normal* wedding. In Ksuisi, we would have had an even better one, maybe with five hundred people. Some people think that we shouldn't celebrate like we did before because we're refugees. And this is like a rich person's party even, which is amazing since we don't have any money. But everybody gave a few lari, and here we have a real wedding!" (see also Dunn 2012a). Like weddings, births also offered a link between past and future: when Mariam Sabashvili's son had a new baby they named him Anzor, after his grandfather. Regenerative cycles, which had been badly disrupted by the war, were beginning to form again and to reconnect people to the larger cosmological order.[7]

Spiritual life had begun to return too: Slowly almost every cottage came to have a shrine inside with cheaply printed copies of icons and small candles. Some IDPs scrounged bricks and cement to make *salotsavebi*, or small prayer shrines, to replace those that had existed in the village. As people began to die in Berbuki and Skra camps, which were more distant from Gori, regional authorities donated land for a cemetery exclusively for the IDP dead, and the IDPs began to build gravesites complete with picnic tables where people feasted their deceased relatives. By Easter 2010 the graveyards were full of people drinking and toasting, pouring wine into the soil and scattering bits of food across it.[8] Although the sterile bones of the humanitarians' abstract space still poked through, they were quickly being covered by the green, lively, unruly traces of village life. The process was clearly makeshift and wobbly, but the destroyed villages seemed to be slowly, unsteadily, resurrecting themselves.

The resurrection of villages, though, did not—and cannot—transform camps into holistic spaces that are reconstructions of what came before. The camp-village is always a degraded and partial form of the village that existed before. There displaced people learn to navigate among multiple worlds, moving among topolgangers with different rules, identities, forms of activity, and relationships, trying to leverage the rules and resources of one domain against the rules and resources of another (Dunn and Cons 2013). In Georgia, as the camps transformed into real places, the IDPs began to navigate among the topolgangers of Karaleti, Tsmindatsqali, and their home villages, becoming increasingly active as the new hybrid system that involved technicity, place of being, and village all on the same terrain became clearer and clearer to them. The people who continued to angle to participate in the project or two launched by the remaining humanitarian NGOs, using their mastery of NGO vocabulary and concepts to write business plans or gain jobs as program facilitators, were moving between the topolgangers of camp and technicity, as were those who sought employment in the increasingly repressive apparatus of the nation-state as spies, soldiers, or police. Others—like the bee guy—moved between the topolgangers of camp and village, trying to replicate farm life in the confines of the cottage gardens or their small plots on the outskirts, or trying to reinstall themselves as craftsmen making window frames or repairing cars. The wages or profits for most of the displaced were miniscule, and almost all of them risked what resources they had in order to do something, anything. Just as for displaced people around the world, the point of work for the Georgian IDPs is not just to survive economically but to keep up an appearance of economic activity as a way of demonstrating their continued social and political utility and of regaining a place in society. Displaced people work as a way of rejoining the world. Rather than remaining passive victims, tied to the state and the surrounding society only by their collective vulnerability and suffering, they seek to use space actively and creatively and to labor as a means of reasserting themselves as individuals (see Agier 2011, 187). But that path was not open to all. A third group, perhaps the largest, remained idle, languishing in the lack of activity and opportunity that characterized the nothingness of camp life.

Placemaking therefore creates difference as much as it (re)creates solidarities, as people with different social networks, skills, and resources leverage them in diverse ways to move among the different worlds of being on the terrain of the camp. Because displaced people draw on their own individual biographies to move among the distinct topolgangers that exist within the space of the camp, many reinstantiate the same hierarchies and social differences that existed before the war rather than creating new social orders (see Betts 2016). Although a new political class emerged in the camp, made up of those people who had become professional IDPs employed by humanitarian agencies, the political leadership of the camp continued to be dominated by those who had been government officials before the war. Likewise those who had been in the social underclass of the village before the war soon found their cottages degrading into squalor as they became unable to pay for electricity, heat, or renovations of the poorly constructed buildings. The partial transformation of the camp into a village allowed for the reestablishment of hierarchies not only of money and power but of taste, comportment, and social class as well. This was not the kind of differentiation feared by the humanitarians, who constantly strove to sort the IDPs based on categories of vulnerability (e.g., the handicapped or children) and to stave off differentiation based on gender or ethnicity (e.g., to prevent sexual violence or violence against the ethnic Ossetians in the camp). But it created wildly different outcomes, nonetheless, reproducing old categories of class and exclusion that were exacerbated by life in the humanitarian condition.

Interestingly, one of the most important forms of differentiation that emerge through placemaking is based on location: camps themselves, which have different proximities to surrounding urban areas and markedly different relationships to the international aid apparatus, take on radically different natures as they are made into inhabitable places. Tserovani, the largest of the camps and also the closest to Tbilisi, was designated early as a camp that would morph not into a village but into a town. The largest beneficiary of humanitarian aid and the "model camp" most often shown to visiting dignitaries and donors, Tserovani was given its own school, kindergarten, two-story municipal office building, clinic, and shopping street, all paid for with donor funding.[9] In a 2015 video an IDP from Akhalgori marveled at the transformation: "They are building more things, they are making more markets . . . it will be just like in Europe!"[10] Skra, built on a former fruit-growing agricultural experiment station a few miles outside of Gori, was quickly transformed into an agriculturally intensive village with the help of farm machinery and infrastructure funded by CARE and, as time went on, the income the IDPs derived from selling the fruit from the already mature orchards there. But other camps languished, unable to construct topolgangers of either town or village. In Khurvaleti, for example, which was far from urban employment in either Gori or Tbilisi and where the land was poor, the only jobs available were doing backbreaking picking for a Turkish-owned commercial farm, which paid heartbreakingly low wages. In Prezeti, high on the mountain ridge where the climate was cold and windy and where there was no irrigation infrastructure, many people abandoned their cottages and returned to Akhalgori (the one region the Russians allowed IDPs to enter),[11] choosing to live in their old homes under Russian occupation rather than continue struggling in the camp. The making of place, so profoundly dependent on imagination and symbolism, is also deeply constrained by the materialities of terrain, topography, and location, and this in itself creates vast differences of opportunity for the displaced.

The Camp as If

Looking at the physical transformation of the camp, it may seem as if some camps really can turn into settlements, as if they really can turn into spaces of inhabitation rather than abstract space. Michel Agier argues for this possibility when he describes the camp as not just a site where the undesirable displaced are confined but also a place that, as it is transformed, can become a public space. In this space displaced people may be able to find their voices and their subjectivity and become once again political and social actors. "Each camp, in this respect, shares in the beginning of the history of the world," he writes (2011, 65). Here Agier seems to echo the hopes embedded in the humanitarian topolganger: the hope that displaced people can somehow be recycled and reintegrated, and somehow become consequential members of the social world rather than simply being confined at its margins.

Yet the camp is always "as if." The topolgangers make it possible for people to live as if it were a village, as if it were a town, as if it were in Europe. In that sense the topolgangers that arise from the terrain of the camp are part of the imaginative forecasting endemic to the future anterior, the "will be state" brought into being by the interaction of the international humanitarian system and the nation-state, as well as the past perfect constructed by IDPs' nostalgic longings (see Frederiksen 2014). Everything is potential, tentative starts, green shoots: the camp is always just on the cusp of becoming a real village like all the others, just like Georgia is always on the cusp of joining NATO and becoming part of Europe. Yet, as Agier remarks, "everything is potential but nothing develops" (2011, 145). The IDPs are never really in a village, never really in a town, never really in Europe, just as Georgia is always offered the possibility of a membership action plan to join NATO or an accession plan for the European Union but never really gets one (RFERL 2014; Civil Georgia 2014).[12] As another woman in the online video about Tserovani said,

> I still think in twenty to thirty years from now, this place could become like Gldani or Mukhiani [two suburbs of the capital—ECD] for Tbilisi. This will become one of these kinds of districts, I think. But it won't be inhabited by people from Akhalgori. It's because you have never been there—Akhalgori is like an orchard. People from Akhalgori won't take root here.

The topolgangers—the humanitarians' technicity, the IDPs' village, the Other Country—also seem not to take root but to lie on the surface of the camp, never becoming fully stable and normal situations or worlds that can be fully relied on. Part of this is due to the economic precarity of the displaced. The businesses that are started are always on the brink of financial collapse (especially when the original microcredit loan is gone). The state job provides a salary, but is at risk of being lost if a family member participates in protests or if the political party that handed it out falls out of power. The meager aid arrives sporadically but is always at risk of disappearing if the government social workers decide that the family has too many possessions to be classified as "socially vulnerable" or if the humanitarians lose interest. The electricity is on, but could be shut off at any time if the donor disappears and the bill can't be paid. The trees are bearing fruit, but the fruit can be destroyed in an instant by a hailstorm, taking a family's capital with it.

But the precarity and uncertainty experienced by internally displaced people is more than the (now quite common) risk of poverty experienced by other groups of people around the world (cf. Allison 2013). It is an existential instability, one peculiar to people who have experienced war and who live in the humanitarian condition. It is a risk that whatever fragile structures of meaning, whatever frail networks of sociality and sense that are built up, might be exploded in an instant. For displaced people around the world, many of whom are held on one side or the other of the border of their own unstable country, that always imminent threat is concrete, not metaphorical. Given that wars tend to be cyclical rather than episodic, there is the ongoing risk that conflict might break out again, destroying whatever the displaced have managed to build in the camp and forcing them once again into an unknown world. In Georgia the Russian Army, which was continually building up more army posts, tank roads, sniper nests, and other military infrastructure just a few kilometers away, kept this possibility always open. The IDPs, whom the Georgian government kept permanently temporary so that they could be mobilized to move back into South Ossetia if the territory could be retaken, were constantly aware of the jeopardy their position near the administrative boundary line posed if the military tide ran the other way, the Russians invaded Georgia proper, and they were killed themselves or displaced once more, forced to flee and leave the graves of their kin behind yet again. In the camp the poles that exist from the beginning remain: a constant enervating tension between death and return, chaos and reintegration, that undergirds life in the humanitarian condition, the topolgangers that represent each possibility flickering on and off and buzzing menacingly like an electric light bulb with a short.

The camp is existentially precarious because it is constantly at risk of nothingness, of falling back into the void. It is as if underneath all the topolgangers, even the Other Country, there is a sinkhole. The sinkhole is always on the cusp of opening and sucking all the other topolgangers into its gaping maw, always on the verge of turning the internally displaced into the eternally displaced, always threatening to transform the normal situation into nothingness. The villages or cities that are resurrected, the meaning-laden connections between elements of everyday life that are built, the spatialized maps of daily practice that are forged, and the life that displaced people can build is one that is profoundly degraded because the process of meaning-making is built over that sinkhole. The ever-present potential for nothingness at the base of the camp is what keeps displaced people from becoming "socially reintegrated," as the humanitarians hope, and what keeps the camp from turning into a "settlement," as the government so wishfully names it, for how can anyone or anything take root over a sinkhole? The very being of the camp, eternally waiting, chronically temporary, and endlessly contingent, is unsettled. It is, as a form of lived experience, constantly and profoundly unsettling.

BRIGHT OBJECTS

Why do corpses catalyze the resettlement of displaced people? Why do dead bodies have the power to bind people together, connect them to particular places, and link them to both past and future? And why can corpses—and other objects like them—spark at least a partial reconstruction of the normal situation? In this meditation I want to think more about why corpses (and some other objects) have these properties, what that means for reestablishing the normal situation for displaced people, and why humanitarianism does not currently facilitate that process. How might humanitarian aid help rather than hinder the remaking of a normal situation, and how can it help refugees resettle themselves rather than keeping them in the eternal limbo of camp life? How might aid better facilitate displaced people's own attempts at remaking meaningful lives? The answer, I think, depends on understanding what Badiou calls the "logics of worlds" (2009), or what the philosopher Levi Bryant calls "onto-cartographies" (2014), and the ways powerful objects such as corpses fit into them.

In his brilliant book *Rubble: The Afterlife of Destruction*, Gaston Gordillo argues that corpses are "bright objects" that can pierce through "everyday opacity to reveal, and to mark in space, the spatial and cultural sedimentation of a historical legacy of violence, whose material residues both attract and repel" (2014, 185). He focuses on the mass graves of indigenous people killed in the colonial encounter, which, although long hidden, continued to hold a terrifying fascination for the people who live among them. The bodies in these graves, now bones and skulls, seemed to exert a kind of gravity that both attracted and repelled the living by virtue of its powerful negativity and compelled them to confront a history of "ruptured objects" and "damaged bodies" that officials and elites would much rather they forget.

Gordillo takes the notion of "bright objects" from the philosopher Levi Bryant (2014), who uses the notion of "luminosity" as a metaphor for thinking about rhizomatic networks of objects, ideas, and persons (see also Gordillo 2014, 189). Bright objects, in comparison to others that are black or dim, are catalysts: they have the ability to connect a great number of other objects together in dense webs of multiplicity, structuring them in relationship to one another and making them into stable assemblages (Bryant 2014, 225). Corpses are particularly bright in this sense. With their special capacity to constitute a dense web of linkages to other objects, including graves, soil, food, tables, wine, villages, shrines, and camps, they create order out of cosmological chaos. In Georgia they connected death in the present with the violence of war in the recent past, creating a narrative of destruction that gave voice to the violence of life in the humanitarian condition. In that sense the corpses in the Georgian IDP camp resonated with the bodies in the mass graves that Gordillo found in Argentina (2014, 187). They affirmatively generated negativity, making it possible to think and speak about the tremendous damage inflicted not only by the war but also by the humanitarian project that claimed to be restoring both bodies and communities (see Klima 2002). In that sense the bodies of the dead were inherently political. By virtue of the way they were cared for, celebrated, buried, and mourned, they showed the local effects of an international geopolitical order and opened a critique of both the local state and humanitarian institutions (see Verdery 1999). In many ways the funereal was not only a summons to the particularities of village communities but also a rejection of the bureaucratic sterility imposed by the humanitarian project on the terrain of the camp.

But corpses do not just produce powerful negativity. They have another side, a positive capacity. As Bryant puts it, bright objects "radiate turbulence that entangle other [objects] with one another and sets them in motion." Bright objects like corpses are thus always about *becoming*, not just *being* (Bryant 2014, 226, 227). In Georgia it was the web of connections sparked by the corpse that gave rise to hybrid forms of daily practice that incorporated elements of the IDPs' old lives in the village with the new practices of life in exile. By linking past and present, the spiritual and the material domains, and the terrain of the camp with the terrain of the village, the corpse became the bright star at the center of a new constellation being born. It was the central node in a world-making project.

The creative power of the corpse comes not only from its incarnation of violence (see Klima 2002; Gordillo 2014, 185) but also from the way it summons care. The bodies of the dead carry with them the love and regard lavished on them when they were living. Proper burial necessitates that they be treated tenderly as they are washed, clothed, fed, and wept over. It requires acts of care, and these spill over both to the mourners in the form of feasts and to the geography of the graveyard, which must be sanctified, tended, and properly maintained at regular intervals. The Georgian Orthodox Easter ceremony embodies this care brilliantly. Whole families go to the gravesites of their relatives, tend to the graves and the headstones, roll Easter eggs dyed with red madder on their soil, and then have enormous and festive feasts while sitting at benches and tables right next to the buried corpses of the dead, caring for them by pouring wine and dropping bits of food into the soil for the Easter feast in the Other Country. The labor of care is what links the corpse with the soil and the food and the terrain of the cemetery. This highlights a key fact: it is care, not violence, that gives the corpse its brightness and reforges the assemblage as a stable and repetitive network. Both the affective labor of care and the practical dimensions of caring for the dead link objects in a stable pattern, and thus spark the world-making process. Corpses are thus what Badiou, following Jacques Lacan, calls "quilting points," stable points in a system of otherwise shifting relations. In the confusing and unstable world of the IDP camp, the properly buried corpse quilts together the camp, the village, and the afterworld, and provides a stable point around which other elements can be organized.

It is thus the corpse, as the paradigmatic bright object, that can answer Badiou's central question in *Logics of Worlds:* "How and why are there worlds rather than chaos?" (2009, 101). This question, which displaced people face in acute form, is for Badiou a problem of existence for everyone. He asks how pure being, which is nothing but indifferent multiplicity, comes to present itself as a consistent and structured world (2009, 36).[1] He argues that "logics of worlds"—another term for the normal situation[2]—act as metastructures that force particular relations within a network of existence, and that this is what makes the world seem both stable and consistent.

So it is the bright object, here the corpse, that catalyzes the reconstruction of the normal situation by creating structured constellations of other elements around itself. In its fleshy materiality, the corpse points out two important points about logics of worlds that Badiou, who dwells in the abstract, is less cognizant of. First, the corpse argues that the logic of the world is corporeal. Where Badiou thinks of the normal situation abstractly, as something that exists in the ether of pure being, the corpse reminds us that for each person the assemblage that makes up the world is first and foremost oriented around the body, and experienced bodily. That's true for the immediate world created around the corpse at the funeral, of course, which is experienced in an embodied way, through crying and wailing, eating and drinking, digging the grave and carrying the corpse. But it is also true of assemblages or situations that are much larger than individual experience. For the IDPs, the situation that makes up international geopolitics—the warring parties, the machines and techniques of violence, the politicized humanitarianism that rushes in afterward—is also experienced in and through the body, not as a macroscale abstraction.

The corpse also signals that the normal situation is always local. The constellation around a bright object is not an abstract diagram, but always an assemblage that is created in the first instance spatially. Levi Bryant starts to hint at this when he thinks about maps of these ontologic constellations as "onto-cartographies," mappable networks of material objects (2014, 111). But oddly, although Bryant sees "onto-cartographies" as material, he doesn't see them as spatial. His constellations appear to exist on an abstract plane rather than within the constraints of particular places. But the corpse shows that the normal situation is organized not just spatially but also very distinctly around place: as Badiou says, a being in a world is only thinkable insofar as it is localized (2009, 113). Therefore the normal situation or the logic of a world is not only oriented to the body but also placed into a concrete onto-topography.[3] This is what Badiou points to when he riffs on Heidegger's assertion that to exist can only be existence relative to a particular world. To be is to *be there* (*être-là*), to be in a particular place, not just to exist in a world but to inhabit it.

For refugees and IDPs displacement means losing the ability to inhabit a place. Their existence is disrupted because they lose the place in which they were to *be there*. Resettlement is therefore something far more existentially profound than just obtaining shelter or employment. It is the regaining of place, the reorientation of the abstract space of the situation into the very localized lived place organized around the body (see Lefebvre 1992, 407). To settle, to *be there*, is to reconstruct the world from a bright object and reinhabit it through the labor of care (see Bachelard 1958, 70).

Viewed through the lens of Orthodox Christian imagery, the rebirth of the normal situation and its reinhabitation might be seen as resurrection. Surely the intent of the humanitarian project is not just to recycle displaced people (see Bauman 2004), but in some sense to resurrect them, to bring them back from social death into the land of the socially and politically living. But the effect of the highly formalized and highly bureaucratized humanitarian system is that resurrection is partial and compromised. Humanitarian projects, with their bureaucratic tendency to universalize individual people into the abstract and homogeneous category of "IDP" or "refugee" (Malkki 1996), tended to suck the particularity out of both the living and the dead. The highly standardized "kit" approach to humanitarian projects also tends to sweep away the particularities of places, turning them not into lived places but into abstract and mass-produced space (see Lefebvre 1974). The dead who walked through the dreams of those living in the camp emblematized this problem. Yes, they were in some sense resurrected, but only in the form of ghosts or shades, wispy and transparent allusions to what had existed before, beings caught in an eternal and unresolvable purgatory. Even as the living IDPs struggled to rebuild the normal situation, to give the new world they found themselves in a stable and distinctive logic, they too found that humanitarian aid did not resurrect them as full, active people but instead trapped them in the purgatory of life in the humanitarian condition. Reconstituting the normal situation requires a bright object set into a distinctive place. But humanitarianism, which conceives of the world through bureaucratic abstraction and capitalist mass production, constantly interferes with the necessary declaration of *hic locus est*. When the humanitarian project transforms the camp into an abstracted technicity, when it creates chaos rather than spelling out the logic of its own world, when it constantly sucks away meaning and leaves only the void, it moves into dialectical relation with the process of becoming essential to resettlement. The result is a constant tension between forces that foster the rebuilding of the normal situation and forces that degrade it and produce disorder. Far from promoting resettlement, this leaves displaced people in a situation that is enduringly unsettling.

ALL THAT REMAINS

Over the eight years that I worked on this book the world changed dramatically—and with it the Georgian IDPs' understanding of what had happened to them and what their place in the larger geopolitical landscape was. The IDPs, like me, discovered that the events following the 2008 war were not anomalies or events particular to the post-Soviet world but part of much larger shifts in national, regional, and international systems. Russian aggression in Georgia turned out to be part of a larger strategy of Russian expansionism, the chaos of aid turned out to be endemic to the global aid system, the yawning pit of nothingness turned out to affect millions of refugees and IDPs around the world, and the struggle for emplacement occasioned an enormous shift in the way the world thought about—and tried to contain—displaced people. The problem of protracted displacement now affected tens of millions of newly displaced people, with no solution on the horizon.

In 2012, in the wake of the revelations of torture at Gldani prison, Mikheil Saakashvili was forced out of power and out of the country. The rise of the new government, led by a billionaire oligarch named Bidzina Ivanishvili and a loose coalition party called Georgian Dream, changed Georgia's geopolitical orientation. Although Ivanishvili did not pull away from Georgia's relationships with the United States, NATO, and the European Union, he began to adopt a much more ambiguous geopolitical orientation in which Georgia, the crumple zone of empire, flirted with Russia while continuing to overtly declare its ambitions to join NATO. Georgia's bid to join the West was clearly over, though: the

European Union and NATO had no appetite for expansion, much less for a conflict with Russia.

The potential for open military conflict in Russia was acutely clear in 2012 when it became evident that the invasion of Georgia had been a dry run for Russia's involvement in Ukraine, where separatist rebels on the Crimean Peninsula and in the Donbas region sought to break away. Russia annexed the Crimean Peninsula, with its strategic deep-water port, outright. But in Donbas it pursued a much more refined version of the strategy it had first piloted in South Ossetia: it funded and armed the rebels, and even sent in soldiers in unmarked uniforms (the notorious "little green men") to fight alongside them, while stringently denying it was involved at all. It was an entirely novel strategy of warfighting: war without war, and occupation without occupation (see Dunn and Bobick 2014). The result, as in Georgia, was the complete destabilization of the legitimate government. With the Russians perched in a separatist region, Ukraine, like Georgia, could not make any serious approach toward joining the European Union or NATO. Russia had begun to successfully re-create a buffer zone between itself and the West at the expense of nearly 1.5 million Ukrainians who became IDPs, joining their Georgian neighbors in protracted displacement.

Western Europe soon had even more serious political problems to face. In 2011 a violent civil war broke out in Syria in the wake of the Arab Spring prodemocracy movements. Soon over 7 million refugees were streaming out of Syria. Over a million Syrians poured into tiny Lebanon, and over 1.4 million Syrians sought refuge in Jordan. With more than 2.5 million Syrian refugees, though, Turkey soon became the largest refugee-hosting country in the world. Although the international humanitarian system led by UNHCR scrambled to set up vast refugee camps, the majority of Syrians refused to enter them, knowing that once there, they were likely to spend down whatever meager resources they had and become stuck indefinitely. UNHCR spent $63.5 million to build a huge camp, Azraq, in the Jordanian desert. It was, just like the Georgian camps, called "the best refugee camp in the world" by UN officials (Hadid and Okur 2014). Yet although it was meant to hold 130,000 refugees, by 2015 it was occupied by only 18,500 people. In Turkey too, refugees refused the camp: over 90% moved to urban areas in search of work rather than becoming dependent on aid in the camp.

Nearly a million of those refugees refused not only the camp but also the endless limbo of displacement altogether, and sought to resettle themselves in Europe. In the summer of 2015 they crowded into flimsy rubber rafts and made a life-threatening crossing of the Aegean Sea, heading for Greece and the European Union. Thousands drowned in this quest to avoid being permanently unsettled, their bodies washing ashore on Greek islands. Those who survived began streaming into Europe by foot, bus, and train. Snaking across Macedonia, Serbia, Hungary, and Austria, they made their way to Germany, France, Sweden, and Denmark, provoking the largest political crisis ever to face the European Union. Hungary, in defiance of the Schengen Treaty, which set out the principle of a borderless Europe, erected fences at its borders to keep out the refugees. Poland refused to accept any refugees. Britain, partly in the hopes of controlling its own immigration policy, voted to leave the European Union. Across Europe the movement of displaced people who refused to remain permanently temporary sparked virulent xenophobia, outright racism, and the rise of right-wing populist parties that won national elections. Even in faraway America, the specter of admitting even a tiny number of Syrian refugees was enough to provoke nativist furor. In the small town in Indiana I moved to, I watched a meeting about refugee resettlement degenerate into a physical altercation as partisans of Donald Trump began shoving prorefugee activists. This was a small version of a national phenomenon: Trump came to power largely on his anti-immigrant, antirefugee platform. In this face of this antirefugee sentiment, the international humanitarian system could only watch helplessly. Around the world Euro-American principles of human rights and the responsibility to protect—which had been easy for donor countries and their proxies, like Saakashvili, to proclaim—crumbled once faced with the actual prospect of refugee resettlement. The entire post–World War II international order was soon in crisis, beset by populist antirefugee movements coming to power across the developed world, many of whom expressed profound opposition to regional and global institutions from the European Union to the United Nations.

The international humanitarian system, struggling to respond, was widely acknowledged to be in crisis as well. The UN's emergency relief coordinator, Stephen O'Brien, famously said that "the system is not broken—but it is broke" (Aly 2016). Broke it definitely was: even though funding was over $25 billion per year, the UN system still had a $15 billion budget shortfall in 2015 and was not able to provide even a minimum of aid to many refugees (UN 2016). The World Food Programme, for example, had to cut rations to refugees around the world, including in Kenya, Uganda, and Lebanon, sometimes to as little as $13.15 per month (Gladstone 2015). But the system was broken as well as broke. As the United Nations itself noted, the practice of giving out subcontracts to provide aid on the basis of competitive bidding meant that aid agencies on the ground had few incentives to coordinate with one another, which led to massive inefficiencies and enormous overhead costs (see chapter 3; see also Curtis 2016). Local NGOs, which were well-suited to access refugee and IDP communities and determine what aid they needed, received less than .05% of global humanitarian funding, whereas large international NGOs and UN agencies, which kept more than half of all funding pledged by international donors, were less able to provide aid that was something rather than nothing (Curtis 2016). Displaced people remained nearly powerless in this system, and engagement with displaced communities remained an "add on" rather than a fundamental part of the aid process (Aly 2016). The chaos of aid, so vividly apparent in the Georgian case, was not an anomaly but an instance of an endemic problem in the global humanitarian system. That chaos not only made aid less helpful for displaced people, but also sharply limited the way donor governments could respond to a political crisis threatening to overwhelm or even destroy the European Union.

The United Nations promised to deliver fundamental reforms of the aid system at two major conferences, the World Humanitarian Summit in May 2016 and the High-Level Leaders' Summit hosted by Barack Obama in conjunction with the UN General Assembly in September 2016. Yet despite these attempts to arrive at what the UN labeled the "grand bargain," there were few new solutions on offer for displaced people. Rather than fundamentally rethink the way that the international system deals with displacement crises, the European Union and the United States continue to attempt to resolve the massive crisis of displacement by holding displaced people offshore in some form of the camp. In Greece, where thousands of refugees were stranded when the Balkan route to the European Union was closed in early 2016, displaced people are being literally incarcerated, held in tents in camps they cannot leave. Conditions for displaced children traveling alone who were being held in Greece were so bad that the NGO Human Rights Watch reported that "children face unsanitary and degrading conditions and abusive treatment" (Riddell 2016). "The Greek government justifies the detention of unaccompanied children as a temporary protection measure in the child's best interest. In practice it is anything but," Human Rights Watch argued (Riddell 2016).

In Turkey, Lebanon, and Jordan, where most refugees have gone to urban areas, international humanitarian donors have paid governments to hold refugees and to prevent their further movement toward Europe. Greece and Italy too are being supported by the European Union and international donors to hold refugees in place and to prevent their further movement. The result is that entire countries have now become giant refugee camps, with topolgangers of suffering and aid based on humanitarian logic now lying atop the terrain of the whole nation-state. These topolgangers, which appear not only in geographically isolated camps but now also in major cities where displaced people are fleeing, are pervaded by the effects of aid and by the existential predicament of the permanently temporary condition inherent to the humanitarian project. In Lebanon, where the government has banned refugee camps altogether, one in four residents—over a quarter of the population!—is a Syrian refugee, and there are refugees in nearly every city and town in the country (Abou Zeid 2014). Yet the Lebanese government has largely denied them the right to permanent residence and legal employment. One-third of the population of Jordan is now made up of refugees, many of whom are trying to eke out a living in Amman. Turkey, with 2.6 million refugees, has become the largest refugee-hosting country in the world, and over 2.4 million of them live in the country's major cities. Greece and Italy, the two major ports of entry for refugees in the European Union, saw over a million arrivals in 2015, many of whom have since become stuck in Athens and Rome. Wealthy donor nations, mostly the United States and Western European countries, have struck bargains with these countries in order to offshore refugees. Turkey, for example, received over $9 billion in aid in 2015–2016, much of it as part of a deal with Germany to prevent refugees from migrating in the European Union. Offshoring is thus not an escape from a camp, but the extension of the logic and practices of the camp to new terrains, including urban environments and the territory of the nation-state.

Humanitarian aid has also continued to fuel the rise of authoritarianism, just as it did in Georgia. In Turkey, where the European Union pledged to funnel more than $7 billion in aid if the Turkish government would assent to the EU's policy of containment and keep refugees on its territory rather than allowing them to move onward toward Greece, Prime Minister Recep Tayyip Erdogan has used aid much in the same way that Georgian President Mikheil Saakashvili did, becoming "openly and arrogantly autocratic, as if to show that he can flout European norms with impunity" (Economist 2015). In 2016 Erdogan countered a coup attempt by cracking down on his enemies, imprisoning thousands of military officers, academics, and journalists (Brown 2016). Devilry, in the form of profound illiberalism, has become part of the response to forced migration.

The systemic failure of humanitarian aid on such a large scale calls into question both the purpose of the aid system and the values that undergird it. According to UNHCR, the purpose of humanitarian aid is to protect displaced people. But it is increasingly obvious that the purpose of the strategies of encampment, offshoring, and containment that form the fundamental logic of the system are not just to protect the displaced but to protect donor countries from the displaced. The humanitarian system does have, at its center, the noble goal of providing a safe haven from violence, poverty, starvation, and death for the displaced people it serves. But overriding that goal and putting strong constraints on the way humanitarians can act is the more politically potent goal of containing the displaced, whether in their country of origin or in the nearby countries they have fled to, in the hopes of protecting wealthy donor countries from having a flood of displaced humanity washing up on its own shores. These two goals, protecting and protecting from, generate a heavy tension that pervades the humanitarian encounter. The point is not that humanitarian aid is corrupt (which is by and large not true) or that life in the humanitarian condition leads inexorably to poverty and despair. Rather, as I have argued in this book, the point is that life in the humanitarian condition is characterized by a tension between being and nothingness, living and just existing, subjectivity and abjectivity, that leaves displaced people stuck in limbo. What creates the "permanently temporary" character of life in the humanitarian condition is the constant interplay between displaced people's own drive to reconstitute a normal situation based on the particulars of place and institutionalized humanitarianism's tendency to create abstract space, to generate political and social chaos, and to create an experience for displaced people that aches of nothingness. The existentialist approach I've used here shows that it is the dialectical tension between the possibility of a degraded, emiserated existence and the hope of reestablishing full political and social life that creates a force field that traps the displaced, leaving them enduringly unsettled.

This is why, over the eight years I have worked on this book, I have steadily resisted the many calls from readers and people who have attended talks I have given based on this material to "point out aid programs that work" or "provide a solution." Sometimes these calls are requests for a happy ending, or at least some relief from the grim, grinding picture portrayed in this book. But more often, I think, they come from the combination of humanitarianism's internal call to do something, the "drive to fix" inherent in the logic of humanitarian action, coupled with the limits that the technocratic, institutionalized framework of the aid system puts not only on action but also on the imagination. When most observers of the humanitarian aid system, whether inside or outside the system, call for a "solution," they want a solution within the confines of the existing institutional structure. Often what they want is a silver bullet: a program like, say, microcredit to start small businesses, or debit cards for direct cash transfers to displaced people, or psychosocial aid that can be enacted within the framework of encampment. These are solutions meant to ameliorate the suffering of the displaced without fundamentally changing the ways that displaced people are held apart from society and prevented from socially reintegrating. But if this book has one central point, it is that the more carefully we look at these kinds of fixes, and the world that humanitarian action produces, the more the easy certainties of the benevolent donor disappear (see also Kraus 2014). Humanitarianism's dual drive to both protect and protect from makes the analysis of humanitarian action and humanitarian logic topsy-turvy: care is also violence, altruism is selfishness, local action becomes an aspect of macrogeopolitical strategy, and the genuine desire to make things better for suffering people can also show up as a weapon of war (see Bornstein and Redfield 2011, 249–53). The urge that drives us to donate $5 to the Red Cross with a click of a smartphone, or to send teddy bears to refugee children, or to buy a pair of shoes because the manufacturer promises to donate another pair, is suddenly compromised (Malkki 2015). So too is the thought of coming up with a better shelter for a camp, yet another program to create soccer leagues for refugee kids, or a community mobilization program for IDP women (see Dunn 2015). Are we really doing any good? Or are we doing harm without even knowing it? Opening the door to these questions is unsettling to anyone who, in good faith, seeks a morally clear path to repair the world.

The only answer that I can see is a fundamental restructuring of the way the international system deals with crises of displacement. Too often the question of "what is to be done" is still being asked at the wrong scale. Nearly every person who asks it assumes that the correct answer is to be found at the level of international aid agencies and NGOs. But the answer is—and must be—at the geopolitical level, because displacement is, in the first instance, a question of political will. To say that the problem is simply not to use forced migration as a tactic of war may seem unrealistically high-minded or hopelessly naive. But the first tenet of the Responsibility to Protect doctrine—the doctrine endorsed by both NATO member states and Russia—is the responsibility to prevent. The International Commission on Intervention and State Sovereignty, which authored R2P, argues that all sovereign states have the responsibility to address both "the root causes and direct causes of internal conflict and other man-made crises putting populations at risk." It continues, "Prevention is the single most important dimension of the responsibility to protect" (ICISS 2001, 13). However unrealistic it is to imagine it, the fact is that the only real solution for crises of displacement is for warring parties to avoid destroying civilian sites, to eschew ethnic cleansing, and to allow people on whatever side of the conflict free access to their homes when the war ends.

Once people are forcibly displaced, the goal of any form of humanitarian aid must be to allow people the ability to reemplace themselves as quickly as possible because this way can exit the limbo of protracted displacement and reestablish the normal situation. Solutions that focus on improving aid delivery to displaced people without focusing on reemplacement are, at best, Band-Aids. Changes like evening out the flow of money so that it does not come in large waves but rather arrives in a steady stream, having aid agencies establish long-term presences in countries with cyclical violence so that aid workers can better develop aid appropriate to the context in which it is distributed, or just keeping displaced people accurately informed of what aid projects would be coming up would make life in the humanitarian condition more bearable. But those tweaks to the system would not keep displaced people from being paralyzed in the long term by the aid that sustains them in the short term. Only granting people the freedom of place—the ability to attach to a place, to use it as the ground for employment, child-rearing, and other daily practices, and to use place as a stable ground for making meaning in a cosmological sense—will allow them to begin their lives again.

The first step in that direction is to eliminate the camp as an institution. Camps (and their urban equivalents, collective centers) are not designed to shelter displaced people or to become a base for restarting their lives. They are designed for the convenience of aid agencies, which have an easier time providing material aid when it can be trucked into a central location. More important, camps are designed for the convenience of host governments, who want to quarantine displaced people in order to keep them out of urban labor markets and to keep them in a situation where they are easy to mobilize and expel when it becomes politically advantageous to do so. Even in IDP situations where the displaced are citizens of the country, host governments have a strong incentive to keep displaced people concentrated together and easy to move. In 2011, for example, Georgia's first-wave IDPs were evicted from the "collective centers" they had been squatting in since 1992 and forcibly resettled in new collective centers in cities on the other side of the country, even though those cities had much higher unemployment rates (Gogidze and Ryan 2011). The IDPs, many of whom had jobs in Tbilisi, lost their livelihoods, social connections, and sense of home as they were forced to move onward. The point is to keep them permanently deportable: able to be moved at a moment's notice, whether simply to expel them or to move them to reclaimed territory. Keeping displaced people indefinitely unsettled is thus not a byproduct of the camp system, it is its entire purpose.

There is a better answer, both for displaced people and for the governments responsible for them: allowing displaced people to resettle themselves in a manner of their own choosing. This means allowing displaced people to choose for themselves where to go in the wake of war, providing them assistance in the places they go, and permitting them to enter the general population rather than keeping them in special, marked places. Residence permits, work permits, and full educational rights in the location where refugees or IDPs are resettling would be obvious parts of a reintegration package, and international donors could help support states in providing those benefits rather than outsourcing care to transient international aid agencies.[1] Providing vouchers to buy or rent housing instead of building shelters, giving out reloadable debit cards instead of making food deliveries, and providing assistance in registering for schools and finding jobs in new locations would make it possible for the displaced to move to locations of their own choosing. This would allow displaced people to leverage their own skills and resources to develop resettlement plans uniquely tailored to their own occupations, family needs, and social relationships. They can move closer to relatives, move to neighborhoods where they can find work, invest in children's educations, buy livestock to restart farms, or purchase equipment to restart careers in skilled trades. In an increasingly diversified global economy, humanitarian aid should be based on a principle of maximal choice. Delivering aid in a way that allows competent adults to make plans for their own lives and to truly resettle rather than being held in a situation of radical dependence is the surest path to a durable solution because it allows displaced people to better understand the logics of the systems they enter into and to remake their own worlds through their own labor and effort. These practices are quickly taking hold in the aid community (see, for example, Hurriyet 2012; UNHCR n.d.), which is contending with refugees who refuse the camps and self-settle in urban areas. But rather than seeing self-resettlement as a second-choice solution, it could become standard practice as a means of avoiding building camps in the first place.

Many host governments strongly resist the notion of self-resettlement for refugees and IDPs. Wealthy Western countries fear refugees will overwhelm them socially and economically. Countries closer to conflict areas fear that a large influx of displaced people will put upward pressure on housing prices and, since they are willing to work for low pay, will depress wage rates. But evidence from Turkey, where most of the displaced have settled outside camps, and Lebanon, which never permitted camps to be built at all, suggests that displaced people bring both short-term and long-term economic benefits to the places in which they self-resettle. In the early years of their displacement, humanitarian aid targeted at self-resettled refugees enters local markets rather than being contained in camps. Rather than having spending on food, housing, clothing, and other forms of humanitarian aid leave the country and go to international companies that sell these items in bulk to agencies that supply camps, self-resettlement allows aid dollars to flow to local merchants, farmers, and owners of rental housing via displaced people. In this situation displaced people are no longer an economic burden, but a valuable consumer market that can stimulate local economic growth (see Zetter 2012). In the long run, displaced people who can self-resettle transition from being just consumers to being productive members of the local economy. As evidence from Somali neighborhoods in Nairobi, Kenya, shows, displaced people can become small- and even large-scale business owners who provide significant economic gains to the places they resettle (Campbell 2006). As Western Europe, with its aging population and labor shortages, seeks a solution to the refugee crisis, it must consider ways to acknowledge not only the moral value of refugees' lives but also the economic and social value of a population allowed to work and flourish and contribute rather than being left in interminable stasis or forced into precarious underground labor.

Planning for local integration through self-settlement does not mean that displaced people or the governments that host them must give up hope that they will ever return. Rather, it is a form of concurrent planning, a concept that has

been successfully used for children in the US foster-care system (who are another kind of displaced person). Like refugees and IDPs, foster children used to be held in limbo for years, waiting to see if they could return to their homes. Deprived of a place to permanently resettle, foster children were placed in orphanages or left to drift from foster home to foster home, neither able to integrate into a new family or community via adoption nor able to permanently return to their families of origin. But since the 1980s the foster-care system has placed an enormous emphasis on the idea of concurrent planning, or planning for adoption/reintegration and for return home at the same time. Children are placed in homes that can adopt them if their parents' rights are terminated; they know from the very beginning that they will be with either one family or the other rather than being left to linger for years in temporary foster homes or in orphanages. Research shows that concurrent planning reduces psychological distress, improves educational outcomes, and in the long term helps foster children avoid negative life events such as teenage pregnancy or incarceration. Having the stability of a place to call home, a place to emotionally attach to and create meaning within, a place within which to rebuild a normal situation, keeps foster children from facing the corrosive effects of being chronically unsettled.

Likewise, pursuing a strategy of concurrent planning for displaced people, in which they are allowed to immediately self-resettle while, at the same time, holding out the hope of returning to their homes, will avoid the most destructive, corrosive aspect of forced migration, which is not eviction but being held in an excruciating permanently temporary condition, always waiting for something to change. This, in the words of many of the IDPs I knew in Georgia, is "just existing," not really "living." Giving up the camp and permitting self-resettlement would mean giving up the fiction that displacement is a temporary condition and would do away with protracted displacement by making reintegration, not repatriation, the durable solution of first resort.

Most important, self-resettlement would allow displaced people to begin the process of emplacement and the spatial reorganization of their economic, political, and spiritual lives. Emplacement is the key means through which displaced people can reestablish a normal situation and begin to really live in their new environments rather than just existing or staying alive in the hope that they can restart their lives after return.[2] The right to settle is about the human right to space and time. It is, fundamentally, the right to attach to place in ways that order the world and make it reasonably stable, comprehensible, and actionable. But it also about the right to temporality, the right to exit the purgatory of displacement and the right to think about and plan for a future. Displaced people, too often deprived of the right to settlement and to permanence, deserve not only freedom from war and death but also from the chaos, nothingness, pressure, and bedevilment of life in the humanitarian condition. This is, more than anything else, a moral claim. But in a world beset with security crises, xenophobic nationalisms, religious fundamentalisms, and other existential threats to a peaceful world order, it is also a practical claim: a claim that by acknowledging the right to place we offer one another the possibility to live, to build, and to grow rather than to merely exist in the rubble of conflict.

Acknowledgments

Books are linked to single authors, but the truth is that every book is a collective project and comes out of the work and ideas of many people. This book is a case in point: it could not have existed without the help, support, collaboration, and brilliance of the people around me.

My greatest debt goes to the people transformed into internally displaced persons (IDPs) by the 2008 Russo-Georgian War. Because political changes in Georgia are wildly unpredictable and because the consequences of talking with an American anthropologist are unknowable, I have avoided using the real names of any person with IDP status. They will of course recognize themselves, but I hope I have concealed the details enough to protect their privacy. I am deeply grateful to the residents of Tsmindatsqali, Khurvaleti, and Skra, and in particular to the people from Ksuisi and Disevi, who welcomed me to their weddings and funerals and supras as well as including me in their everyday lives. Special thanks go to my research assistant, Olga Zoziashvili, and her family, and to my friends Maia, Mzia, Etera, Tamuna, Gela, Inga, and Nona, who taught me about Georgian history and IDP life.

In Georgia I was supported by a wonderful and warm community in both Tbilisi and Gori. My deepest gratitude goes to Tamuna Robakidze, a dear friend whose life was as beautiful as it was short. She took care of my son and I, taught us both Georgian, and loved us as if we were her own family. I am also grateful to Tamriko Razmadze, Manana Robakidze, Pridon Kiria and Lia Kapanadze, Beppe Karlsson, Louise Bermsjo, Daniel McBrayer, Temo Sabashvili, George Welton, Timothy Blauvelt, Hans Gutbrod, Till Bruckner, Davit Toklikishvili, Tamuna Karosanidze, and the people at Transparency International. In the world of humanitarian NGOs I am indebted to the straightforwardness and insightfulness of Christoph Bierworth, Nino Shushania, Jonathan Puddifoot, and Tea Korzadze. For ideas and intellectual companionship, I thank Ketevan Khutsishvili, Lika Tsuladze, Erin Koch, and especially Veta Lazarashvili, who helped concoct many of the ideas in chapter 5. Beth Mitchneck, Joanna Regulska, and Peter Kabachnik were extraordinarily generous in sharing their data and insights about IDPs in Georgia. Ramaz Kurdadze spent endless hours teaching me the notoriously difficult grammar of the Georgian language. I am especially indebted to Hannah Mintek, whose haunting and elegiac photographs grace this book. Her artist's eye is only equalled by her moxie.

In the United States I have been fortunate to have magnanimous colleagues and friends. At the University of Colorado at Boulder, I would like to thank Emily Yeh, Tim Oakes, Najeeb Jan, Joe Bryan, and Caitlin Ryan, who all read portions of the manuscript. Austin Cowley was a valiant research assistant at home and in Georgia. At Indiana University I thank Dan Knudsen, Rebecca Lave, Ryan Wyeth, Seraphima Mixon, Olga Kalentzidou, Joanna Niżyńska, Padraic Kenney, Sara Friedman, Laura Plummer, and Ilana Gershon. I am grateful to Martin Demant Frederiksen and Katrine Gotfredsen for collegiality and uninterrupted time in Copenhagen to think about nothingness. I am particularly grateful to Jason Cons, who read the whole manuscript and gave both hard truths and valuable encouragement. Other important colleagues include Yael Navaro, Bruce Grant, Gaston Gordillo, and Jeffrey Mantz. Maggie Boys offered valuable help in editing. Martha Lampland kept me going when I lost my voice, both literally and figuratively, after fieldwork. Roger Haydon, my editor at Cornell University Press, reminded me that my own voice was worth writing in. His support has made all the difference.

This book was written with the generous support of the Fulbright Commission, the International Research and Exchanges Board, Indiana University, and the University of Copenhagen. The drastic cuts in funding to these institutions means it will be harder and harder to conduct research on the former Soviet Union. I hope this book will convince readers that the work they fund is important and worth support.

Without Bryan Dunn, Barbara Miller, and George Miller, there is no way this book could have been written. You all reminded me that love and life go on, even in the face of great hardship. I am also grateful to Sally Purath. Jane Stout cheered me on in the last push to finish. Thank you for the examples you set for finding joy in living—my gratitude can never be as huge as all you've given me, but I'm going to try.

The person who was the absolutely most important in the writing of this book was my son, Aaron Dunn, who was five years old when I brought him to Georgia. He learned another language, went to his first year of school in Tbilisi, and taught me to eat khinkali without spilling any soup on the plate. When the other moms in Colorado asked me what kind of camp Aaron was going to for the summer, and I answered "refugee camp," he took it right in stride. For his adventurous spirit, dry sense of humor, loving heart, and incredible curiosity, this book is dedicated to him.

Notes

CHAPTER 1. THE CAMP AND THE CAMP

1. I also benefited enormously from the work of my student and colleague, Austin Cowley, who spent the summer of 2012 in Khurvaleti.

2. Strictly speaking, under the Responsibility to Protect (R2P), states are only obliged to prevent atrocities such as genocide or ethnic cleansing. As Pandolfi (2003) argues, however, R2P has taken on an expansive sense, in which any state that is deemed by Western donor nations as having failed to "properly" care for the citizenry may find Western development and humanitarian aid agencies taking over functions that were formerly the purview of the nation-state.

3. With the help of two IDP research assistants and the anthropologist Veta Lazarashvili, I later conducted an additional forty formal interviews with IDPs using Q-sort, a formal interview method that asks respondents to rank statements on a Likert scale and to discuss their rationales for agreeing or disagreeing with the statements. These interviews were transcribed, translated, and formally coded to give a statistically validated picture of the physical, political, and social problems the IDPs themselves found most difficult.

CHAPTER 2. WAR

This chapter was written with invaluable research assistance from Ryan Wyeth and Seraphima Mixon. I am grateful to both of them.

1. I thank Adam Levy for this image.

2. If the name Machabeli rings familiar to Americans, it is because of Prince Georges Matchabelli, a member of the Georgian noble family who emigrated to the United States in 1921 and became a perfumer. His fragrances were later acquired by the Vicks Chemical Company and widely distributed—so much so that in the fall of 1954 General Motors gave away over a million bottles of Prince Matchabelli perfume to promote the 1955 Chevrolet models (Kimes and Ackerson 1987, 114). In the 1970s a Prince Matchabelli fragrance, Charlie, was promoted as the signature perfume of the feminist movement.

3. Svanetia and Abkhazia were not joined to the *guberniya* of Georgia until much later—1858 and 1864, respectively (Tsereteli 2014, 77).

4. Today roughly 90% of South Ossetians are Orthodox Christians, while 10% remain Muslim. In North Ossetia only about half the population is Christian, with the remainder practicing Islam or an indigenous Ossetian religion.

5. Welt (2014, 224), using documents published in the 1950s and 1960s, offers the figure of twenty thousand. Saparov (2015, 70), working from a 1933 document, puts the figure at thirty-five thousand.

6. Rayfield argues that Gamsakhurdia was shot in the back of the neck by Russian special forces operating at the behest of Shevardnadze.

7. There are disputes about when exactly the war started: on August 7 or August 8. Because those dates are linked to questions about who shot first and therefore who bears moral responsibility for the war, and because I do not know the truth, I say merely "early August" here.

INTERTEXT ONE. THE NORMAL SITUATION

1. I was not in the kindergartens and other temporary shelters in the three months immediately following the war, where perhaps IDPs discussed the events of the war in more detail.

2. For Badiou, only mathematics expresses pure ontology (Meillassoux 2011, 1). So the first violence I do to Badiou is to introduce human action into pure ontology. When I say "we" structure the inherent multiplicity of the world into the count-as-one, I'm already introducing an actor that Badiou does not.

3. By focusing on Badiou's ontology, I deliberately set aside the current vogue for object-oriented ontology (OOO), which asks about the liveliness of animals, objects, and ecologies that surpasses their relationship with human beings (see, for example, Kohn 2013). For the existentialist questions of meaning and action that concern me here, human-oriented ontology seems sufficient. But for a discussion of the independent lives of material objects and their relations to war and displacement, see Navaro-Yashin (2012).

4. It is hard to tell if the main characters are fictional or real in novels so heavily premised on autobiography.

CHAPTER 3. CHAOS

1. See, for example, *National Geographic Adventure* magazine's profile of its "adventurer of the year," Ashley Jonathan Clements, a humanitarian aid worker the magazine dubbed "Dynamo in the Disaster Zone." Clements, a twenty-seven-year-old worker for World Vision, was lauded for shuttling "into emerging disaster zones, often ahead of other humanitarian groups and mainstream press, to scout situations, drum up global support with photos and video, and get aid flowing in the right directions. Then he rolls up his shirtsleeves." Among other feats, Clements flew to Georgia in the wake of the 2008 war, touching down "before the bullets stopped flying, to assist the 80,000 [*sic*!] or so Ossetian and Georgian refugees who had fled to Tbilisi. There he prepped them for winter, handing out blankets and helping to establish cooking facilities, which delivered food to some 25,000 people" (Pollock 2008).

2. Two more settlements were added after 2009.

3. Families with fewer than three members were not assigned cottages but moved into apartments created from renovated schools or military barracks. This led some families to split their children up and place them with grandparents in the hope of getting an additional cottage—a practice that often led to the fracturing of the extended families at the heart of the Georgian kinship system and the long-term separation of parents and children.

4. The word "system" as applied to humanitarianism perhaps implies structure and rationality that isn't there. As Weiss (2013, 96) writes of humanitarian agencies, "Indeed, 'system' is a misnomer unless the adjective 'feudal' accompanies it. Each organization within the business ferociously guards its independence."

CHAPTER 4. NOTHING

1. Although, of course, they often give less than they claim to, and do things that are not very useful—see Sullivan 2015 for an example from Haiti.

2. In fact most of the pasta given out by the WFP was purchased in Turkey, but none of the IDPs I interviewed could identify its place of origin.

3. I thank Maggie Boys for this framing.

4. Because of its proximity to Gori, the regional center, residents of Tsmindatsqali had an easier time getting government jobs. My informal survey estimated that by 2011 about 70% of the adult residents lacked waged work. But in the outlying settlements the

situation was dire: an employee of the municipal government estimated for me that more than 90% of residents lacked paid work.

5. This information comes from a CARE International Internal document entitled "MSA (Monitoring, Study and Analysis) Report Draft," which analyzes the effectiveness of the Enhancing Rural Livelihoods in the Adjacent Area project and the Job Creation through Enhancing Small-Sized Enterprise Development project.

6. Some of these funded organizations did endure: kiosks, a restaurant that served the hot, cheesy bread called *khachapuri*, and a paper plant in Tserovani settlement, for example. But these businesses were not, on the whole, very visible, and outside Tserovani, the camp closest to Tbilisi, I rarely saw any in operation (see also Nikuradze 2014).

7. Ronald Asmus (2010) confirms some of these rumors. He calls Saakashvili a "notorious night owl," and describes how important political decisions were made after midnight at *supras* (ritual banquets) held with political officials, see also T. de Waal 2010, 196).

8. The IDPs' suspicions were confirmed after 2012 when Saakashvili was forced out of power by his rival Bidzina Ivanishvili. After the change of government, key officials from the Saakashvili government, including the minister of the interior Vano Merabishvili and the minister of health Zurab Chiaberashvili, were convicted of using their offices to steal money from the budget in order to buy votes and to run Ponzi schemes (see Vartanyan 2014).

9. In Anthony Marra's novel *A Constellation of Vital Phenomena* (2013), a displaced six-year-old Chechen girl puts it perfectly. She announces, "I'm still a minimalist." "Do you know what that is?" asks an adult. "It's a nicer way to say you have nothing," she answers.

INTERTEXT 2. VOID

1. That is, in the space of appearance. But as I mentioned in Intertext 1, I don't think there's any use in separating "pure being" from a "space of appearance," so for those of us who are interested in the application of philosophy to concrete cases, what is represented is always represented in a concrete time and place.

CHAPTER 5. PRESSURE

The research for this chapter was done with the kind help of Veta Lazarashvili, a Georgian medical anthropologist who has worked extensively on public health issues among displaced people. I also benefited from the help of my research assistants, Olga Zosiashvili and Tamuna Shoshitashvili.

1. I have to signal three significant exceptions to this general principle in Georgia. The German aid agency Gesellschaft Für Zusammenarbeit (GTZ) resisted the government's politically driven push to get IDPs housed immediately, and instead took more than a year to build a settlement that looked more like an American suburb than like a refugee camp. It had winding streets, trees, even a church, and was so well built that people could live there for decades. The World Food Programme, along with the Georgian Ministry of Agriculture, handed out tools and seeds for people to plant crops, but unfortunately both were of such low quality that they were not used for long. The most helpful NGO of them all was Heifer International, which contracted with the French agency Première Urgence Internationale to give out livestock. There were no expensive needs-assessment surveys, no endless training programs, and no paperwork: IDPs were simply asked if they preferred bees, chickens, or a goat. This small program made some of the biggest economic differences in the camps.

2. Some of the Georgian casualties were apparently caused by the Georgian Army, which used Israeli cluster bombs that failed to hit their targets and instead fell on Georgian villages (Schwirtz 2008).

3. I want to acknowledge here the skilled leadership and enormous personal care for the IDP community shown by Christoph Bierwirth, the Senior Protection Officer at UNHCR Georgia. More than anyone else in the aid community, Bierwirth understood the problem of humanitarian abandonment and tried, with an increasingly limited budget, to assist the IDPs during the period in which aid was tapering off and other NGOs were leaving. He had a sophisticated understanding of what the Georgian government was likely to do for the IDPs—I relied on him for much of my own understanding of the situation—and was himself worried about what would happen to them in the long run.

4. Of course, as discussed in chapter 2, the Russians did not fully retreat behind the borders of South Ossetia. They remained in Akhalgori region, which had never historically been attached to South Ossetia but which was strategically important territory for gaining access to the East-West highway that bisected Georgia.

5. The establishment of the South Ossetian administrative boundary line as an international border proceeded even more intensely in 2012 and 2013 when Russian forces established smaller bases at Eredvi and Disevi, two villages that had been ethnically cleansed, installed permanent snipers' nests along the boundary, and began putting up fences to block roads and footpaths. They also installed Smersh multiple-rocket launching systems, which, since they could fire 70–90 kilometers, were within range of Tbilisi. See UNHCR 2013.

6. Unemployment in Khurvaleti was reduced in 2013 when IDPs there were hired as field hands by a Turkish company who had purchased nearby agricultural lands. This was an interesting reversal of traditional migrant labor in agriculture: usually people escaping poverty and violence travel to the fields to engage in backbreaking low-wage work (see, e.g., Holmes 2013). Here because the IDPs were spatially blocked, migrant capital and thus the fields themselves came to them.

7. For example, CARE International's SIIMS program was offered in settlements in the province of Shida Kartli, but not in any of the settlements inside neighboring Mtskheta-Mtiani, which was deemed to be the responsibility of a different agency.

8. Another woman, who had been splashed by boiling water and had severe burns, scoffed at the notion that she should go to the doctor. "Why go to the doctor when you can't afford the medicine?" she said, instead covering her burns in a mixture of greasy cream and toothpaste.

9. Convulex is valproic acid, an anticonvulsant sold in the United States under the trade name Depakote. A typical child's dose, 125 mg per day, costs about USD $50 per month for the generic version.

10. The Kapanadzes' grandson spent almost a year on Convulex, which left him drugged and too groggy to develop movement or language normally. According to Dr. Tracey Wilkinson, a pediatrician at Indiana University Health, Convulex is not ordinarily prescribed for hydrocephaly. Worse, it turned out that the child did not even have hydrocephaly. Why the drug was prescribed to him remains a mystery to me, but it caused him significant developmental delays.

11. I owe this explanation of the compound effects of poor diet and stress on the body to the anthropologist and physician Timothy McCajor Hall, MD.

12. The strong boundary that humanitarians draw between war-related deaths and those seen as "natural" was driven home to me at a conference I attended at the Tbilisi Marriott on "New Directions in the IDP Action Plan" in June 2010, which was sponsored by the Ministry for Refugees and Accommodation and attended by many of the NGOs focused on aid to IDPs. In a panel on IDP health where I presented, I was told by a representative of UNICEF that hypertension and diabetes were "not war related" and "not related to IDP status," and so not within the purview of projects focusing on IDPs.

CHAPTER 6. THE DEVIL AND THE AUTHORITARIAN STATE

1. Manning (2015) points out that all manner of beings haunt rural Georgia: among others, there is the *kaji*, or goblin, which infests people's roofs, breaks into their houses, throws things at them, and steals their belongings; the *devi*, a multiheaded horned ogre; the *ali*, a dangerous and seductive succubus; and the *chinka*, a small childlike mischievous spirit.

2. About 10% of ethnic Ossetians in South Ossetia consider themselves Muslim.

3. The anthropologist Ketevan Gurchiani confirmed for me that this is also specifically true in Georgian Orthodoxy. I am grateful for her assistance.

4. See, for example, papers on Korea, Nigeria, Haiti, and the United States in Sanders and West 2003. The pervasiveness of conspiracy theories among right-wing activists in the United States, of course, is also an example.

5. I am grateful to Paul Manning for bringing this to my attention.

6. For more on conspiracy theories in Georgia, see Pelkmans 2006: 186–93.

7. The agency's complete name is Sakartvelos Erovnuli Ushishroebis Sabcho, or the Georgian National Security Council, but it is commonly referred to as Ushishroeba, or "security."

8. The apartment I rented in Tbilisi in 2009 was, coincidentally, directly underneath Molashvili's apartment. We lived there when he returned from prison and heard about his political travails from the neighbors. When his son was arrested we heard about it directly from the Molashvilis, who blasted the television until 4 or 5 am and shouted at one another at such volume that we heard their conversations quite clearly through our ceiling.

INTERTEXT 3. THE STATE AND THE STATE

1. Johnson, paraphrasing Eduard Bernstein, writes, "The danger of a 'truly miraculous belief in the creative power of force' . . . is that you begin by doing violence to reality in theory, and end by doing violence to people in practice. What distinguishes the new communism is that its leading partisans are fully aware of that potential . . . *and embrace it as a strategy* (Johnson 2012).

CHAPTER 7. DEATH

1. I thank Maggie Boys for this phrasing.

2. The exception to the general rule of run-down village poverty appears to be the village of Kurta, about 9 kilometers northeast of Tskhinvali, which became the site of the Provisional Administration of South Ossetia, an alternative government sponsored by the Georgian state. Under Saakashvili, the Georgian government invested more than 1.8 million Georgian lari (about USD $900,000) in major infrastructural improvements, including expensive renovations of a hospital and a cinema and the installation of a bank branch complete with what was then a novelty in South Ossetia, an ATM machine.

3. Rebecca Gould (personal communication) points out that Chechens returning to Chechnya after displacement in Kazakhstan and Kyrgyzstan did much the same thing, disinterring the bones of their dead from the Eurasian steppe and bringing them back to the Caucasus so that they would be buried in their proper place.

4. One of my most important ties to the IDPs at Tsmindatsqali was forged as money was collected for the funeral. Since the amounts given by each person were being recorded and publicly discussed, I didn't want to give an inappropriately large sum. After all, this was a mutual insurance scheme in which villagers paid for each other's' burials by giving at one family's funeral and then later expecting a return contribution from the beneficiaries at a subsequent funeral in the donor's family. As the only foreigner in attendance,

with no family around me, I was obviously not participating in mutual insurance, which would transform my contribution into a gift that could not be reciprocated. To avoid this awkwardness, and yet to still contribute, what I did was pay for the contributions of Maia Abaeva and two other IDPs. The fact that I gave a large sum was duly noted—as was the fact that I saved face for the people whose donations I financed. The result was an enduring closeness with Anzor Kapanadze's family, for which I am incredibly grateful.

5. This is a bare-bones list of the usual toasts given at a *supra*. Many more toasts can be added, and the order can be varied by event (e.g., the order is different at a wedding than at a birthday). There is also some regional variation in the order and number of toasts.

6. The Georgian word *gardatsvaleba* uses the root word *tsvla*, to transform, and the prefix *garda*, which refers to moving across or transgressing boundaries. Death is thus a "transformation of the state of life" in which the soul is liberated from the body rather than the end of life. I thank Nutsa Batiashvili and Maya Razmadze for their help with the nuances of this term.

7. I owe the idea of the link between regenerative cycles and cosmological order to Georgina Ramsay.

8. Although it had been rumored that the Russians would open the border for that one day so that the IDPs could visit their village graves, the military situation remained unresolved and the IDPs had to content themselves with the spatial reconstructions offered by the topolgangers they had built.

9. Much of the money for building Tserovani was ostensibly paid for by the Georgian government's Municipal Development Fund, but this was largely money from international donors that had been routed through the national budget.

10. The video was produced by the Danish NGO MyMedia, which supports local journalists in seven countries including Georgia. The author of the video is not named, and the intended audience, given that it is titled in English but full of uncaptioned and untranslated Georgian speech, is unclear. The video is at https://www.youtube.com/watch?t=75&v=6P9vCGYjpLY.

11. The situation of Akhalgori was more complicated than for the rest of Russian-occupied territory. Akhalgori is not in South Ossetia, but was occupied by the Russian Army because the region provided strategic military access to Tbilisi, the capital city. Unlike IDPs from South Ossetia, who were prohibited from returning, IDPs from Akhalgori, who were mainly in Tserovani and Prezeti, were allowed to cross the administrative boundary line and move back and forth from the camps to their lands in Akhalgori.

12. As the speaker of the Georgian parliament, Davit Usupashvili, said, "Membership Action Plan—this magical word MAP—for many, many Georgians means much more than it really is, because it has become a symbol of answering on a question: 'Does free world need Georgia or not? Does free world keep its promise that Georgia will become a NATO member or not?'" (quoted in Civil Georgia 2014).

INTERTEXT 4. BRIGHT OBJECTS

1. That is, Badiou turns his attention away from pure ontology to a much more complicated and messy phenomenology, one that places the forces of entropy and stability, rather than "truth," at the heart of his philosophy.

2. As I mentioned in the first meditation, Badiou's distinction between ontology and phenomenology, or between the realm of pure being and the world as we live in it, seems of little use to me. For Badiou the distinction is important because it changes the language in which he can think about the metastructure of existence. He argues that while the metastructure that links abstract elements together in the realm of pure being, which he calls the "state of the situation," can only be expressed through mathematics (particularly set theory), the metastructures of everyday life, which he calls "logics of worlds,"

can be expressed in terms of mapped relations among specific things. If that is clear as mud, take heart: drawing a clear difference between being-itself and being-in-the-world is not essential to understanding what Badiou is getting at. The important point is that making a functioning world—or a "sense of a meaningful universe in which people act" (Verdery 1999, 34)—requires the formulation of a structured network of things linked to one another in semantically or functionally meaningful ways.

3. Here I part company with Bryant, who argues that worlds are not localizable because they always exceed individual subjectivities (Bryant 2014, 112).

CHAPTER 8. ALL THAT REMAINS

1. This approach is not new: The European Union, for example, pushed Turkey to give work permits to Syrian refugees in 2016 as a means of preventing their onward trek to Europe (Gurses and Ozcan 2016). But it should be widespread, and it should happen early in the resettlement process rather than forcing displaced people to wait for years before being able to seek legal employment and neighborhood, not camp, housing.

2. Members of the Georgian government or the international aid community in Georgia would argue that the Georgian government did in fact plan on the displacement of the people from South Ossetia being permanent. The reason that the government built cinderblock houses in the new settlements—and in fact called them settlements rather than camps—was that there was little expectation of return. And yet the very fact that the new settlements were placed along the border, largely devoid of churches and schools and other infrastructure (with the exception of Tserovani), and designed to group the IDPs together rather than allowing them to blend into already existing villages or cities was because the government held some hope that they could return and wanted to keep them easy to mobilize.

References

Abou Zeid, Mario. 2014. "A Time Bomb in Lebanon: The Syrian Refugee Crisis." http://carnegie-mec.org/diwan/56857.

Abrams, Phillip. 1988. "Notes on the Difficulty of Studying the State." *Journal of Historical Sociology* 1, no. 1: 58–89.

Agamben, Giorgio. 1994. "We Refugees." *Symposium* 49, no. 2: 114–19.

——. 1998. *Homo Sacer: Sovereign Power and Bare Life*. Palo Alto, CA: Stanford University Press.

——. 2000. *Means without End*. Minneapolis: University of Minnesota Press.

——. 2002. *Remnants of Auschwitz: The Witness and the Archive*. New York: Zone Books.

Agier, Michel. 2002. "Between War and City: Towards an Urban Anthropology of Refugee Camps." *Ethnography* 3, no. 3: 317–41.

——. 2010. "Humanity as an Identity and Its Political Effects: A Note on Camps and Humanitarian Government." *Humanity* 1, no. 1: 29–46.

——. 2011. *Managing the Undesirables: Refugee Camps and Humanitarian Government*. London: Polity.

——. 2015. "What Camps Tell Us about the World to Come." *Humanity* 7, no. 3: 459–68.

Allison, Anne. 1991. "Japanese Mothers and Obentos: The Lunchbox as Ideological State Apparatus." *Anthropological Quarterly* 64, no. 4: 195–208.

——. 2013. *Precarious Japan*. Durham, NC: Duke University Press.

Althusser, Louis. 1971. *Ideology and State Apparatuses*. New York: Monthly Review Press.

Aly, Heba. 2016. "Q&A: 'UN Doesn't Have to Change,' says UN Relief Chief." http://bit.ly/1XKGtCe.

American Friends of Georgia. 2010. "Life after War: AFG Visits a Border Village Caught in the South Ossetian Conflict." www.afgeorgia.org/life-after-war/.

Antidze, Margarita. 2008. "Georgian Army Replaces Kalashnikov with US Rifle." *Reuters*. http://www.reuters.com/article/2008/01/18/us-georgia-army-idUSANT847080 20080118.

Aptsiauri, Goga. 2013. "Georgian Villagers Irate as Fence Goes up on South Ossetia Boundary." http://www.rferl.mobi/a/georgia-russia-ossetia/25131531.html.

Arendt, Hannah. 1943. "We Refugees." *Menorah Journal* 31: 69–77.

——. 1951. *The Origins of Totalitarianism*. New York: Harcourt Brace Jovanovich.

Asheville Global Review. 2005. "Interview with Alain Badiou." www.lacan.com/badash.html.

Asmus, Ronald. 2010. *The Little War That Shook the World: Georgia, Russia and the Future of the West*. New York: Palgrave MacMillan.

Bachelard, Gaston. 1958 (1994). *The Poetics of Space*. New York: Beacon.

Badiou, Alain. 2002. *Ethics: An Essay on the Understanding of Evil*. London: Verso.

——. 2003. *St. Paul: The Foundation of Universalism*. Stanford, CA: Stanford University Press.

——. 2006. *Being and Event*. London: Continuum.

——. 2009. *Logics of Worlds*. New York: Continuum.

Bahrampour, Tara. 2008. "An Uncertain Death Toll in Georgia-Russia War." *The Washington Post*, August 25. http://articles.washingtonpost.com/2008-08-25/world/36858240_1_georgians-ossetian-officials-tskinvali.

Barnett, Michael. 2010. *The International Humanitarian Order*. London: Routledge.
——. 2011. *Empire of Humanity: A History of Humanitarianism*. Ithaca, NY: Cornell University Press.
Barnett, Michael, and Thomas Weiss, eds. 2008. *Humanitarianism in Question: Politics, Power, Ethics*. Ithaca: Cornell University Press.
——. 2008. "Humanitarianism: A Brief History of the Present." In Barnett and Weiss, *Humanitarianism in Question*, 1–48.
Barry, Ellen. 2008. "Soviet Union's Fall Unraveled Enclave in Georgia." *New York Times*, September 7, A6. http://www.nytimes.com/2008/09/07/world/europe/07alborova. html?_r=0.
——. 2009. "Georgia Challenges Report That Says It Shot First." *New York Times*, October 1. http://www.nytimes.com/2009/10/01/world/europe/01russia.html?_r=0.
——. 2010. "Georgia Holds 13, Saying They Spied for Russia." *New York Times*, November 6, p. A8. http://www.nytimes.com/2010/11/06/world/europe/06georgia. html?_r=0.
——. 2011. "Out of a Swelter Come Apocalyptic Visions." *New York Times*, August 2, A8. http://www.nytimes.com/2011/08/03/world/europe/03plagues.html.
——. 2012. "On Black Sea Swamp, Big Plans for Instant City." *New York Times*, April 22. http://www.nytimes.com/2012/04/22/world/europe/in-georgia-plans-for-an-instant-city.html.
Bauman, Zygmunt. 2004. *Wasted Lives: Modernity and Its Outcasts*. New York: Polity.
BBC. 2008. "South Ossetia Evacuates Children." http://news.bbc.co.uk/2/hi/europe/7539282.stm.
——. 2009. "Q & A: Georgia Conflict a Year On." news.bbc.co.uk/2/hi/europe/8186356. stm.
——. 2015. "Migrant Crisis: Migration to Europe Explained in Graphics." http://www. bbc.com/news/world-europe-34131911.
Bedwell, Helena. 2008. "Russia, Georgia Begin War Games as Tensions Escalate." http:// www.bloomberg.com/apps/news?pid=newsarchive&sid=a.mv7C.Q97s4.
Benhabib, Seyla. 2004. *Negotiating Republican Self-Determination and Cosmopolitan Norms*. Berkeley: University of California Press. http://tannerlectures.utah.edu/_ documents/a-to-z/b/benhabib_2005.pdf.
Benton, Lauren. 2009. *A Search for Sovereignty: Law and Geography in European Empires, 1400–1900*. Cambridge: Cambridge University Press.
Berlant, Lauren. 2011. *Cruel Optimism*. Chapel Hill, NC: Duke University Press.
Betts, Alexander 2016. *Refugee Economies: Forced Displacement and Development*. Cambridge: Cambridge University Press.
Beyer, Judith. 2006. "Revitalisation, Invention and Continued Existence of Kyrgyz Aksakal Courts: Listening to Pluralistic Accounts of History." *Journal of Legal Pluralism and Unofficial Law* 38, nos. 53–54: 141–76.
——. 2014. "'There Is This Law': Performing the State in the Kyrgyz Court of Elders." In *Ethnographies of the State in Central Asia: Performing Politics*, edited by Madeleine Reeves, Johan Rasanayagam, and Judith Beyer, 99–124. Bloomington: Indiana University Press.
Biehl, Joao, Byron Good, and Arthur Kleinman. 2007. "Introduction: Rethinking Subjectivity." In *Subjectivity: Ethnographic Investigations*, edited by Joao Biehl, Byron Good, and Arthur Kleinman, 1–24. Berkeley: University of California Press.
Boltanski, Luc. 1993. *Distant Suffering: Morality, Media and Politics*. Cambridge: Cambridge University Press.
Bonner, Elena. 1995. Nationalism, Ethnic Strife and Human Rights. *John Marshall Law Review* 28: 769–74.

Borenstein, David. 2007. *How to Change the World: Social Entrepreneurs and the Power of New Ideas.* London: Oxford University Press.

Borenstein, Eliot. 2014a. *Conspiracy as Information.* Washington, DC: Council for European Studies.

———. 2014b. "Why Conspiracy Theories Take Hold in Russia." *The World Post.* www.huffingtonpost.com/eliot-borenstein/why-conspiracy-theories_b_5626149.html.

Bornstein, Erica. 2001. "Child Sponsorship, Evangelism and Belonging in the Work of World Vision Zimbabwe." *American Ethnologist* 28, no. 3: 595–622.

———. 2012. *Disquieting Gifts: Humanitarianism in New Delhi.* Stanford, CA: Stanford University Press.

Bornstein, Erica, and Peter Redfield, eds. 2011. *Forces of Compassion: Humanitarianism between Ethics and Politics.* Santa Fe, NM: SAR Press.

———. 2011a. "Afterward: Humanitarianism and the Scale of Disaster." In Bornstein and Redfield, *Forces of Compassion,* 249–53.

———. 2011b. "An Introduction to the Anthropology of Humanitarianism." In Bornstein and Redfield, *Forces of Compassion,* 3–30.

Böröcz, József. 2000. "Informality Rules." *Eastern European Politics and Societies* 14, no. 2: 348–80.

Bosteels, Bruno. 2011. *Badiou and Politics.* Durham, NC: Duke University Press.

Bracken, Patrick. 2002. *Trauma: Culture, Meaning and Philosophy.* London: Whurr Publishers.

Brookings Institution. 2010. *IASC Framework for Durable Solutions for Internally Displaced Persons.* Washington, DC: Brookings Institution. http://www.brookings.edu/reports/2010/0305_internal_displacement.aspx.

———. 2011. *From Responsibility to Response: Assessing National Approaches to Internal Displacement.* Washington, DC: Brookings Institution. http://www.brookings.edu/reports/2011/11_responsibility_response_ferris.aspx.

Brown, Matthew. 2016. "Hundreds Are Being Arrested as Turkey's Erdogan Cracks Down on Journalists, Academics." http://ab.co/1ROBPJb.

Bruckner, Pascal. 1986. *The Tears of the White Man: Compassion as Contempt.* New York: The Free Press.

Bryant, Levi. 2014. *Onto-Cartography: An Ontology of Machines and Media.* Edinburgh: Edinburgh University Press.

Bukkvoll, Tor. 2009. "Russia's Military Performance in Georgia." *Military Review* (November–December): 57–62.

Burbank, Jane. 2006. "An Imperial Rights Regime: Law and Citizenship in the Russian Empire." *Kritika: Explorations in Russian and Eurasian History* 7, no. 3: 397–431.

Butler, Judith, and Gayatri Spivak. 2010. *Who Sings the Nation-State?* London: Seagull Books.

Byron, Michael. 2005. "Simon's Revenge, or Incommensurability and Satisficing." *Analysis* 65, no. 4: 311–15.

Calhoun, Craig. 2008. "The Imperative to Reduce Suffering: Charity, Progress and Emergencies in the Field of Humanitarian Action." In Barnett and Weiss, *Humanitarianism in Question,* 73–98.

———. 2010. "The Idea of Emergency: Humanitarian Action and Global (Dis)Order." In Fassin and Pandolfi, *Contemporary States of Emergency,* 29–58.

Campbell, Elizabeth H. 2006. "Urban Refugees in Nairobi: Problems of Protection, Mechanisms of Survival, and Possibilities for Integration." *Journal of Refugee Studies* 19, no. 3: 396–413.

CARE International. 2009. "Making a Difference: Annual Report 2009." http://98.139.
236.92/search/srpcache?p=CARE+international+making+a+difference+annual+
report+2009&ei=UTF-8&hspart=mozilla&hsimp=yhs-002&fr=yhs-mozilla-002&
u=http://webcache.googleusercontent.com/search?q=cache:WtleDRRbyEoJ:
http://www.care-international.org/files/files/publications/CARE-International-
Annual-Report-2010%281%29.pdf%20CARE%20international%20making%20
a%20difference%20annual%20report%202009&icp=1&.intl=us&sig=9JuLlH5Zs
9Eu5Ax2o2heYA--.

———. 2010. *Post-Emergency Development Newsletter #4*. http://www.care-caucasus.org.
ge/photos/Emergency newsletter 4 ENG.pdf.

Caucasus Institute for Peace (CIPDD). (2009). "After August 2008: Consequences of the
Russian-Georgian War." www.cipdd.org/index.php?lang_id=ENG&sec_id=7&info_
id=316.

Chamayou, Grégoire. 2012. *Manhunts: A Philosophical History*. Durham, NC: Duke
University Press.

Chauffeur, Celia, and Tarel Gusep. 2004. "Investigation: Tide Turning for a Political Symbol, the Iveria Hotel." www.caucaz.com/home_eng/breve_contenu.php?id 91.

Cheterian, Vicken. 2008. *War and Peace in the Caucasus: Ethnic Conflict and the New
Geopolitics*. New York: Columbia University Press.

Chigoev, M. 2011. "Some Aspects of Solving Problems of Refugees and Internally
Displaced Persons in Light of Georgian-Ossetian Relations." In *Georgian-South
Ossetian Conflict: Researching Peace*, edited by Susan Allen Nan, 1–67. Fairfax, VA:
George Mason University. http://pointofviewdialogue.com/en/images/georgian-
south ossetian conflict_oss-2.pdf.

Chilton, Paul, and M. Ilyan. 1993. "Metaphor in Political Discourse: The Case of the
'Common European House.'" *Discourse and Society* 4, no. 1: 7–31.

Civil Georgia. 2009. "UNGA Passes Georgia IDP Resolution." http://www.civil.ge/eng/
article.php?id=21447.

———. 2011. "Saakashvili Plans to Build 'New City' on the Black Sea Coast" (in Georgian).
http://www.civil.ge/geo/article.php?id=24882.

———. 2014. "Usupashvili's Blunt Warning over NATO MAP." http://www.civil.ge/eng/
article.php?id=26857.

Cloke, Paul. 1988. *Policies and Plans for Rural People: An International Perspective*. London: Routledge.

Cohen, Roberta. n.d. "Reconciling R2P with IDP Protection." http://www.brookings.
edu/~/media/research/files/articles/2010/3/25 internal displacement cohen/0325_
internal_displacement_cohen.pdf.

Cohen, Roberta, and Francis M. Deng. 1998. *Masses in Flight: The Global Crisis of Internal Displacement*. Washington, DC: Brookings Institution Press.

Cole, Jennifer, and Deborah Durham. 2008. "Globalization and the Temporality of
Children and Youth." In *Figuring the Future*, edited by Jennifer Cole. and Deborah
Durham, 3–24. Santa Fe, NM: SAR Press.

Comaroff, John. 1991. "Humanity, Ethnicity, Nationality." *Theory and Society* 20, no. 5:
661–87.

Committee For Justice. 2012. "Angelina Jolie Sends Gifts and a Special Message to IDP
Children in Georgia." http://cfj.ge/en/media/new/view/336.

Conlon, Deirdre. 2010. "Ties That Bind: Governmentality, the State and Asylum in Contemporary Ireland." *Environment and Planning D* 28: 95–111.

Cons, Jason, and Kasia Paprocki. 2010. "Contested Credit Landscapes: Micro-Credit,
Self-Help and Self-Determination in Rural Bangladesh." *Third World Quarterly*
31, no. 4: 637–54.

Corso, Molly. 2010. "Georgia: 2011 Budget Is Big on Bucks, Small on Public Details."
http://www.eurasianet.org/node/62604.

——. 2012. "Georgia: War IDPs Fight Ongoing Battle with Poverty." http://www.eurasianet.
org/node/65764.

Cresswell, Tim. 2004. *Place: A Short Introduction*. Hoboken, NJ: Wiley-Blackwell.

Croft, Adrian. 2014. "NATO Will Not Offer Georgia Membership Step, Avoiding Russia
Clash." http://www.reuters.com/article/2014/06/25/us-nato-enlargement-idUSKB
N0F00IJ20140625.

Crowley, S. 1994. "Barriers to Collective Action: Steelworkers and Mutual Dependence in
the Former Soviet Union." *World Politics* 46, no. 4: 589–615.

——. 1997. "Coal Miners and the Transformation of the USSR." *Post-Soviet Affairs* 13,
no. 2: 167–95.

Curtis, Kimberly. 2016. "Can One 'Grand Bargain' Fix a Broken Humanitarian System?"
UNDispatch, May 26. http://bit.ly/1RKvnWs.

Daniel, C. 2005. "Bush Backs Georgia as 'Beacon for Democracy.'" *Financial Times*. www.
ft.com/cms/s/0/3cc8ba4e-c128-11d9-943f-00000e2511c8.html#axzz2gsM6OUfi.

Daniel, E. Valentine, and John Chr. Knudsen. 1995. "Introduction." In *Mistrusting Refugees*, edited by E. Valentine Daniel and J.C. Knudsen, 1–13. Berkeley: University of
California Press.

Danish Refugee Council. 2010. *IDPs—Overview and Trends*. http://www.drc.dk/
conventions-and-definitions/definitions/idps-overview-and-trends/.

Das, Veena, and Deborah Poole, eds. 2004. *Anthropology in the Margins of the State*. Santa
Fe: School for American Research Press.

de Certeau, Michel. 1984. *The Practice of Everyday Life*. Berkeley: University of California
Press.

del Valle, Hernan, and Sean Healy. 2013. "Humanitarian Agencies and Authoritarian
States: A Symbiotic Relationship?" *Disasters* 37, S2: S188–S201.

Delaney, David. 2010. *The Spatial, the Legal, and the Pragmatics of World-Making: Nomo-
spheric Investigations*. London: Routledge.

Deleuze, Gilles, and Felix Guattari 1988. *A Thousand Plateaus: Capitalism and Schizo-
phrenia*. London: Athlone.

d'Encausse, Hélène Carrère. 1993. *The End of the Soviet Empire: The Triumph of the
Nations*. New York: Basic Books.

Deng, Francis, et al. 1996. *Sovereignty as Responsibility: Conflict Management in Africa*.
Washington, DC: Brookings Institution.

de Waal, Alex. 2010. "An Empancipatory Imperium? Power and Principle in the Humanitarian International." In Fassin and Pandolfi, *Contemporary States of Emergency*,
295–316.

de Waal, Thomas. 2010. *The Caucasus: An Introduction*. New York: Oxford University
Press.

Diasamidze, T., ed. 2004. *Apkhazetis da samkhret osetis avtonomiuri regionebis statusi
sakartvelos shemadgenlobashi (1917–1988): Politikur-samartlebrivi aktebis krebuli*
[Status of the Abkhazian and South Ossetian Autonomous Regions within the
Composition of Georgia (1917–1988)]. Tbilisi: Center for Regional Research.

Diken, Bülent, and Carsten Bagge Laustsen. 2006. "The Camp." *Geografiska Annaler:
Series B, Human Geography* 88, no. 4: 443–52.

Dudoignon, Stéphane, and Christian Noack, eds. 2014. *Allah's Kolkhozes: Migration, De-
Stalinisation, Privatisation and the New Muslim Congregations in the Soviet Realm
(1950s–2000s)*. Berlin: Klaus Schwartz Verlag.

Dunn, Elizabeth. 2004. *Privatizing Poland: Baby Food, Big Business and the Remaking of
Labor*. Ithaca, NY: Cornell University Press.

——. 2008. "Postsocialist Spores: Disease, Bodies and the State in the Republic of Georgia." *American Ethnologist* 35, no. 2: 243–58.

——. 2012a. "A Gift from the American People." *Iowa Review* 42, no. 2: 37–48.

——. 2012b. "The Chaos of Humanitarianism: Adhocracy in the Republic of Georgia." *Humanity* 3, no. 1: 1–23.

——. 2014. "Notes towards an Anthropology of Nothing: Humanitarianism and the Void in the Republic of Georgia." *Slavic Review* 73, no. 2: 288–306.

Dunn, Elizabeth Cullen, and Michael S. Bobick. 2014. "The Empire Strikes Back: War without War and Occupation without Occupation in the Russian Sphere of Influence." *American Ethnologist* 41, no. 3: 405–13.

Dunn, Elizabeth Cullen, and Jason Cons. 2013. "Aleatory Sovereignty and the Rule of Sensitive Spaces." *Antipode* 46, no. 1: 92–109.

Easterling, Keller. 2014. *Extrastatecraft: The Power of Infrastructure Space.* London: Verso.

Easterly, William. 2006. *The White Man's Burden: Why the West's Efforts to Aid the Rest Have Done So Much Ill and So Little Good.* London: Penguin.

Economist. 2015. "Migration to Europe: Death at Sea." http://www.economist.com/blogs/graphicdetail/2015/09/migration-europe-0.

Edkins, Jenny. 2000. "Sovereign Power, Zones of Indistinction, and the Camp." *Alternatives* 25, no. 1: 3–25.

ELHRA. 2010. *Professionalising the Humanitarian Sector.* www.elrha.org/uploads/Professionalising_the_humanitarian_sector.pdf.

English, Robert. 2008. "Georgia: The Ignored History." *New York Review of Books*, November 6. http://www.nybooks.com/articles/archives/2008/nov/06/georgia-the-ignored-history/?pagination=false.

Etzioni, Amitai. 2006. "Sovereignty as Responsibility." *Orbis* 50, no. 1: 71–85.

Farmer, Paul. 2004a. "An Anthropology of Structural Violence." *Current Anthropology* 45, no. 3: 305–25.

——. 2004b. *Pathologies of Power: Health, Human Rights and the New War on the Poor.* Berkeley: University of California Press.

Fassin, Didier. 2007. "Humanitarianism as Politics of Life." *Public Culture* 19, no. 3: 499–520.

——. 2010. "Heart of Humaneness: The Moral Economy of Humanitarian Intervention." In Fassin and Pandolfi, *Contemporary States of Emergency*, 269–94.

——. 2012. *Humanitarian Reason: A Moral History of the Present.* Berkeley: University of California Press.

——. 2014. "The Parallel Lives of Philosophy and Anthropology." In *The Ground Between: Anthropologists Engage Philosophy*, edited by Veena Das, Arthur Kleinman, and Bhrigupati Singh, 50–70. Durham, NC: Duke University Press.

Fassin, Didier, and Mariella Pandolfi, eds. 2010. *Contemporary States of Emergency: The Politics of Military and Humanitarian Intervention.* New York: Zone Books.

——. 2010. "Introduction: Military and Humanitarian Government in the Age of Intervention." In Fassin and Pandolfi, *Contemporary States of Emergency*, 9–28.

Fassin, Didier, and Richard Rechtman. 2009. *Empire of Trauma: An Inquiry into the Condition of Victimhood.* Princeton, NJ: Princeton University Press.

Fearon, James D. 2008. "The Rise of Emergency Relief Aid." In Barnett and Weiss, *Humanitarianism in Question*, 49–72.

Feldman, Ilana. 2007. "The Quaker Way: Ethical Labor and Humanitarian Relief." *American Ethnologist* 34, no. 4: 689–705.

——. 2008a. "Ad Hoc Humanity: Peacekeeping and the Limits of International Community in Gaza." *American Anthropologist* 112, no. 3: 416–29.

——. 2008b. *Governing Gaza: Bureaucracy, Authority and the Work of Rule 1917–1967.* Durham, NC: Duke University Press.

——. 2011. "The Humanitarian Circuit: Relief Work, Development Assistance, and CARE in Gaza, 1955–67." In Bornstein and Redfield, *Forces of Compassion,* 203–26.

——. 2012. "The Humanitarian Condition: Palestinian Refugees and the Politics of Living." *Humanity* 3, no. 2: 155–72.

——. 2014. "What Is a Camp? Legitimate Refugee Lives in Spaces of Long-Term Displacement." *Geoforum* 66: 244–52.

Felgenhauer, Pavel. 2009. "The Russian Military Concentration in the Caucasus." *Eurodialogue,* July 15. http://eurodialogue.org/The-Russian-Military-Concentration-In-The-Caucasus.

Ferguson, James. 1994. *The Anti-Politics Machine: "Development," Depoliticization and Bureaucratic Power in Lesotho.* Minneapolis: University of Minnesota Press.

Finnstrom, Sven. 2008. *Living with Bad Surroundings: War, History and Everyday Moments in Northern Uganda.* Durham, NC: Duke University Press.

Foucault, Michel. 1984. "Of Other Spaces: Utopias and Heterotopias." *Architecture/ Movement/Continuity* (October). web.mit.edu/allanmc/www/foucault1.pdf.

——. 2007. *Security, Territory, Population: Lectures at the Collège de France.* New York: Picador.

Frederiksen, Martin. 2013. *Young Men, Time and Boredom.* Philadelphia, PA: Temple University Press.

——. 2014. "Heterochronic Atmospheres: Affect, Materiality, and Youth in Depression." In *Ethnographies of Youth and Temporality,* edited by Anne Line Dalsgard, 81–96. Philadelphia: Temple University Press.

Freese, Theresa. n.d. "Georgia: Revolutions in the Regions." http://www.eurasianet.org/georgia/shida/story.html.

Fukuyama, Francis. 1992. *The End of History and the Last Man.* New York: Free Press.

Gachechiladze, R. G., M. A. Nadzhafaliyev, and A. D. Rondeli. 1984. "The Regional Development Problems of Transcaucasia." *Geoforum* 15, no. 1: 65–73.

Gall, Carlota. 1995. "New Georgia to Move toward West." *Moscow Times,* http://www.themoscowtimes.com/sitemap/free/1995/11/article/new-georgia-to-move-toward-west/332450.html (accessed September 15, 2012).

Gall, Carlota, and Thomas de Waal. 1998. *Chechnya: Calamity in the Caucasus.* New York: New York University Press.

Gazzaev, V. E. 2010. "Osetiya-Gruziya: Istoriya vzaimootnosheniy i prichiny konflikta [Ossetia-Georgia: History of Relations and Causes of Conflict]." http://www.iriston.com/nogbon/news.php?newsid=404.

Geostat. 2010. "Foreign Direct Investment." http://geostat.ge/index.php?action=page&p_id=140&lang=eng.

Gilbert, Andrew. 2006. "The Past in Parenthesis: (Non)Post-Socialism in Post-War Bosnia-Hercegovina." *Anthropology Today* 22, no. 4: 14–20.

Gladstone, Rick. 2015. "As Supplies Dwindle, World Food Program Cutting Rations to Refugees in Kenya." *New York Times,* June 12. http://nyti.ms/2pZgeOi.

Gleason, Abbott. 1997. *Totalitarianism: The Inner History of the Cold War.* Oxford: Oxford University Press.

Global Humanitarian Assistance. 2011. *GHA Report 2011.* www.globalhumanitarianassistance.org/wp-content/uploads/2011/07/gha-report-2011.pdf.

——. 2015. *Global Humanitarian Assistance Report.* http://www.globalhumanitarianassistance.org/report/gha-report-2015/.

Gogidze, L., and Caitlin Ryan. 2011. "Fact-Checking the State of the Nation Address: IDPs." http://www.transparency.ge/en/node/1107.

Goltz, Thomas. 2009. "The Paradox of Living in Paradise: Georgia's Descent into Chaos." In *The Guns of August 2008: Russia's War in Georgia*, edited by Svante Cornell and S. Frederick Starr, 10–28. Armonk, NY: M. E. Sharpe.

Gordillo, Gaston. 2002. "The Breath of Devils: Memories and Places of an Experience of Terror." *American Ethnologist* 29, no. 1: 33–57.

———. 2004. *"Landscapes of Devils: Tensions of Place and Memory in the Argentinean Chaco."* Durham, NC: Duke University Press.

———. 2014. *Rubble: The Afterlife of Destruction*. Durham, NC: Duke University Press.

Gotfredsen, Katrine. 2013. *Evasive Politics: Paradoxes of History, Nation and Everyday Communication in the Republic of Georgia*. PhD diss., University of Copenhagen. http://anthropology.ku.dk/research/new_publications/phd-dissertation-evasive-politics/.

Government of Georgia 2007. "Decree #47 of the Government of Georgia—On Approving the State Strategy for Internally Displaced Persons (Persecuted)." www.internal-displacement.org/.../State+Strategy+for+IDP+-+ENG.pdf.

———. 2009. "State Strategy for IDPs." http://relief.migration.ge/intranet/index.php.

———. 2010. "Adoption of the Action Plan for the Implementation of the State Strategy on IDPs during 2009–2012." http://bit.ly/2nPrydv.

Grant, Bruce. 2004. "An Average Azeri Village." *Slavic Review* 63, no. 4: 705–31.

———. 2014. "The Edifice Complex: Architecture and the Political Life of Surplus in the New Baku." *Public Culture* 26, no. 3: 501–28.

Greenberg, Jessica. 2011. "On the Road to Normal: Negotiating Agency and State Sovereignty in Postsocialist Serbia." *American Ethnologist* 113, no. 1: 88–100.

Greene, Thomas. 1998. "Internal Displacement in the North Caucasus, Azerbaijan, Armenia and Georgia." In *The Forsaken People*, edited by Roberta Cohen and Francis M. Deng, 233–96. Washington, DC: Brookings Institution Press.

Gross, Jan T. 1988. *Revolution from Abroad: The Soviet Conquest of Poland's Western Ukraine and Western Belorussia*. Princeton, NJ: Princeton University Press.

Gurses, E., and Mert Ozkan. 2016. "Turkey Plans to Introduce Work Permits for Refugees, Minister Says." Reuters. http://www.reuters.com/article/us-europe-migrants-turkey-idUSKCN0UP0QP20160111.

Hallward, Peter. 2003. *Badiou: A Subject to Truth*. Minneapolis: University of Minnesota Press.

Hammarberg, T. 2013. *Dealing with Illegal Surveillance: Preliminary Advice*. http://transparency.ge/en/node/3242.

Hammond, Laura. 2004. *This Place Will Become Home: Refugee Repatriation to Ethiopia*. Ithaca, NY: Cornell University Press.

Harding, Luke. 2012. "Georgia's President Saakashvili Concedes Election Defeat." *Guardian*, October 2. London. www.theguardian.com/world/2012/oct/02/georgia-president-saakashvili-election-defeat.

Harild, Niels, and Asger Christiansen. 2010. *The Development Challenge of Finding Durable Solutions for Refugees and Internally Displaced People: A World Development Report Background Note*. Washington, DC: World Bank. http://siteresources.worldbank.org/EXTSOCIALDEVELOPMENT/Resources/244362-1265299949041/6766328-1265299960363/WDR-Background-Note-development-challenge-Displacement.pdf

Harrell-Bond, Barbara, Efthinia Vouitra, and Mark Leopold. 1992. "Counting the Refugees: Gifts, Givers, Patrons and Clients." *Journal of Refugee Studies* 5, nos. 3–4: 205–25.

Hart, Jason. 2002. "Children and Nationalism in a Palestinian Refugee Camp in Jordan." *Childhood* 9, no. 1: 35–47.

———. 2008. "Displaced Children's Participation in Political Violence: Towards A Greater Understanding of Mobilisation." *Conflict, Security, and Development* 8, no. 3: 278–93.

Hautzinger, Sarah, and Jean Scandlyn. 2013. *Beyond Post-Traumatic Stress: Homefront Struggles with the Wars on Terror.* Walnut Creek, CA: Left Coast Press.

Higgins, Noelle, and Kieran O'Reilly. 2009. "The Use of Force, Wars of National Liberation, and the Right to Self-Determination in the South Ossetian Conflict." *International Criminal Law Review* 9, no. 1: 567–83.

High, Holly. 2006. "'Work Together, Act Together, for the Common Good, Solidarity!': Village Formation in Southern Laos." *Sojourn* 21, no. 1: 22–45.

Hilhorst, Dorothea. 2002. "Being Good at Doing Good? Quality and Accountability of Humanitarian NGOs." *Disasters* 26, no. 3: 193–212.

Hirsch, F. 2005. *Empire of Nations: Ethnographic Knowledge and the Making of the Soviet Union.* Ithaca, NY: Cornell University Press.

Hoffman, David. 2003. *Stalinist Values: The Cultural Norms of Soviet Modernity, 1917–1941.* Ithaca, NY: Cornell University Press.

Holmes, Seth. 2013. *Fresh Fruit Broken Bodies: Migrant Workers in the United States.* Berkeley: University of California Press.

Human Rights Watch. 2009. "Up in Flames: Humanitarian Law Violations and Civilian Victims in the Conflict Over South Ossetia." http://www.hrw.org/sites/default/files/reports/georgia0109_brochure_web.pdf.

Humphrey, Caroline. 2008. "Reassembling Individual Subjects: Events and Decisions in Troubled Times." *Anthropological Theory* 8, no. 4: 357–80.

Hunter, Shireen. 2006. "Borders, Conflict and Security in the Caucasus: The Legacy of the Past." *SAIS Review* 26, no. 1: 111–25.

Hurriyet. 2012. "Debit Cards Come to Aid of Syrian Refugees in Turkey." http://www.hurriyetdailynews.com/debit-cards-come-to-the-aid-of-syrian-refugees-in-turkey.aspx?pageID=238&nid=36321.

Husserl, Edmund. 1970. *The Crisis of European Sciences and Transcendental Phenomenology: An Introduction to Phenomenological Philosophy.* Evanston, IL: Northwestern University Press.

Hyndman, Jennifer. 2000. *Managing Displacement: Refugees and the Politics of Humanitarianism.* Minneapolis: University of Minnesota Press.

Igniateff, Michael. 2003. *Human Rights as Politics and Idolatry.* Princeton, NJ: Princeton University Press.

Independent. 1994. "Gamsakhurdia 'Was Murdered,'" January 25. http://www.independent.co.uk/news/world/gamsakhurdia-was-murdered-1402394.html.

Ingold, Tim. 2003. "The Temporality of Landscape." *World Archaeology* 25, no. 2: 152–74.

Internal Displacement Monitoring Center. 2006. "Georgia: IDPs' Living Conditions Remain Miserable, as National Strategy Is Being Developed: A Profile of the Internal Displacement Situation." Geneva: Norwegian Refugee Council.

———. 2012. *Partial Progress towards Durable Solutions for IDPs.* http://www.internal-displacement.org/8025708F004CE90B/%28httpCountries%29/F62BE07C33DE4D19802570A7004C84A3?OpenDocument.

———. 2015. Ukraine IDP Figures Analysis. http://www.internal-displacement.org/europe-the-caucasus-and-central-asia/ukraine/figures-analysis.

International Commission on Intervention and State Sovereignty. 2001. *The Responsibility to Protect.* http://www.responsibilitytoprotect.org/index.php/about-rtop/learn-about-rtop.

International Committee of the Red Cross. n.d. "The Seven Fundamental Principles." http://www.ifrc.org/who-we-are/vision-and-mission/the-seven-fundamental-principles/.

——. 1995. "The Code of Conduct for the International Red Cross and Red Crescent Movement and NGOs in Disaster Relief." http://www.ifrc.org/Docs/idrl/I259EN.pdf.

International Council of Voluntary Agencies (ICVA). 2005. "What's All This Cluster Talk?" *ICVA Bulletin* 7, no. 3. http://www.icva.ch/doc00001467.html.

International Crisis Group. 2007. *Georgia's South Ossetia Conflict: Make Haste Slowly.* Europe Report. http://www.crisisgroup.org/en/regions/europe/south-caucasus/georgia/183-georgias-south-ossetia-conflict-make-haste-slowly.aspx.

——. 2008a. *Georgia: Risks of Winter.* https://www.crisisgroup.org/europe-central-asia/caucasus/georgia/georgia-risks-winter.

——. 2008b. *Russia vs. Georgia: The Fallout.* https://www.crisisgroup.org/europe-central-asia/caucasus/georgia/russia-vs-georgia-fallout.

——. 2009. *Russia-Georgia: Still Insecure and Dangerous.* https://www.crisisgroup.org/europe-central-asia/caucasus/georgia/georgia-russia-still-insecure-and-dangerous.

International Fact Finding Mission on the Conflict in Georgia. 2009. "Report on the Conflict in Georgia." www.ceiig.ch/pdf/IIFFMCG_Volume_I.pdf.

International Monetary Fund. 2015. World Economic Outlook Database. April. https://www.imf.org/external/pubs/ft/weo/2015/01/weodata/index.aspx.

Interpress News. 2010. "Bernard Kouchner Visited IDPs in Koda." http://www.interpressnews.ge/en/video.html?view=video&video=57.

Jackson, Michael. 2005. *Existential Anthropology.* New York: Berghahn Books.

——. 2013. *Lifeworlds: Essays in Existential Anthropology.* Chicago: University of Chicago Press.

James, Erica C. 2010. *Democratic Insecurities: Violence, Trauma and Intervention in Haiti.* Berkeley: University of California Press.

James, William. 1890. *The Principles of Psychology.* New York: Henry Holt and Company.

Jasny, N. 1949. *The Socialized Agriculture of the USSR: Plans and Performance.* Stanford, CA: Stanford University Press.

Jersild, Austin. 2002. *Orientalism and Empire: North Caucasus Mountain Peoples and the Georgian Frontier, 1845–1917.* Montreal: McGill-Queen's University Press.

John Paul II. 1981. *Laborem Exercens.* http://w2.vatican.va/content/john-paul-ii/en/encyclicals/documents/hf_jp-ii_enc_14091981_laborem-exercens.html.

Johnson, Alan. 2012. "The New Communism: Resurrecting the Utopian Delusion." http://www.worldaffairsjournal.org/article/new-communism-resurrecting-utopian-delusion.

Jojua, T. 2007. "Istoriografiya Tskhinvalskogo Regiona (Yuzhnaya Osetiya) [Historiography of the Tskhinvali Region (South Ossetia)]." In *Istoriograficheskiy dialog vokrug nepriznannykh gosudarstv: Pridnestrove, Nagorny Karabakh, Armeniya, Yuzhnaya Osetiya i Gruziya [Historiographical Dialogue around the Unrecognized Governments: Transnistria, Nagorno-Karabakh, Armenia, South Ossetia, and Georgia],* 84–112. Hokkaido: Slavic Research Center.

Jomarjidze, N. 2011. "Problems in the Border Areas." http://dfwatch.net/problems-in-the-border-areas-2008.

Jones, Lynne. 2014. "Does Everyone Who Suffers Trauma Have PTSD?" *Aeon.* http://aeon.co/magazine/living-together/does-everyone-who-suffers-trauma-have-ptsd.html.

Jones, Stephen. 2005. *Socialism in Georgian Colors: The European Road to Social Democracy, 1883–1917.* Cambridge, MA: Harvard University Press.

——. 2013. *Georgia: A Political History since Independence.* London: I. B. Tauris.

———, ed. 2014. *The Making of Modern Georgia, 1918–2012: The First Georgian Republic and Its Successors*. London: Routledge.

Jönsson, Elin, and Elin Ackerman. 2009. *Direct Cash Transfer and Food Security in Georgia*. Lund: Nationalekonomiska Institutionen vid Lunds Universitet.

Kabachnik, Peter. 2012. "Wounds That Won't Heal: Cartographic Anxieties and the Quest for Territorial Integrity in Georgia." *Central Asian Survey* 31, no. 1: 45–60.

Kabachnik, Peter, Joanna Regulska, and Beth Mitchneck. 2010. "Where and When Is Home? The Double Displacement of Georgian IDPs from Abkhazia." *Journal of Refugee Studies* 23, no. 3: 315–36.

Kahn, Carrie. 2011. "Haitians Take Rubble Removal into Own Hands." http://www.npr.org/2011/01/12/132844805/haitians-take-rubble-removal-into-own-hands.

Kalin, Walter. 2006. *Georgia Must Act on Promises to End Displacement Crisis*. Brookings Institution Working Papers. http://www.reliefweb.int/rw/rwb.nsf/db900sid/KHII-6PG5DG?OpenDocument.

Kennedy, David. 2004. *The Dark Sides of Virtue*. Princeton, NJ: Princeton University Press.

Kharashvili, Julia, Tamar Tsivtsivadze, Nino Zhvania, Gia Cheladze, Gia Kobalia, Tea Lekveshvili, and Giorgi Uridia. 2003. "Study of IDP Rights." http://www.undp.org.ge/Projects/new_approach.html.

Kimes, Beverly Rae, and Robert C. Ackerson. 1987. *Chevrolet: A History from 1911*. Minneapolis, MN: Automobile Quarterly.

King, Charles. 2008. *The Ghost of Freedom: A History of the Caucasus*. Oxford: Oxford University Press.

Klein, Naomi. 2007. *The Shock Doctrine: The Rise of Disaster Capitalism*. New York: Henry Holt.

Kleinman, Arthur, Veena Das, and Margaret Lock, eds. 1994. *Social Suffering*. Berkeley, CA: University of California Press.

Klima, Alan. 2002. *The Funeral Casino: Meditation, Massacre, and Exchange with the Dead in Thailand*. Princeton, NJ: Princeton University Press.

Klumbytė, Neringa. 2010. "The Soviet Sausage Renaissance." *American Anthropologist* 112, no. 1: 22–37.

Koch, Erin. 2008. "Beyond Suspicion." *American Ethnologist* 33, no. 1: 50–62.

———. 2013. *Free Market Tuberculosis: Managing Epidemics in Post-Soviet Georgia*. Nashville, TN: Vanderbilt University Press.

Kochieva, I., and A. Margiev. 2008. "Proshlo 68 let . . . [68 Years Have Gone by . . .]." In Pavlovsky, *Den Katastrofy—888*, 3–152.

Kohn, Eduardo. 2013. *How Forests Think: Towards an Anthropology beyond the Human*. Berkeley: University of California Press.

Kornai, Janos. 1992. *The Socialist System: The Political Economy of Communism*. Princeton, NJ: Princeton University Press.

Kowal, S. 2011. "Systematic Project Design for Organizational Capacity Development." http://usaideducationworkshop.com/conf/creg6.nsf/files/D1624B87DC90914586 25793C00746577/$file/Kowal PPT.pdf.

Krause, Monika. 2014. *The Good Project: Humanitarian Relief NGOs and the Fragmentation of Reason*. Chicago: University of Chicago Press.

Kristeva, Julia. 1982. *Powers of Horror: An Essay in Abjection*. New York: Columbia University Press.

Kwon, Heonik. 2008. *Ghosts of War in Vietnam*. Cambridge: Cambridge University Press.

Lampland, Martha. 2010. "False Numbers as Formalizing Practices." *Social Studies of Science* 40, no. 3: 377–404.

———. 2016. *The Value of Labor: The Science of Commodification in Hungary, 1920–1956*. Chicago: University of Chicago Press.

Lanchava, N. 2005. "Resisting the Devil—First, in the Name of the Savior." (in Georgian) http://www.orthodoxy.ge/sakhli/tsin_agudeqit_eshmaks.htm.

Lapidus, Gail. 1991. "The Structural Context of Soviet Ethno-Nationalism." *Theory and Society* 20, no. 5: 705–9.

Larsen, Soren C., and Jay T. Johnson. 2012. "Toward an Open Sense of Place: Phenomenology, Affinity, and the Question of Being." *Annals of the Association of American Geographers* 102, no. 3: 632–46.

Latour, Bruno. 1987. *Science in Action*. Cambridge, MA: Harvard University Press.

Ledeneva, Alean. V. 2006. *How Russia Really Works: The Informal Practices That Shaped Post-Soviet Politics and Business*. Ithaca, NY: Cornell University Press.

LeFebvre, Henri. 1992. *The Production of Space*. New York: Wiley.

Leibniz, Gottfried Wilhelm. 1998 [1714]. *Philosophical Texts*. Oxford: Oxford University Press.

Lenin, Vladimir Ilyich. 1916. "The Right of Nations to Self-Determination." www.marxists.org/archive/lenin/works/1916/jan/x01.htm.

Lévi-Strauss, Claude. 1966. *The Savage Mind*. Chicago: University of Chicago Press.

Li, Tania. 2007. *The Will to Improve: Governmentality, Development and the Practice of Politics*. Durham, NC: Duke University Press.

Lischer, S. K. 2007. "Military Intervention and the Humanitarian 'Force Multiplier.'" *Global Governance* 13: 99–118.

Lofgren, Orvar, and Billy Ehn. 2010. *The Secret World of Doing Nothing*. Berkeley: University of California Press.

Lomsadze, Giorgi. 2013. "Ericsson Technology Enables Georgian Eavesdropping on Cell Phones." http://www.eurasianet.org/node/67707.

Long, K. 2011. *Permanent Crises? Unlocking Protracted Displacement for Refugees and Internally Displaced Persons*. Oxford: Refugee Studies Centre. http://www.rsc.ox.ac.uk/files/publications/policy-briefing-series/pb-unlocking-protracted-displacement-2011.pdf.

Malek, Martin. 2009. "Georgia and Russia: The Unknown Prelude to the Five Day War." *Caucasian Review of International Affairs* 3, no. 2: 227–32. http://www.cria-online.org/7_10.html.

Malkki, Liisa. 1992. "National Geographic: The Rooting of Peoples and the Territorialization of National Identity among Scholars and Refugees." *Cultural Anthropology* 7, no. 1: 24–44.

——. 1995. *Purity and Exile: Violence, Memory and National Cosmology among Hutu Refugees in Tanzania*. Chicago: University of Chicago Press.

——. 1996. "Speechless Emissaries: Refugees, Humanitarianism and Dehistoricization." *Cultural Anthropology* 11, no. 3: 377–404.

——. 2015. *The Need to Help*. Durham, NC: Duke University Press.

Malpas, Jeffrey. 2012. *Heidegger and the Thinking of Place: Explorations in the Topology of Being*. Cambridge: MIT Press.

Mamdani, Mahmood. 2009. *Saviors and Survivors: Darfur, Politics, and the War on Terror*. New York: Doubleday.

Manning, Paul. 2007. "Rose Colored Glasses?: Color Revolutions and Cartoon Chaos in Postsocialist Georgia." *Cultural Anthropology* 22, no. 2: 171–213.

——. 2008. "The Hotel/Refugee Camp Iveria: Symptom, Monster, Fetish, Home." www.dangerserviceagency.org.

——. 2012. *Strangers in a Strange Land: Occidentalist Publics and Orientalist Geographies in Nineteenth-Century Georgian Imaginaries*. Brighton, MA: Academic Studies Press.

——. 2015. "When Goblins Come to Town: The Ethnography of Urban Hauntings in Georgia." In *Monster Anthropology in Australasia and Beyond*, edited by Yasmine Musharbash and Geir Henning Presterudstuen, 1–16. New York: Palgrave Macmillan.

Maren, Michael. 2002. *The Road to Hell: The Ravaging Effects of Foreign Aid and International Charity*. New York: Simon and Schuster.

Marra, Anthony. 2013. *A Constellation of Vital Phenomena*. New York: Hogarth.

Mauss, Marcel. 1954. *The Gift: Forms and Functions of Exchange in Primitive Societies*. New York: W. W. Norton.

Mbembe, Achille. 2003. "Necropolitics." *Public Culture* 15, no. 1: 11–40.

McCauley, M. 1994. "Obituary: Zviad Gamsakhurdia." *Independent*. http://www. independent.co.uk/news/people/obituary-zviad-gamsakhurdia-1396384.html.

McFalls, Laurence. 2010. "Benevolent Dictatorship: The Formal Logic of Humanitarian Government." In *Contemporary States of Emergency: The Politics of Humanitarian and Military Intervention*, edited by Didier Fassin and Mariella Pandolfi, 317–44. New York: Zone Books.

Mchedlishvili, N. 2013. "After Years of Secret Tapes, Georgia Mulls How to Destroy Them." RFE/RL. http://www.rferl.org/content/georgia-secret-tapes-destroy/25019275.html.

Mearsheimer, John J. 2014. "Getting Ukraine Wrong." *New York Times*, March 13. https:// www.nytimes.com/2014/03/14/opinion/getting-ukraine-wrong.html.

Medvedev, S. 2007. *The Crisis in EU-Russia Relations: Between "Sovereignty" and "Europeanization."* Moscow: Higher School of Economics. https://www.hse.ru/ data/2010/05/07/1217274096/WP14_2007_02.pdf.

Meillassoux, Quentin. 2011. "History and Event in Alain Badiou." *Parrhesia* 12: 1–11.

Mercy Corps. 2014. "In Crowded Lebanon, Syrian Refugees Are Forced to Shelter in Unlikely Places." https://www.mercycorps.org.uk/articles/lebanon-syria/ crowded-lebanon-syrian-refugees-are-forced-shelter-unlikely-places.

Meyers, Diana Tietjens. 2011. "Two Victim Paradigms and the Problem of 'Impure' Victims." *Humanity* 2, no. 2: 255–75.

Mieczkowski, Z. 1966. "The Economic Regionalization of the Soviet Union in the Lenin and Stalin Period." *Canadian Slavonic Papers* 8: 89–124.

Miéville, China. 2009. *The City & The City*. New York: Del Rey.

Millennium Challenge Corporation. 2011. "The Road to Better Aid: An Emerging Bipartisan Consensus." http://www.mcc.gov/pages/press/release/the-road-to-better-aid-an-emerging-bipartisan-consensus.

Milner, James, and Gil Loescher. 2011. *Responding to Protracted Refugee Situations: Lessons from a Decade of Discussion*. Forced Migration Policy Briefings. Oxford: Refugee Studies Centre. http://www.rsc.ox.ac.uk/publications/policy-briefings/ RSCPB6-RespondingToProtractedRefugeeSituations.pdf.

Minca, Claudio. 2005. "The Return of the Camp." *Progress in Human Geography* 29, no. 4: 405–12.

——. 2015. "Geographies of the Camp." *Political Geography* 49: 74–83.

Ministry of Foreign Affairs of the Russian Federation. 2008b. "Statement by Russia's Ministry of Foreign Affairs on Kosovo." Moscow. http://archive.mid.ru/bdomp/ brp_4.nsf/e78a48070f128a7b43256999005bcbb3/041c5af46913d38ac32573f30027 b380!OpenDocument.

Mitchell, Timothy. 1991. "America's Egypt: Discourse of the Development Industry." *Middle East Report* 169 (March–April): 18–36.

——. 2002. *The Rule of Experts: Egypt, Techno-Politics, Modernity*. Berkeley: University of California Press.

Mitchneck, Beth, Olga Mayorova, and Joanna Regulska. 2009. "'Post'-Conflict Displacement: Isolation and Integration in Georgia." *Annals of the Association of American Geographers* 99, no. 5: 1022–32.

Miyazaki, Hirokazu. 2006. *The Method of Hope: Anthropology, Philosophy and Fijian Knowledge.* Stanford, CA: Stanford University Press.

Mol, Annemarie. 2002. *The Body Multiple: Ontologies of Medical Practice.* Durham, NC: Duke University Press.

Monaghan, A. 2015. "A 'New Cold War'?: Abusing History, Misunderstanding Russia." http://www.chathamhouse.org/sites/files/chathamhouse/field/field_document/20150522ColdWarRussiaMonaghan.pdf.

Mosse, David. 2004. *Cultivating Development: An Ethnography of Aid Policy and Practice.* London: Pluto Press.

Mountz, Alison. 2004. "Embodying the Nation-State: Canada's Response to Human Smuggling." *Political Geography* 23: 325–45.

Moyn, Samuel. 2010. *The Last Utopia: Human Rights in History.* Cambridge, MA: Belknap Press.

Mühlfried, Florian. 2010. "Citizenship and War: Passports and Nationality in the 2008 Russian-Georgian Conflict." *Anthropology Today* 26, no. 2: 8–13.

——. 2015. "A Taste of Mistrust." *Ab Imperio* 4: 63–68.

Mundt, Alex, and Elizabeth Ferris. 2008. *Durable Solutions for IDPs in Protracted Situations.* Washington, DC: Brookings Institution.

Nash, J. 1979. *We Eat the Mines and the Mines Eat Us: Dependency and Exploitation in Bolivian Tin Mines.* New York: Columbia University Press.

Navaro-Yashin, Y. 2012. *The Make-Believe Space: Affective Geography in a Post-War Polity.* Durham, NC: Duke University Press.

Nazpary, Joma. 2001. *Post-Soviet Chaos: Violence and Dispossession in Kazakhstan.* London: Pluto Press.

Nelson, Diane. 2009. *Reckoning: The Ends of War in Guatemala.* Durham, NC: Duke University Press.

Nemtsova, Anna. 2008. "How Mikheil Saakashvili Miscalculated in Georgia." *Newsweek,* August 22. http://www.newsweek.com/how-mikheil-saakashvili-miscalculated-georgia-88107.

Nicolls, Martina. 2010. *Pre-Monitoring Review of IDP Data and Information.* Washington, DC: US Department of State. http://www.state.gov/documents/organization/193716.pdf.

Nikuradze, M. 2014. "Tserovani—The Village of Refugees from 2008 War." http://dfwatch.net/tserovani-the-village-of-refugees-from-2008-war-37778-28842.

Nilsson, N. 2009. "Georgia's Rose Revolution: The Break with the Past." In *The Guns of August 2008: Russia's War in Georgia,* edited by Svante Cornell and S. Frederick Starr, 85–103. Armonk, NY: M. E. Sharpe.

Nockerts, Regina. 2008. "A Theory of Obligation." *Journal of Humanitarian Assistance.* http://sites.tufts.edu/jha/archives/138.

Norris, Christopher. 2009. "Badiou on Set Theory, Ontology and Truth." *Polish Journal of Philosophy* 3, no. 2: 51–72.

Nye, Joseph S., Jr. 2005. *Soft Power: The Means to Success in World Politics.* New York: Public Affairs.

OCHA. 2008a. "Key Messages and Decisions—HCM of 11 August." www.relief.migration.ge.

——. 2008b. "New Settlements: Internally Displaced." http://www.reliefweb.int/rw/fullMaps_Sa.nsf/luFullMap/2D4F2BDC6FC80607C12575610033A848/$File/map.pdf?OpenElement.

——. 2008c. "Georgia Crisis: Flash Appeal." ochaonline.un.org/humanitarianappeal/webpage.asp?Page=1692.

——. n.d.-a. "The Consolidated Appeal Process." www.unocha.org/cap/about-the-cap/faqs#t57n1957.

——. n.d.-b. "The Four Pillars of Humanitarian Reform." ochaonline.un.org/OchaLink Click.aspx?link=ocha&docId=1146894.

O'Neill, Bruce. 2014. "Cast Aside: Boredom, Downward Mobility, and Homelessness in Post-Communist Bucharest." *Cultural Anthropology* 29, no. 1: 8–31.

Ong, Aiwha. 1987. *Spirits of Resistance and Capitalist Discipline*. Albany: State University of New York Press.

Ong, Aiwha, and Stephen Collier. 2005. *Global Assemblages: Technology, Politics and Ethics as Anthropological Problems*. London: Blackwell.

Orford, Anne. 2010. "The Passions of Protection: Sovereign Authority and Humanitarian War." In Fassin and Pandolfi, *Contemporary States of Emergency*, 335–56.

Ortner, Sherry. 2016. "Dark Anthropology and Its Others: Theory since the Eighties." *Hau* 16, no. 1. http://www.haujournal.org/index.php/hau/article/view/hau6.1.004.

Ostrovsky, A. 2004. "How to Be a Founding Father." *Financial Times*. http://www.ft.com/cms/s/0/6e074e40-d20e-11d8-85fc-00000e2511c8.html#axzz3jjiPSAlG.

Pandolfi, Mariella. 2000. "L'industrie humanitaire: Une soverainete mouvante et supra-coloniale." *Multitudes* 3: 97–105.

——. 2003. "Contract of Mutual (In)Difference: Governance and the Humanitarian Apparatus in Contemporary Albania and Kosovo." *Indiana Journal for Global Legal Studies* 10, no. 1: 369–81.

——. 2010. "From Paradox to Paradigm: The Permanent State of Emergency in the Balkans." In Fassin and Pandolfi, *Contemporary States of Emergency*, 153–72.

Pavlovsky, G., ed. 2008. *Den Katastrofy—888: Ostanovlenny genotsid v Yuzhnoy Osetii* [*Day of the Catastrophe—888: The Prevented Genocide in South Ossetia*]. Moscow: Evropa.

Pelkmans, Mathijs. 2006. *Defending the Border: Identity, Religion and Modernity in the Republic of Georgia*. Ithaca, NY: Cornell University Press.

Percy, Benjamin. 2012. "On the Ground." *New York Times*, BR1. http://www.nytimes.com/2012/10/07/books/review/the-yellow-birds-by-kevin-powers.html.

Petryna, Adriana. 2002. *Life Exposed: Biological Citizens after Chernobyl*. Princeton, NJ: Princeton University Press.

Piccio, Lorenzo. 2013. "A Billion Dollars for 5 Million People." https://www.devex.com/news/a-billion-dollars-for-5-million-people-80819.

Pollock, Lucas. 2008. "Dynamo in the Disaster Zone." *National Geographic Adventure*. http://adventure.nationalgeographic.com/2008/12/best-of/ashley-clements-text.

Polman, Linda. 2010. *The Crisis Caravan: What's Wrong with Humanitarian Aid?* New York: Macmillan.

Povinelli, Elizabeth. 2008. "The Child in the Broom Closet: States of Killing and Letting Die." *South Atlantic Quarterly* 107, no. 3: 509–30.

——. 2011. *Economies of Abandonment: Social Belonging and Endurance in Late Liberalism*. Durham, NC: Duke University Press.

Power, Michael. 1997. *The Audit Society: Rituals of Verification*. Oxford: Oxford University Press.

Powers, Kevin. 2012. *The Yellow Birds*. New York: Hachette.

Prazauskas, A. 1991. "Ethnic Conflicts in the Context of Democratizing Political Systems: Theses." *Theory and Society* 20, no. 5: 581–602.

Prcić, Ismet. 2011. *Shards*. New York: Black Cat.

Public Defender of Georgia. 2009. *The Situation of Human Rights and Freedoms in Georgia*. http://www.ombudsman.ge/index.php?page=21&lang=1.

Pupavac, Vanessa. 2004. "Psychosocial Interventions and the Demoralization of Humanitarianism." *Journal of Biosocial Science* 36: 491–504.

——. 2010. "Between Compassion and Conservatism: A Genealogy of Humanitarian Sensibilities." In Fassin and Pandolfi, *Contemporary States of Emergency*, 491–504.

Quesada, James. 1998. "Suffering Child: An Embodiment of War and Its Aftermath in Post-Sandinista Nicaragua." *Medical Anthropology Quarterly* 12, no. 1: 51–73.

Ramadan, Adam. 2013. "Spatialising the Refugee Camp." *Transactions of the Institute of British Geographers* 38: 65–77.

Ranciere, Jacques. 2004. "Who Is the Subject of the Rights of Man?" *South Atlantic Quarterly* 103, nos. 2–3: 297–310.

Rayfield, Donald. 2012. *Edge of Empire: A History of Georgia.* London: Reaktion Books.

Redfield, Peter. 2005. "Doctors, Borders, and Life in Crisis." *American Ethnologist* 20, no. 3: 320–61.

——. 2008a. "Sacrifice, Triage, and Global Humanitarianism." In Barnett and Weiss, *Humanitarianism in Question*, 196–214.

——. 2008b. "Vital Mobility and the Humanitarian Kit." In *Biosecurity Interventions*, edited by Stephen J. Collier and Andrew Lakoff, 147–72. New York: Columbia University Press.

——. 2012. "Bioexpectations: Life Technologies as Humanitarian Goods." *Public Culture* 24, no. 1: 157–84.

——. 2013. *Life in Crisis: The Ethical Journey of Doctors Without Borders.* Berkeley: University of California Press.

RFERL. 2006. "Saakashvili Calls for Georgia to Be Admitted into NATO." http://www.rferl.org/content/article/1065431.html.

——. 2010. "Georgian IDPs Sew Mouths Shut in Eviction Protest." http://www.rferl.org/content/Georgian_IDPs_Sew_Mouths_Shut_In_Eviction_Protest_/2137496.html.

——. 2012. "Georgia, South Ossetia, Both Claim Preparations for New Hostilities." http://www.rferl.org/content/georgia-south-ossetia-trade-accusations-of-preparing-for-war/24716583.html.

——. 2014. "Georgia Sets Sights on NATO Membership Action Plan." http://www.rferl.org/content/caucasus-report-georgia-nato/25232112.html.

RIA-Novosti. 2008. "Russia Hands over Control of Georgia Buffer Zones to EU." http://web.archive.org/web/20081012093601/http://en.rian.ru/world/20081009/117637460.html.

Riddell, Rebecca. 2016. "'Why Are You Keeping Me Here?': Unaccompanied Children Detained in Greece." https://www.hrw.org/report/2016/09/08/why-are-you-keeping-me-here/unaccompanied-children-detained-greece.

Rieff, David. 2003. *A Bed for the Night: Humanitarianism in Crisis.* New York: Simon and Schuster.

Rigi, Jakub. 2007. "The War in Chechnya: The Chaotic Mode of Domination, Violence, and Bare Life in the Post-Soviet Context." *Critique of Anthropology* 27, no. 1: 37–62.

Rimple, Paul. 2012. "Saakashvili's Party Loses as Georgian Democracy Takes Step Forward." *Christian Science Monitor.* http://www.csmonitor.com/World/Europe/2012/1002/Saakashvili's-party-loses-as-Georgian-democracy-takes-step-forward-video.

Robbins, Joel. 2013. "Beyond the Suffering Slot: Toward an Anthropology of the Good." *Journal of the Royal Anthropological Institute* 19, no. 3: 447–62.

Robinson, Andrew. 2014. "Alain Badiou: The State." *Ceasefire Magazine.* https://ceasefiremagazine.co.uk/alain-badiou-state/.

Rogers, Douglas. 2009. *The Old Faith and the Russian Land: A Historical Ethnography of Ethics in the Urals.* Ithaca, NY: Cornell University Press.

———. 2014. *Comments on Borenstein's "Conspiracy as Information."* Washington, DC: Council for European Studies.

Roitman, Janet. 2004. *Fiscal Disobedience.* Princeton, NJ: Princeton University Press.

Rondeli, Alexander. 2014. "The Russian-Georgian War and Its Implications for Georgian State Building." In Jones, *The Making of Modern Georgia, 1918–2012*, 35–48.

Roxburgh, Angus. 2012. "Merkel Herself Hand-Wrote a Pledge That Read 'We Agree Today That Georgia and Ukraine Shall One Day Become Members of NATO.'" In *The Strongman: Vladimir Putin and the Struggle for Russia*, 223–28. New York: I. B. Tauris Publishers.

Rudolph, J. 2014. "How Putin Distorts the Responsibility to Protect in Ukraine." http://opencanada.org/features/the-think-tank/comments/how-putin-distorts-r2p-in-ukraine/.

Rudoren, Jodi. 2013. "A Desert Cold and Wet Multiplies the Misery of Syrian Refugees." *New York Times*, January 12. http://www.nytimes.com/2013/01/13/world/middleeast/fleeing-warfare-syrians-find-more-misery-in-refugee-camp.html?hp&_r=0.

Saakashvili, Mikheil. n.d. "Lazica: Chven Vashenebt Akhal Kalaki." https://www.youtube.com/watch?v=fZ4gyoG2hPs.

———. 2006. "The Path to Energy Security." *Washington Post*, January 8. http://www.washingtonpost.com/wp-dyn/content/article/2006/01/08/AR2006010801167.html.

———. 2009. "President Saakashvili's Written Statement." http://www.civil.ge/eng/article.php?id=20702.

———. 2011. "Annual Address to Parliament." http://www.president.gov.ge/en/PressOffice/Documents?p=6142&i=1.

Sabanadze, Natalia. 2014. "Georgia's Ethnic Diversity: A Challenge to State-Building." In Jones, *The Making of Modern Georgia, 1918–2012*, 119–40.

Sammut, Dennis. 2001. "Population Displacement in the Caucasus: An Overview." *Central Asian Survey* 20, no. 1: 55–62.

Sanders, Todd, and Harry G. West, eds. 2003. "Transparency and Conspiracy: Ethnographies of Suspicion in the New World Order. Durham: Duke University Press.

Santayana, George. 1924. *Soliloquies.* London: Scribner.

Saparov, Arsène. 2010. "From Conflict to Autonomy: The Making of the South Ossetian Autonomous Region 1918–1922." *Europe-Asia Studies* 62, no. 1: 99–123.

Saparov, Arsène. 2014. *From Conflict to Autonomy in the Caucasus: The Soviet Union and the Making of Abkhazia, South Ossetia, and Nagorno Karabakh.* London: Routledge.

Sartre, Jean-Paul. 1943. *Being and Nothingness: An Essay in Phenomenological Ontology.* London: Citadel.

Scheper-Hughes, Nancy, and Margaret Lock. 1987. "The Mindful Body: A Prolegomenon to Future Work in Medical Anthropology." *Medical Anthropology Quarterly* 1, no. 1: 6–41.

Schoenberg, N. E., and E. M. Drew. 2002. "Articulating Silences: Experiential and Biomedical Constructions of Hypertension Symptomatology." *Medical Anthropology Quarterly* 16, no. 4: 458–75.

Schueth, Samuel. 2012. "Apparatus of Capture: Fiscal State Formation in the Republic of Georgia." *Political Geography* 31, no 3: 133–43.

Schwirtz, Michael. 2008. "Georgia Fired More Cluster Bombs Than Thought, Killing Civilians, Report Finds." *New York Times*, November 6. www.nytimes.com:/2008/11/06/world/europe/06cluster.html.

Scott, James C. 1998. *Seeing Like a State: How Certain Schemes to Improve the Human Condition Have Failed.* New Haven, CT: Yale University Press.

———. 2010. *The Art of Not Being Governed: An Anarchist History of Upland Southeast Asia.* New Haven, CT: Yale University Press.

Seife, Charles. 2000. *Zero: The Biography of a Dangerous Idea.* London: Penguin.

Sengupta, S. 2015. "60 Million People Fleeing Chaotic Lands, U.N. Says." *New York Times,* June 18. http://www.nytimes.com/2015/06/18/world/60-million-people-fleeing-chaotic-lands-un-says.html?hp&action=click&pgtype=Homepage&module=second-column-region&region=top-news&WT.nav=top-news&_r=0.

Shatirishvili, M. 2010. *Efficiency Analysis of USG Cash Transfer Assistance Program.* http://www.state.gov/documents/organization/193590.pdf.

Simon, Herbert. 1955. "A Behavioral Model of Rational Choice." *Quarterly Journal of Economics* 69, no. 1: 99–118.

Simon, Jonathan. 2009. *Governing through Crime: How the War on Crime Transformed American Democracy and Created a Culture of Fear.* Oxford: Oxford University Press.

Slade, Gavin. 2012. "Georgia's War on Crime: Creating Security in a Post-Revolutionary Context." *European Security* 21, no. 1: 37–56.

Slezkine, Yuri. 1994. "The USSR as a Communal Apartment, or How a Socialist State Promoted Ethnic Particularism." *Slavic Review* 53, no. 2: 414–52.

Slim, Hugo. 2006. "Claiming a Humanitarian Imperative: NGOs and the Cultivation of Humanitarian Duty." In *Human Rights and Conflict: Exploring the Links between Rights, Law and Peacebuilding,* edited by Julie Mertus and Jeffrey W. Helsing, 159–75. Washington, DC: United States Institutes of Peace.

Sontag, Deborah. 2012. "Years after Haiti Quake, Safe Housing a Dream for Many." *New York Times,* August 16. http://www.nytimes.com/2012/08/16/world/americas/years-after-haiti-quake-safe-housing-is-dream-for-multitudes.html?_r=1&hp.

Spiotta, Dana. 2011. "Leaving Bosnia (and Not)." *New York Times,* BR 16. http://www.nytimes.com/2011/10/23/books/review/shards-by-ismet-prcic-book-review.html.

Stalin, Joseph. 1954. "Marxism and the National Question." In *Collected Works of J. V. Stalin,* 2: 300–381. Moscow: Foreign Languages Publishing House. Marxists Internet Archive, https://www.marxists.org/reference/archive/stalin/works/1913/03.htm. Accessed March 4, 2017.

Steavenson, Wendell. 2008. "Marching through Georgia." *New Yorker,* December 15, 64.

Stein, Janice. 2008. "Humanitarian Organizations: Accountable—Why, to Whom, for What and How?" In Barnett and Weiss, *Humanitarianism in Question,* 124–42.

Steinberg, Mark D., and Catherine Wanner. 2013. *Religion, Morality and Community in Post-Soviet Societies.* Bloomington: Indiana University Press.

Sullivan, Laura. 2015. "In Search of The Red Cross' $500 Million in Haiti Relief." Washington, DC: National Public Radio. http://www.npr.org/2015/06/03/411524156/in-search-of-the-red-cross-500-million-in-haiti-relief?utm_source=facebook.com&utm_medium=social&utm_campaign=npr&utm_term=nprnews&utm_content=20150603.

Sumbadze, Nana, and Giorgi Tarkhan-Mouravi. 2003. "Working Paper on IDP Vulnerability and Economic Self-Reliance." Tbilisi. www.undp.ge/news/EconomicSelfReliance.pdf.

Swain, Frank. 2013. "Russians Who Raised the Dead." *Salon.* http://www.salon.com/2013/06/14/russians_who_raised_the_dead/.

Sydney Morning Herald. 2008. "Putin Calls Kosovo Independence 'Terrible Precedent.'" http://www.smh.com.au/news/world/putin-calls-kosovo-independence-terrible-precedent/2008/02/23/1203467431503.html.

Szakolczai, Arpad, and Agnes Horvath. 1991. "Information Management in Bolshevik-Type Party States: A Version of the Information Society." *East European Politics & Societies* 5, no. 2: 268–305.

Tabula. 2013. "Hammarberg Issues Recommendations on Illegal Surveillance." http://www.tabula.ge/en/story/73206-hammarberg-issues-recommendations-on-illegal-surveillance-materials.

Tagliavini, Heidi, et al. 2009. *Report of the Independent International Fact Finding Mission on the Conflict in Georgia.* Brussels: Council of the European Union. Brussels: Council of the European Union. http://mpil.de/files/pdf4/IIFFMCG_Volume_II1.pdf.

Tarkhan-Mouravi, Giorgi. 2009. *Assessment of IDP Livelihoods in Georgia: Facts and Policies.* http://www.unhcr.org/4ad827b12.pdf.

Taussig, Michael. 1980. *The Devil and Commodity Fetishism.* Chapel Hill: University of North Carolina Press.

Taylor, Charles. 1989. *Sources of the Self: The Making of Modern Identity.* Cambridge, MA: Harvard University Press.

Terry, F. 2002. *Condemned to Repeat: The Paradox of Humanitarian Action.* Ithaca, NY: Cornell University Press.

Theodorou, M. 2006. "Theorizing Architectural Resistance." www.oppositional architecture.com/CFOA 2006/Paper CFOA 2006.pdf.

Ticktin, Miriam, n.d. *The Offshore Camps of the European Union: At the Border of Humanity.* New School Working Papers. New York: New School.

———. 2006. "Where Ethics and Politics Meet: The Violence of Humanitarianism in France." *American Ethnologist* 33, no. 1: 33–49.

———. 2011. *Casualties of Care: Immigration and the Politics of Humanitarianism in France.* Berkeley: University of California Press.

Tilly, Charles. 1996. "Invisible Elbow." *Sociological Forum* 11, no. 4: 589–601.

Tishkov, Valeri. 1991. "The Soviet Empire after Perestroika." *Theory and Society* 20, no. 5: 603–29.

Topchishvili, R. 2009. *Georgian-Ossetian Historical Review.* Institute of Historical Studies, Ivane Javakhishvili State University. https://histinstitute.files.wordpress.com/2009/04/osebitopchishvili1.pdf.

Totadze, A. 2006. *Osebi Sakartveloshi: Miti da realoba (Ossetians in Georgia: Myth and Reality).* Tbilisi: Universali.

Transparency International. 2011. "National Integrity System: Georgia." transparency.ge/nis/2011/law-enforcement.

———. 2013a. "Open Letter to the Government of Georgia on Unchecked Telephone Tapping Made by the Ministry of Internal Affairs via Mobile Operators." http://transparency.ge/en/node/3082.

———. 2013b. "Secret Surveillance and Personal Data Protection: Moving Forward." http://transparency.ge/en/post/press-release/conference-secret-surveillance-and-personal-data-protection-moving-forward.

Tsereteli, M. 2014. "Georgia as a Geographical Pivot: Past, Present, and Future." In Jones, *The Making of Modern Georgia, 1918–2012,* 74–93.

Tsing, Anna Lowenhaupt. 1993. *In the Realm of the Diamond Queen.* Princeton, NJ: Princeton University Press.

Tuan, Yi-Fu. 1974. *Topophilia: A Study of Environmental Perception, Value and Attitudes.* New York: Columbia University Press.

Tuite, Kevin. 2010. "The Autocrat of the Banquet Table: The Political and Social Significance of the Georgian Supra." In *Language, History and Cultural Identities in the Caucasus,* edited by K. Vamling, 9–35. Caucasus Studies 2. Papers from the conference, June 17–20 2005, Malmö University, Sweden. Malmö: Malmö University.

Turner, Simon. 2005. "Suspended Spaces: Contested Sovereignties in a Refugee Camp." In *Sovereign Bodies: Citizens, Migrants and States in the Postcolonial World,* edited by Thomas Blom Hansen and Finn Stepputat, 312–32. Princeton, NJ: Princeton University Press.

Turner, Terence. 1986. "Production, Exploitation, and Social Consciousness in the 'Peripheral Situation.'" *Social Analysis* 19: 91–115.

Turton, David. 2003. *Conceptualising Forced Migration*. Refugee Studies Centre Working Paper. Oxford: Oxford University.

United Nations. 2008. *Georgia: Summary of Joint Needs Assessment Findings*. http://documents.worldbank.org/curated/en/961861486983389566/Georgia-Summary-of-joint-needs-assessment-findings.

——. 2011. "UN-Led Effort Helps Haitians Clear Half of Quake Rubble in Large-Scale Operation." http://www.un.org/apps/news/story.asp?NewsID=40026#.Uc5zrkLOXww.

——. 2016. "Too Important to Fail: Addressing the Humanitarian Financing Gap." http://bit.ly/1RKvnWs.

United Nations Association of Georgia. 2008. *National Integration and Tolerance in Georgia Assessment Survey Report*. Tbilisi: United Nations Association of Georgia. http://www.una.ge/pdfs/publications/survey_report_eng.pdf.

United Nations Children's Fund. 2008. "Calmness and Love for Displaced Breast Feeding Mothers in the New Temporary Shelter." www.unicef.org/georgia/reallives_10695.html.

United Nations Development Program. 2010. "Gender Equality Resource Centre Offers Training for Youth." http://www.undp.org.ge/index.php?lang_id=ENG&sec_id=22&info_id=832.

United Nations High Commission for Refugees. n.d. "Biometric Cash Assistance." http://innovation.unhcr.org/labs_post/cash-assistance/.

——. 2006. "Global Appeal 2007: Strategies and Programs." http://www.unhcr.org/static/publ/ga2007/ga2007toc.htm.

——. 2007. "Statute of the Office of the High Commission for Refugees." http://www.unhcr.org/protect/PROTECTION/3b66c39e1.pdf.

——. 2009. "UNHCR Annual Report Shows 42 Million People Uprooted Worldwide." www.unhcr.org/4a2fd52412d.html.

——. 2010. "Haiti Earthquake Funding Tracker." www.reliefweb.int/rw/fts/nsf/doc105?OpenForm&rc=2&emid=EQ-2010-000009-HTI.

——. 2011. *UNHCR Global Report*. http://www.unhcr.org/4fc880b9b.pdf.

——. 2012. "Report on Participatory Assessments for the Extension of the IDP Action Plan." www.internal-displacement.org/.../UNHCR+Particip+Assessm+GEO.pdf.

——. 2013. "Status of Internally Displaced Persons and Refugees from Abkhazia, Georgia and the Tskhinvali Region/South Ossetia, Georgia." www.unhcr.org/51c05a419.pdf.

——. 2015. "Worldwide Displacement Hits All-Time High as War and Persecution Increase." http://www.unhcr.org/558193896.html.

United Nations Humanitarian Mission to South Ossetia. 2008. *Mission Report: Humanitarian Assessment Mission*. http://www.parliament.ge/files/1185_20708_481490_SOssetia_Mission_Report_16-20_Sept_2008_Final_for_distr.pdf.

United States Agency for International Development. 2004. "USAID Assistance to Internally Displaced Persons Policy." www.usaid.gov/policy/ads/200/200mbc.pd.

——. 2008. "Cash Transfer Grant Agreement between the Government of the United States of America, Acting through the United States Agency for International Development, and the Government of Georgia." http://www.state.gov/documents/organization/120560.pdf.

———. 2010. "Efficiency Analysis of USG Cash Transfer Assistance." http://www.state.gov/documents/organization/193590.pdf.

United States Department of State. 2008. "Cash Transfer Grant Agreement." http://www.state.gov/documents/organization/120560.pdf.

Van den Hemel, Ernst. 2008. "Included but Not Belonging: Badiou and Ranciere on Human Rights." *Krisis* 3. www.krisis.eu/content/2008-3/2008-3-03.hemel.pdf.

Van der Leeuw, Charles. 1998. *Storm over the Caucasus: In the Wake of Independence.* New York: St. Martin's Press.

Vartanyan, Olesya, and Ellen Barry. 2014. "If History Is a Guide, Crimeans' Celebration May Be Short Lived." *New York Times*, March 19. http://www.nytimes.com/2014/03/19/world/europe/south-ossetia-crimea.html?.

Vartanyan, Olesya, and Michael Schwirtz. 2009. "Georgia and an Enclave Trade Accusations." *New York Times*, August 5. www.nytimes.com/2009/08/05/world/europe/05georgia.html.

Vashakidze, G. 2008. "Koba's Refugees: We Will Return." *Sakartvelos Respublika*, p. 12.

Verdery, Katherine. 1996. *What Was Socialism and What Comes Next?* Princeton, NJ: Princeton University Press.

———. 1999. *The Political Lives of Dead Bodies.* New York: Columbia University Press.

———. 2014. *Secrets and Truths: Ethnography in the Archive of Romania's Secret Police.* Budapest: Central European University Press.

Vonnegut, Kurt. 1969. *Slaughterhouse-Five.* New York: Delacorte.

Walker, Chris, and Morgan Hartley. 2013. "NSA on Steroids: Georgia Republic's Mass Surveillance." http://www.theglobalist.com/nsa-on-steroids-mass-surveillance-in-georgia-republic/.

Wallace, J. 2014. "Workers of the World, Faint!" *New York Times*, January 17. https://www.nytimes.com/2014/01/18/opinion/workers-of-the-world-faint.html.

Walters, Christopher, and R. Cortina. 2007. *Psychosocial Education as a Viable Mental Health Rehabilitator for Internally Displaced Persons: A Case Study on the Republic of Georgia.* International Educational Development. New York: Columbia University Press.

Ware, Kallistos. 1979. *The Orthodox Way.* Yonkers, NY: St. Vladimir's Seminary Press.

Wawrzonek, M. 2014. "Ukraine in the 'Gray Zone': Between the 'Russkiy Mir' and Europe." *East European Politics and Societies* 28, no. 4: 758–80.

Weber, Max. 1930. *The Protestant Ethic and the Spirit of Capitalism.* London: Penguin.

Weiss, Thomas. 2013. *Humanitarian Business.* New York: Polity.

Weizman, Eyal. 2011. *The Least of All Possible Evils.* London: Verso.

Welt, Cory. 2010. "The Thawing of a Frozen Conflict: The Internal Security Dilemma and the 2004 Prelude to the Russo-Georgian War." *Europe-Asia Studies* 62, no. 1: 63–97.

———. 2014. "A Fateful Moment: Ethnic Autonomy and Revolutionary Violence in the Democratic Republic of Georgia (1918–1921)." In *The Making of Modern Georgia, 1918–2012*, edited by Stephen Jones, 205–31.

Williams, Christian A. 2012. "Silence, Voices and the Camp." *Humanity* 3, no. 2: 65–80.

Woodward, Susan. 1995. *Balkan Tragedy: Chaos and Dissolution after the Cold War.* Washington, DC: Brookings Institution Press.

Yamskov, A. N. 1991. "Ethnic Conflict in the Transcaucasus: The Case of Nagorno-Karabakh." *Theory and Society* 20, no. 5: 631–60.

Yurchak, Alexei. 2014. "Little Green Men: Russia, Ukraine, and Post-Soviet Sovereignty." http://anthropoliteia.net/2014/03/31/little-green-men-russia-ukraine-and-post-soviet-sovereignty/?utm_content=buffer5465b&utm_medium=social&utm_source=facebook.com&utm_campaign=buffer.

Zamira, K. 2005. *Osta sakitkhi da kartuli sinamdvile 1921–1940 tslebshi: Shida kartlis magalitze (The Ossetian Question and Georgian Reality, 1921–1940: On the Example of Shida-Kartli)*. Tbilisi: Khatula LLC.

Zetter, Roger 1991. "Labelling Refugees: Forming and Transforming a Bureaucratic Identity." *Journal of Refugee Studies* 4, no. 1: 39–63.

——. 2012. "Are Refugees an Economic Burden or a Benefit?" *Forced Migration Review* 41: 50–52.

Zürcher, Christoph. 2007. *The Post-Soviet Wars: Rebellion, Ethnic Conflict, and Nationhood in the Caucasus*. New York: New York University Press.

Index

Pages numbers followed by *f*, *n*, or *nn* indicate figures or notes.

CPSIA information can be obtained
at www.ICGtesting.com
Printed in the USA
LVHW01s0234021018
591861LV00002B/6/P